The PEN, the SWORD, and the LAW

MCGILL-QUEEN'S IBERIAN AND LATIN AMERICAN CULTURES SERIES
SERIES EDITOR: NICOLÁS FERNÁNDEZ-MEDINA

The McGill-Queen's Iberian and Latin American Cultures Series is committed to publishing original scholarship that explores and re-evaluates Iberian and Latin American cultures, connections, and identities. Offering diverse perspectives on a range of regional and global histories from the early modern period to twenty-first-century contexts, the series cuts across disciplinary boundaries to consider how questions of authority, nation, revolution, gender, sexuality, science, epistemology, avant-gardism, aesthetics, travel, colonization, race relations, religious belief, and media technologies, among others, have shaped the rich and complex trajectories of modernity in the Iberian Peninsula and Latin America.

The McGill-Queen's Iberian and Latin American Cultures Series promotes rigorous scholarship and welcomes proposals for innovative and theoretically compelling monographs and edited collections.

1 Populism and Ethnicity
  Peronism and the Jews of Argentina
  Raanan Rein
  Translated by Isis Sadek

2 What Would Cervantes Do?
  Navigating Post-Truth with Spanish Baroque Literature
  David Castillo and William Egginton

3 The Pen, the Sword, and the Law
  Dueling and Democracy in Uruguay
  David S. Parker

The PEN, the SWORD, and the LAW

Dueling and Democracy in Uruguay

DAVID S. PARKER

McGill-Queen's University Press
Montreal & Kingston · London · Chicago

© McGill-Queen's University Press 2022

ISBN 978-0-2280-1102-6 (cloth)
ISBN 978-0-2280-1234-4 (ePDF)
ISBN 978-0-2280-1235-1 (ePUB)

Legal deposit second quarter 2022
Bibliothèque nationale du Québec

Printed in Canada on acid-free paper that is 100% ancient forest free (100% post-consumer recycled), processed chlorine free

This book has been published with the help of a grant from the Federation for the Humanities and Social Sciences, through the Awards to Scholarly Publications Program, using funds provided by the Social Sciences and Humanities Research Council of Canada.

We acknowledge the support of the Canada Council for the Arts.

Nous remercions le Conseil des arts du Canada de son soutien.

Library and Archives Canada Cataloguing in Publication

Title: The pen, the sword, and the law : dueling and democracy in Uruguay / David S. Parker.

Names: Parker, D. S. (David Stuart), 1960- author.

Series: McGill-Queen's Iberian and Latin American cultures series ; 3.

Description: Series statement: McGill-Queen's Iberian and Latin American cultures series ; 3 | Includes bibliographical references and index.

Identifiers: Canadiana (print) 20210369507 | Canadiana (ebook) 20210369590 | ISBN 9780228011026 (cloth) | ISBN 9780228012344 (ePDF) | ISBN 9780228012351 (ePUB)

Subjects: LCSH: Dueling – Uruguay – History. | LCSH: Honor – Uruguay – History. | LCSH: Democracy – Uruguay – History.

Classification: LCC CR4595.U7 P37 2022 | DDC 394/.809895 – dc23

This book was designed and typeset by Peggy & Co. Design in 11/14 Adobe Garamond Pro.

Contents

Figures and Tables   vii
Preface and Acknowledgments   ix

Introduction   3
1   The Laws of Honor   19
2   Dueling as Politics and the Politics of Dueling   55
3   Impunity to Legality: Dueling and the Law, 1860s–1930s   92
4   Resurgence and Recriminalization, 1950s–1992   132
Appendix: Methodology   167

Notes   179
Bibliography   213
Index   227

Figures and Tables

Figures

1.1	Statue to Giuseppe Garibaldi, Montevideo	26
1.2	*Carta-poder*	33
1.3	Duel between Enrique Areco and Luis Batlle Berres	37
1.4	*Acta previa* of the Areco-Batlle Berres duel	38–39
1.5	Director of combat issuing instructions in a fencing duel	41
2.1	Juan Carlos Gómez	56
2.2	Nicolás Calvo	57
2.3	Salvatore "Totó" Nicosía	71
2.4	Washington Bermúdez, editor of *El Negro Timoteo*	86
2.5	José Batlle y Ordóñez	91
3.1	Luis Alberto de Herrera, caricature	109
3.2	Juan Andrés Ramírez	113
3.3	Washington Beltrán	117
3.4	Duel between César Batlle Pacheco and Eduardo de Castro	126
3.5	Duel between Baltasar Brum and Colonel Alberto Riverós	126
3.6	Decision of an honor tribunal	129
4.1	Julio Maria Sanguinetti	141
4.2	General Líber Seregni	146
4.3	Uruguay's last duel, between the generals Líber Seregni and Juan P. Ribas	146

Tables

A1 Duels or Incidents Researched for This Book, Involving an Uruguayan or Fought in Uruguay   171

A2 Duels, c. 1890–Early 1920, Recorded in "Actualidad: Estadística del duelo," *El Plata*, 14 April 1920   177

Preface and Acknowledgments

This book was slow to take form. My children, Francesca and Robert, now both adults, were four and six during the sabbatical in Uruguay and Argentina when I began research on this project. Very few sources were digitized, and the only way to reproduce newspapers from the extraordinary collection at the Hemeroteca of Uruguay's Biblioteca Nacional was to have them microfilmed. On a follow-up visit, I was among the first to bring a digital camera into the Hemeroteca, setting up alongside microfilm photographer Miguel Marabotto. The long and winding path toward writing this book started with two journal articles and a book chapter, limited excerpts of which appear here in revised form: "El código penal y las 'leyes caballerescas': Hacia el duelo legal en el Uruguay, 1880–1920," *Anuario IEHS*, no. 14 (1999): 295–311; "Law, Honor, and Impunity in Spanish America: The Debate over Dueling, 1870–1920," *Law and History Review* 19, no. 2 (2001): 311–41; and "Gentlemanly Responsibility and Insults of a Woman: Dueling and the Unwritten Rules of Public Life in Uruguay, 1860–1920," in *Gender, Sexuality, and Power in Latin America since Independence*, edited by Katherine Elaine Bliss and William E. French (Lanham, MD: Rowman & Littlefield, 2007), 109–32.

After publishing these shorter pieces, I set the research aside to work on other projects, but three things kept reminding me insistently why Uruguay's duelists should not remain exiled forever to my filing cabinets of notes and the virtual dusty shelves of my computer. First, although Uruguayans are aware of their history of dueling and of their unique law that legalized the practice, this is a story that readers in English-speaking countries likely do not know and might find intriguing. Second, every time I talked about what I had encountered in the archives, I realized how much it clashed with people's inherited preconceptions of the duel, stereotypes that persisted despite my own earlier writings and those of others. And finally, there were simply too many astounding, ironic, funny, and poignant anecdotes to keep to myself. Readers in English deserve to meet David Buchelli and Salvatore Nicosía, Juan Carlos Gómez and Nicolás Calvo, Washington Bermúdez and Lieutenant Schilemberg, Enrique Romero Jiménez and José Paul y Angulo, Virgilio Sampognaro and Washington Paullier, José Batlle y Ordóñez and Washington Beltrán – and all the other characters who make up the cast of this book.

Any research and writing process as drawn out as this one incurs many debts of gratitude, going back so far in time that I know I have forgotten many deserving people. An invitation from Eduardo Zimmermann instigated my first trip to the Rio de la Plata – I had previously worked in Peru and Chile – and it was on that initial visit that a vague hunch led me to the Archivo General de la Nación in Buenos Aires, where I came across the hilarious report of a deliberately inconclusive police investigation into an alleged 1873 duel between Jacobo Varela and Julio Benítez. From that moment, I was hooked. Later Eduardo would introduce me to Gerardo Caetano, who would be my guide and teacher in Uruguay.

Prior to starting work in earnest in Montevideo and Buenos Aires, I began at the Lillian Goldman Law Library at Yale University, whose fine international law collection and helpful staff set me on the right path and made possible a grant application to the Social Sciences and Humanities Research Council of Canada. Additional thanks go as well to Sterling Library at Yale and Widener Library at Harvard. SSHRC funding made possible ten uninterrupted months of research in South America, family in tow. Thanks to the generosity of Dr Caetano, I established an affiliation in Montevideo with CLAEH, the Centro Latino-Americano de Economía Humana, which provided library and internet access, assistance, and colleagueship. My thanks go to all of CLAEH's administrative staff and affiliated scholars. The following institutions in Montevideo were essential to the research: the Biblioteca Nacional de Uruguay, with special recognition to the Hemeroteca and its staff; the Biblioteca del Poder Legislativo, where employees and even another patron, Escribano Osimani, took an interest in what I was doing and made contacts on my behalf; the Archivo Histórico and Archivo Judicial of the Archivo General de la Nación; and the Museo Histórico Nacional.

Also in Montevideo, I would like to extend special appreciation to Dr Rubén Domínguez Cabot for allowing me access to the private papers of late fencing master Cándido Domínguez and permission to photograph them. Employees at Tevé Ciudad took the time to burn to DVD copies of their nine-part documentary series, *Uruguay de Duelo: Ofensores y Ofendidos*, which originally aired in 2003. Two congressmen and a former president, José Díaz, Daniel Díaz Maynard, and Julio Maria Sanguinetti, generously agreed to interviews. Other scholars who shared their time and ideas along the way, in person, by email, or both, include John Charles Chasteen, Leandro Kierszenbaum, Gerardo Leibner, Anton Rosenthal, Richard Walter, and the late Ricardo Marletti Strada.

In Argentina, in addition to Eduardo Zimmermann, special appreciation goes to Sandra Gayol. We shared materials and often discussed our findings while she was researching her own excellent book on Argentine dueling. Libraries and archives in Argentina that facilitated my research included the Biblioteca Nacional, the Biblioteca del Congreso, the Biblioteca of the Facultad de Derecho at the Universidad de Buenos Aires, and the Archivo General de la Nación. Thanks also to Dora Barrancos, Jorge Cermesone, Víctor O. García Costa, Ricardo Salvatore, the late Francisco Lucchetti, fencing instructor at the Club Gimnasia y Esgrima, and Lieutenant Colonel Leonhardt for the gift of his copy of the Ferreto honor code. Doris, Jorge, Diego, and Tamara were my family's second family for three months in their warm Belgrano home.

Conference papers that ended up in the manuscript in revised form, draft chapters, or the entire book draft have benefited from the critical scrutiny of Sandra Gayol, Pablo Piccato, Guillermo Silva Grucci, my colleague Nancy van Deusen, Richard Ratzlaff at McGill-Queen's University Press, two anonymous readers, and copyeditor Maureen Garvie. Referees for academic promotion read the manuscript prior to publication and weighed in with useful advice as well: Joel Wolfe, Paulo Drinot, Dennis Gilbert, Ricardo López-Pedreros, and an anonymous fifth. Thanks also to Rosana Delgado at the Archivo General de la Nación, Clara von Sanden at the Museo Histórico Nacional, Fabián Centurión at *Diario El País*, and Guillermo Silva Grucci, for assistance in obtaining photographs to accompany the text. This book is a better one for the contributions of all who collaborated in one way or another over such a long period of time. My sincerest thanks to everyone I have mentioned, and my apologies to those I inadvertently have omitted. The book is dedicated to all of you.

The PEN, the SWORD, and the LAW

Introduction

In 1992, the Uruguayan Senate approved a bill passed two years earlier in the House of Representatives to make dueling illegal. Not 1892, but 1992. To be more precise, the senators voted to repeal a 1920 law that had decriminalized all duels that followed a specified protocol. In both houses, the repeal won by comfortable margins, but recriminalization did not go unopposed. "If we repeal the *Ley de Duelos*," warned Senate president Gonzalo Aguirre Ramírez, "how will we prevent insults and defamation? What will we do if tomorrow someone insults someone else and this leads to an incident involving gunshots or blows?"[1] Seven years later in a 1999 interview, former president Julio Maria Sanguinetti concluded that the recriminalization of dueling had been a mistake: without the duel as a "psychological inhibition" against character assassination, he argued, the quality of political debate had descended to new lows.[2] As recently as 2017, the ex-president and former guerrilla José Mujica expressed sentiments almost identical to Sanguinetti's.[3]

Uruguay's 1920 *Ley de Duelos* (Law of Duels) was unique in the world. Although duels had occurred with relative impunity in many parts of Europe and the Americas – in a few countries up into the 1950s, 1960s, and 1970s – only Uruguay chose the radical step of formally legalizing the practice. One goal of this book is to explain the context in which that legalization occurred, a question that involves several parts. First, why did so many Uruguayans view dueling as a necessary part of political life? How did advocates justify the duel, and what purpose, or purposes, did the duel actually serve? Why were the duel's many opponents not only powerless to stop the practice but unable even to prevent its legalization? These questions open a window onto the day-to-day culture of politics, the press, and the evolving public sphere in late nineteenth- and twentieth-century Latin America. They also directly address the complicated relationship between law and society.[4] Prior to 1920, how did Uruguayan elites reconcile the obvious tension between state formation and the expanding dominion of the rule of law on the one hand, and their permissive attitude toward this unique violent crime on the other? How did political leaders, as experts in the law, live with their own blatant violations of that law? What juridical theories underpinned the decriminalization of dueling and justified this single remarkable exception to Uruguay's criminal statutes on murder or assault? How did the duel's abolitionists finally turn the tide, and why did it take until 1992?

This book's answers to those questions tend not to emphasize – or at least not to overemphasize – the idea of honor, constructions of masculinity, or the consolidation of an elite, although all of these themes appear.[5] One thing that distinguishes the argument presented here is my deliberate choice not to focus on the duel as a manifestation in microcosm of some deep cultural essence, or as a marker of some epochal transformation of attitudes toward violence or in class or gender relations.[6] Dueling reflected and reinforced a particular set of values and shared understandings of how people should live their lives, to be sure, but the explanation for the rise of dueling in mid- to late-nineteenth-century Uruguay and its persistence into the late twentieth century lies elsewhere. Take the concept of honor, for example. Too often the relationship between dueling and honor has been treated in a way that borders on tautological. Why did people duel? Because they were excessively protective of their honor. How do we know that they were excessively protective of their honor? Because they fought duels. Clearly, the idea of honor was essential to the mindset of the duelist. In the almost two hundred duels or near-duels that provide the raw material for this book, one would be hard pressed to find a single case in which the protagonists did not invoke honor. Dueling manuals were known as "honor codes," duels were fought on the "field of honor," and the insults or accusations that led to duels were called "offenses against honor." Uruguayans described honor as their most cherished value, more precious than life itself. They repeatedly expressed their willingness to die for honor and their refusal to live without it.

Yet honor can take many forms and be expressed in many ways. In late colonial Latin America, plebeians often settled interpersonal conflicts at knifepoint, but elite dueling was rare.[7] Does that mean eighteenth-century aristocrats were unconcerned with honor? Hardly: denunciations for defamation or insult (*injuria*) fill colonial archives.[8] The question then becomes why, in the nineteenth and early twentieth centuries, political elites in Uruguay and many other places chose to abandon the courtroom and to set off instead for the field of honor whenever their public image came under attack. Why did comparatively tame insults spark a duel in one situation, while more brutal profanities were ignored or forgiven in another? Why were so many duels the result of deliberate provocation? Tempting though it may be to seek explanations in changing ideas of honor, changing constructions of masculinity, changing attitudes toward violence, or changes to the social structure, this book puts forward a simpler explanation: the duel offered a utilitarian solution to deep but essentially practical problems of political conflict in a young republic.[9] The duel provided a peculiar kind of customary law to police the boundaries of journalism and public speech, at a time when weak states and fragile legal systems were perceived to be incapable of managing the rising competition for power and prominence.

In other words, the duel and its attendant honor code provided a set of quasi-legal norms that regulated political discourse. They filled a void because a large number of powerful people believed that the existing statutes and state institutions of law enforcement were not up to the task of crafting legitimate, enforceable rules that would allow democratic debate to flourish while discouraging personal invective.[10] This book shows how the dueling codes – the so-called codes of honor – provided this alternative legality; it explains why so many Uruguayans, like many Europeans and Latin Americans elsewhere, came to view dueling as a necessary evil, as a safeguard of civility in the public sphere. Understanding the duel as a practical response to democracy's built-in tensions rather than as some archaic throwback to the age of chivalry helps to explain why dueling became such a fundamental part of political life in a place like Uruguay, which, I would argue, had possibly the most democratic, most egalitarian, and least aristocratic political culture on the South American continent.

My reason for choosing Uruguay as the principal location for this study should now be clear. Uruguay, the only country to decriminalize the duel, was a bastion of liberalism in Latin America, a land of successful immigrants and seemingly boundless opportunities, a pioneer of social reform and political experimentation, all in all an inhospitable place for aristocratic pretension. If a case can be made for the duel's liberal pedigree, Uruguay is the place to make it. Still, this book does not limit its scope to one bank of the Rio de la Plata. Examples from neighboring Argentina appear frequently, for several reasons. First of all, for most of the period under study, the ties between Montevideo and Buenos Aires were so numerous and so strong that it makes sense to consider them as two parts of a single region. No sector of society lived those connections more intimately than the political class, as each of the many so-called revolutions sent a new wave of exiles across the estuary. When Argentine expatriates landed in Montevideo, they reestablished their newspapers and continued debating as if they had never left home; occasionally their polemics led to duels fought on Uruguayan soil. Uruguayans in Buenos Aires, some of whom lived fully binational lives with homes and members of their extended families in both places, did the same.[11] When exiles carried out journalistic guerrilla warfare against the government that had expelled them, it did not take long for the papers – and the insults – to cross the Rio de la Plata on the next day's steamer. Not infrequently, these cross-border arguments turned into cross-border duels.

Second, the proximity of Uruguay to Argentina facilitated what one pundit described as dueling tourism.[12] For many years it was not unusual for Uruguayans to duel in Buenos Aires or for Argentines to duel in Colonia or Montevideo in order to escape police repression. Prior to 1920, the traffic went both ways, taking advantage of the convenient fact that dueling, despite being a crime in both countries, did not figure among the extraditable offenses listed in the 1877 bilateral treaty.[13] After legalization of dueling in Uruguay, that tourism became a one-way affair. Even Argentine duelists who did not leave home claimed to have done so, falsely reporting Uruguay as the venue of duels that insiders knew had actually been fought in some Buenos Aires backyard or Palermo Park.[14]

The frequency of cross-border dueling highlights the existence of a common dueling culture in both places, and in so doing puts the legal history of the duel and its regulation into sharper relief. Argentines also debated the legality of dueling, to the point of proposing reforms in Congress on several occasions. But there the decriminalization advocates never won the day, despite counting in their ranks some of the country's most influential jurists. The two different legal responses to a shared dueling culture and a common set of dilemmas creates a sort of natural historical experiment with a control group, giving us a broader perspective on the context and impact of Uruguay's unique decision to legalize.

Dueling in the Rio de la Plata: A Brief Background

In the pastoral, underpopulated Viceroyalty of Buenos Aires, dueling among members of the urban elite was rare in the colonial era. By the 1860s, however, the duel with all its formal protocol had become an established institution on both sides of the Rio de la Plata. We do not have an exact chronology of the rise of Uruguayan dueling in the first half of the 1800s, but the better-known history of Argentina suggests scenarios. Argentine authors maintain that dueling first became common in the unsettled years of the early nineteenth century, in the immediate aftermath of emancipation from Spain. Independence hero General José de San Martín introduced among his officers the principle that military honor obliged them to accept any challenge and to challenge any affront. General José Maria Paz lamented in his memoirs that military duels became commonplace as a result.[15] At the same time, however, the civil authorities in Buenos Aires issued several edicts reaffirming the criminality of the duel and promising severe repression of a practice that, in their words, was "proscribed by our religion, our laws, and our customs."[16] If the governments of the 1810s and '20s did not successfully repress dueling, dictator Juan Manuel de Rosas (1830–50) did; he went so far as to close Buenos Aires's one fencing school.[17] Only after the fall of Rosas did dueling reemerge in Argentina, with a vigor far outstripping the earlier era.[18]

Uruguay was directly affected by events in Argentina, even if it did not necessarily follow an identical path. Uruguay did not have a dictator with the power and longevity of Rosas: indeed, Montevideo was a haven for anti-Rosas exiles, a city roiling with plots, intrigues, press polemics, and open civil war from 1839 to 1851. Yet despite this seemingly fertile climate, few duels appear in the documentary record prior to about 1850. Their absence could simply be a function of the poverty of the documentation for those unsettled years, but it more likely reflects the changing nature of dueling between the first and second halves of the nineteenth century. Early-century duels lacked the formality and publicity that so characterized late-century duels. For example, after a famous and deadly 1814 duel fought in Buenos Aires between two Chilean military officers, General Juan Mackenna was found the next morning lying dead in pool of blood. Although his opponent's second would later claim that a physician had been in attendance and that both seconds had dutifully attempted to prevent the duel, the grisly aftermath tells a different story.[19] If these were the conditions of early-century duels, it should surprise no one that they would be poorly documented. As a result, we have no way of knowing for sure whether elite dueling was entirely absent from early nineteenth-century Uruguay or whether it was just hidden from view.

We do know, however, that the duel emerged as a visible, well-documented practice and a subject of intense debate after mid-century. Uruguay's first recorded fatality in a formal duel, conducted in accordance with the gentlemanly honor codes of the day, occurred in 1866, when José Cándido Bustamante shot his former friend Servando Martínez. The institutionalization of formal, public, protocolar elite dueling in Uruguay mirrored what was going on in post-Rosas Argentina and also followed the example of continental Europe, where the duel was experiencing its own resurgence.[20] It was Europe, after all, that offered Argentines and Uruguayans an ideal to emulate and the means to attain that ideal, what Mexican historian Pablo Piccato aptly called the "technology of honor."[21] French and Italian fencing masters found themselves in great demand in Spanish America, and many forged successful careers. Andrés Facundo Cesario, the first European master to arrive in Buenos Aires and open a school, had come from Gibraltar in 1833; in 1870–71, he was joined by the Italian Juan Bay and the Frenchman La Marie. In 1897, the world-famous Italian champion Eugenio Pini established a fencing school in Buenos Aires for officers of the armed forces.[22] While all of these masters promoted fencing as an art and a sport, no small proportion of their business came from journalists and politicians interested in preparing themselves for the eventual duel. The first internationally recognized Uruguayan fencing master was Montevideo-born Nicolás Revello, who began teaching in 1903, making him a rough contemporary of Pini.[23] And in both countries the pool of duelists was enriched by the arrival of political exiles, especially Spaniards and Italians, some of whom became important players in the world of journalism.[24]

As Robert Nye has pointed out, French dueling in the later nineteenth century also bore little resemblance to that of earlier times. Late-century duels were increasingly tamed and regularized, as Europeans adopted the strict 1836 dueling code of the Comte de Chateauvillard, and fencing became a sport of gentlemen, part of a young elite male's cultural formation.[25] It was this new, more civilized European dueling that provided the model for Latin Americans. Violence was channeled and controlled by protocol in ways that made fatalities or severe injuries the exception. But if deaths in elite duels were exceedingly rare – documented dueling fatalities occurred in Uruguay in 1866, 1880, 1893, 1908, 1920, and 1921 – they remained frequent enough that no generation lacked its one or two tragic memories, and that was surely enough to remind people of the duel's deadly potential. Other duels, while not fatal, resulted in serious injuries; in addition, dueling deaths in Europe, Argentina, and elsewhere were inevitably reported in the papers and became a part of Uruguayans' collective consciousness.[26] The highly publicized deaths of Argentines Pantaleón Gómez in 1880 and Lucio Vicente López in 1894 were topics of conversation on both banks of the Rio de la Plata.[27]

In the early twentieth century, duels in Uruguay became more frequent rather than less so, and for Argentina that appears to have been the case as well.[28] At minimum, a hundred duels were fought in Argentina between 1904 and 1927, thirty of them with pistols.[29] In Uruguay, the frequency of dueling reached its apogee around World War I: close to fifty duels were recorded during a period of only seven years, from 1914 to 1920.[30] Despite the increasing frequency of duels, the absolute number of deaths or serious injuries remained roughly constant, meaning that the proportion of duels with grave consequences was falling. That trend was significant, as we will see. Duels were never particularly numerous in the Rio de la Plata when compared to late nineteenth-century Germany, France, or Italy (Italy reported an average of 269 duels *per year* through the 1880s).[31] Even in its early twentieth-century heyday, dueling in Uruguay was nowhere near as ubiquitous as in parts of continental Europe, nor did the number of duels in Uruguay ever remotely approach the number of homicides or cases of manslaughter.[32] But that does not make formal elite dueling insignificant. First, for every duel actually fought, there were many more "incidents" involving challenges (*desafíos*) and the naming of seconds: violence was often averted thanks to the seconds' successful mediation and/or the parties' willingness to give and accept "satisfaction" in the form of an apology or retraction. As a general rule, the honor codes regulated the conduct of politicians, journalists, and other public men whenever they engaged in political controversies; even when those conflicts did not occasion duels or challenges, the dueling codes played no small role in setting norms of behavior and limits on what could and could not be said in debate.

Second, the importance of dueling lies in the social and political prominence of its practitioners. Famous names in Uruguayan dueling include, in approximate chronological order, Juan Carlos Gómez, José Cándido Bustamante, José Pedro Varela, Francisco Bauzá, Carlos Maria Ramírez, Alberto Palomeque, Eugenio Garzón, Eduardo Acevedo Díaz, Carlos Roxlo, José Batlle y Ordóñez, Washington Beltrán, Luis Alberto de Herrera, Leonel Aguirre, Juan Andrés Ramírez, Baltasar Brum, Luis Batlle Berres, Julio Maria Sanguinetti, Jorge Batlle, and Líber Seregni, and the list could go on. It is a list that includes no fewer than seven men who eventually became president of the republic, leaders of all three of Uruguay's dominant political parties, noted poets and writers, top military officials, government ministers, chiefs of police, and scores of senators and members of the House of Representatives. The congressmen, protected from prosecution by their parliamentary immunity, appear on balance to have had the fewest scruples about dueling while in exercise of their office. Ministers and other public officials often had to resign their posts temporarily in order to duel; the several occasions when sitting presidents either dueled or engaged in dueling preliminaries raised the grave specter of institutional crisis.[33] Uruguay's best-known duel – one of Latin America's most famous – ended the life of Washington Beltrán, rising star and leading light in the party of opposition, killed at the hand of former president José Batlle y Ordóñez, the governing party's patriarch and architect of the modern Uruguayan state. Beltrán's death remains an indelible part of national collective memory.[34] In short, while dueling may not have preoccupied the everyday lives of ordinary people, it did preoccupy the political class, with far-reaching consequences. It is impossible to comprehend the operation of the public sphere without looking at how the duel and its governing honor code shaped the culture of Uruguayan politics.

Third, Uruguay's unprecedented decision to legalize the duel underscored both its importance in the minds of the political class and the unique dilemma posed by this peculiar form of elite lawlessness. The debates surrounding legalization offer a privileged window through which to glimpse Uruguayans' diverse and conflicting ideas about the role of the legislator, the duties and powers of the state, and the nature of the law. Finally, the persistence of the duel well into the second half of the twentieth century is as unusual as it is revealing. Uruguay's last-known duel was fought in December 1971 between two generals, one of whom, Líber Seregni, had just finished running for president at the head of a left-wing electoral alliance. That the presidential candidate for a coalition that included Marxist revolutionaries would feel compelled to challenge a critic to a duel speaks to the unique role that dueling continued to play in the political life of the nation.

Organization and Major Themes of the Book

The book's first two chapters focus on the intimate yet complex relationship between dueling and public life, focusing mostly though not exclusively on the years prior to 1920, when the duel was made legal. Chapter 1 explains how the code of honor functioned as something akin to a parallel legal code, designed to deter politicians and journalists from crossing the line into invective and character assassination. If in the heat of an argument someone did exceed the bounds of civility, the conventions of the dueling codes were supposed to act as a reconciliation mechanism, channeling violent passions down a controlled path and restoring the self-restraint that had temporarily been lost. Although the honor codes often worked as designed, almost as frequently they did not. Chapter 2 investigates why this was the case, by looking at the many motives that could incite men to duel. The chapter shows why and how competing politicians used and abused the rules of honor in order to control their public image, promote their careers, and silence and/or discredit their rivals. Duels, challenges, insults, and provocations were powerful and frequently employed weapons in high-stakes political games.

Chapter 2 also explores the kinds of disputes that arose when duelists and seconds adjudicated conflicts within the quasi-legal framework of the honor codes. As they applied "dueling law" to specific circumstances, Uruguayans found themselves debating fundamental questions about the norms of public discourse and the limits of democracy. Was a particular statement a just cause for a duel or not? Did a man alleged to have committed a crime have the right to challenge his accuser to a duel, or did he first need to prove his innocence in a court of law? Could a sitting president practice journalism and polemicize in print if as president he was not permitted to duel? In order to answer those kinds of questions and thus determine whether a duel was justified, the seconds entered – with surprising frequency – into a thicket of complex issues, including the line between legitimate debate and personal attack, the responsibilities of elected and appointed officials, the qualifications for participation in the public forum, the rights and responsibilities of a free press, and the boundary between dissent and sedition.

Chapter 3 deals with how Uruguayans confronted dueling as a moral and legal question, and why Congress chose in 1920 to decriminalize it. The chapter examines the ebb and flow of opposition to the duel, the arguments pro and con, and the on-again, off-again, ultimately fruitless effort by the authorities to prevent duels and prosecute duelists. The chapter looks at the 1919–20 legalization debate in the context of ongoing efforts to modernize criminal codes and institutions and in general to extend the rule of law. I argue that decriminalization, paradoxically, can be interpreted as a triumph of legal reform and proof of the growing precedence of codified law over informal customary law. Chapter 3 ends with a look at the immediate – and ambiguous – impact of legalization, which brought a dangerous spike in high-profile duels taking on all the quality of public spectacles but also created procedures that would in time prevent many duels from happening.

Chapter 4 traces the trajectory of dueling in Uruguay from passage of the 1920 Ley de Duelos to the law's repeal in 1992. The chapter looks at the decline of dueling from the 1930s through World War II, the duel's resuscitation between the 1950s and early 1970s as a polarized nation lurched toward military dictatorship, and the definitive end of dueling in the 1990s following Uruguay's return to democracy. I argue that before recriminalization could pass, dueling culture needed to atrophy to the point of near disappearance. Uruguayans had to come to the collective conclusion that the duel was a ridiculous remnant of the past rather than a necessary institution that solved real problems. But in order for that to happen, opponents of the duel needed also to find answers to the underlying concerns that had long justified the duel, offering streamlined legal procedures to deal with insult and defamation. The recriminalization vote reignited old debates about the limits of press freedom, what rules should exist to moderate discourse in the political sphere, the line between legitimate critique and character assassination, and what recourse public figures might employ in defense of their reputations. As interviews in the press with Sanguinetti and Mujica in 1999 and 2017 made clear, not everyone was satisfied with how, in the absence of the duel, Uruguay would henceforth answer those questions, thereby underscoring their continued salience.

Democracy and Partisan Conflict in Uruguay

Uruguayans are invited to skip this section, but for readers who lack familiarity with the country, my intention is to provide a rough interpretive sketch of Uruguayan political history in order to make better sense of the context in which dueling arose and flourished. The sketch begins with the central paradox identified by many scholars but best captured by Fernando López-Alves: that a nineteenth century "ravaged by wars and personalism" in the form of ongoing violent competition between two rival political factions, the Blancos and the Colorados, not only evolved into an unusually stable and comparatively progressive two-party liberal democracy in the twentieth century but, it can be argued, the former created the preconditions for the consolidation of the latter.[35]

The Colorados (reds) and Blancos (whites) were so named for the color of the identifying ribbons that their soldiers wore on the battlefield during a civil conflict known as the Guerra Grande, or Great War (1839–51). Led respectively by their founders Fructuoso Rivera and Manuel Oribe, the Colorados and Blancos were distinguished less by ideology than by regionalism and geopolitical loyalties. The Blancos allied themselves with Argentine dictator Juan Manuel de Rosas and were strongest in Uruguay's interior provinces, while the Colorados defended the capital Montevideo and received support from Rosas's enemies in exile, from brigades of foreigners including one led by Giuseppe Garibaldi, and from the Empire of Brazil. Of the two factions, the Colorados were undoubtedly the more liberal and cosmopolitan: many imagined themselves the party of civilization and progress against Blanco "barbarism."[36] But the Blancos could not really be called conservatives, or at least they did not resemble the classic conservatives that emerged in so many other Latin American countries. They were not militantly pro-clerical, nor did they fight on behalf of traditional institutions or the Spanish heritage. Instead they preached a rustic, somewhat xenophobic libertarianism that insisted on local autonomy and resistance to perceived Colorado overreach.[37]

After the Peace of 1851 put an end to the Guerra Grande "without victors or vanquished," subsequent outbreaks of partisan violence were frequent but usually short-lived affairs that alternated with negotiated power-sharing agreements. The various peace accords created conditions that permitted the Colorados to control the national government for the vast majority of the time, in exchange for ceding a number of departmental governments to the Blancos. In the heat of politics, those truces periodically broke down, and each of the resulting revolutions might shift the power equilibrium one way or the other and lead to renegotiated treaty terms. But even when resulting in serious bloodshed, these were never wars of total elimination, perhaps because questions of power were amenable to compromise in ways that radically incompatible ideological worldviews might not have been.[38]

Complicating the panorama of nineteenth-century Blanco-Colorado conflict was the tension between each party's *doctores*, the educated elites, and their grassroots base of armed, mobilized militiamen and *caudillo* warlords. The power-sharing agreements not only guaranteed Blanco rule in a number of rural departments but they also cemented Blanco control over local patronage, which translated into the ability to elect congressmen and senators. These politicians lived and worked in Montevideo where they interacted with their Colorado counterparts, men with whom they shared affinities of class and education, political antagonism notwithstanding. Out of this milieu, and fortified by a general desire for progress, order, and democratic institution building, there arose intermittent movements to marginalize the caudillos and the militias in order to create modern parties of ideas led by serious men of means and principles. Colorado doctors, too, found themselves often at odds with their own strongmen and willing to cross party lines, at least under certain conditions. On several occasions, these doctors initiated armed uprisings of their own, though more typically this kind of fusionism, also known as *principismo*, played out in efforts to build third-party alternatives to the Blanco-Colorado duopoly. (The best known was the Constitutional Party, formed in 1880). Yet these anti-party initiatives, be they violent or peaceful, were repeatedly destined to fail because their gentlemanly leaders, famously described as "a General Staff without an army," could never wean the masses from primordial Blanco or Colorado identities that had been forged on the battlefield, secured by patronage, and passed from father to son over generations.[39]

Nevertheless, Uruguayan politics did evolve in the late nineteenth century as the regular military gradually strengthened as a force for state building. With rising budgets and better organization and armaments – in part the legacy of Uruguay's participation in the Paraguayan War (1865–70) – the national army began to amass firepower that the militias and caudillos would find ever harder to contest. As the state's administrative capacity also grew, military-backed Colorado governments such as that of Colonel Lorenzo Latorre (1876–80) embarked on a modernization agenda that included the expansion of free secular public education, a reform that over time would lead Uruguay to one of the highest literacy rates in Latin America.[40] Latorre also succeeded, uniquely, in maintaining good relations with both Blanco and Colorado doctors while faithfully holding to the terms of the April 1872 power-sharing agreement and thus keeping the Blanco caudillos in check.[41] For the most part, though, the string of military governments of the later nineteenth century relied on Colorado patronage networks for political support and on Colorado doctors for expertise, while the Blancos, their doctors, and their patronage networks participated as minority partners at the national level while continuing to dominate politics in the provinces under their control. This dynamic helps explain López-Alves's paradox that nineteenth-century conflict created the preconditions for later stability: "It was in the intermeshing of parties and the military, in the shared loyalties of generals and officers who were simultaneously military men and partisans, that the polity evolved into a liberal democracy."[42]

The final step in that evolution was the transition to full civilian rule, which was ultimately consolidated under the government of José Batlle y Ordóñez. Batlle, a Colorado from a long political line, had participated in the failed Quebracho Revolution against General Máximo Santos in 1886, a bipartisan rebellion fighting – as they saw it – for democracy against a dictator. After a gradual return to constitutional rule with the November Conciliation and the election of General Máximo Tajes as Santos's successor, a string of Colorado civilian presidents began with Julio Herrera y Obes (1890–94). The government that followed Herrera, however, ended up sparking (or at least was unable to prevent) yet another old-style partisan rebellion, led by the last of the great Blanco caudillos, Aparicio Saravia, starting in March 1897 and lasting six months. Saravia declared war yet again after Batlle y Ordóñez's election in 1903, and thus it was on Batlle's watch that government forces finally killed Saravia and defeated his gaucho army at the Battle of Masoller the following year.[43] In so doing, José Batlle y Ordóñez, a controversial but monumental force in Uruguayan history and a prominent figure in this book, set the stage for the new kinds of political battles that would characterize the twentieth century.

As things stood by the end of Batlle's first administration (1903–07), Uruguayan politics had developed a singular set of characteristics. The Colorados remained entrenched as a more or less permanent governing party, but within an increasingly competitive political order. They were accused – with some justification – of using state patronage, the armed forces, and the police as partisan resources, as Colorado police chiefs, justices of the peace, and political bosses allegedly prioritized Colorado electoral fortunes over the impartial administration of justice. The Blanco party, which from 1872 onward had officially adopted the name Partido Nacional, developed into a semi-permanent party of opposition while ably leveraging the not-inconsiderable resources that power sharing afforded them. If the Colorados justified their political dominance as bringing civilization, progress, and enlightenment to an otherwise backward and unruly country, the Blancos or Nacionalista perceived themselves as the party of the people against a corrupt ruling machine, as defenders of the provinces against the capital, and as champions of the secret ballot, genuine democracy, individual freedoms, and the rule of law against Colorado electoral fraud and self-dealing.[44]

The interesting point here is the paradox that civil war and caudillo power had created over time the conditions for a kind of rough democratization. Competition between two diverse patronage-based political parties, each commanding intense partisan loyalty and each with its own dense clientelist networks, nurtured a certain social connectedness bordering almost on egalitarianism. Uruguayans were likely to think of themselves as born Blanco or born Colorado, and that birthright gave them access to people with influence and thus to the protections that patrons could bestow on clients. This dynamic was aided by scale: as a small country where everyone knew everyone, Uruguay was and remains the kind of place where a visiting historian can arrange to interview an ex-president with just an introduction or two through the right contacts. By the early twentieth century, those same mechanisms of party clientelism were being employed to access government jobs and contracts, public services, legal representation, or any number of other kinds of favors, including – if conditions required – seconds for a duel.

Uruguay's transformation from a country "ravaged by wars and personalism" to a successful liberal democracy was accompanied by its gradual but inexorable transformation from a frontier nation of ranches and wide-open spaces to a predominantly urban society filled with European immigrants and, increasingly, their educated, Uruguay-born offspring. Montevideo had always been the center of Colorado power, but Batlle y Ordóñez was particularly cognizant of the fact that whatever party was more successful at capturing this flood of new urban voters would have an unprecedented opportunity to consolidate electoral dominance. So in his second administration (1911–15), after a four-year sojourn in Europe, Batlle embarked on an ambitious program of political and social welfare reform from above, unique for its time in Latin America and progressive even by European standards. Batlle's legislative agenda dominated debate in Uruguay for nearly a generation and included everything from civil divorce and abolition of the death penalty to the eight-hour workday, old age pensions, and Batlle's signature political reform, replacement of the presidential system with a Swiss-inspired plural executive called the Colegiado.[45]

Batlle's reforms, and the social forces that his movement, *batllismo*, both unleashed and sought to harness, brought fundamental changes to the dynamic of partisan conflict in Uruguay. New and modern concerns of class-based interest politics injected themselves into Blanco-Colorado electoral competition in ways that were unexpected and lasting. First and foremost, resistance to Batlle's reformism in general and to the Colegiado in particular split the Colorados into militantly pro-Batlle (*batllista*) and anti-Batlle factions. Conservative status-quo Colorados, who were many, found common cause with conservative status-quo Blancos, and together they delayed or watered down some reforms and stymied others. This superimposition of social, ideological, and class conflicts onto Uruguay's historically bifurcated partisan politics elevated the intensity of internal party struggles but also created new opportunities for cross-party cooperation and strategic line-crossing.[46] Generally these shifting factional alliances were tactical and temporary, coalescing around a single issue or in opposition to some unpopular initiative or leader, but deeper and more durable fusions were also possible. The best example here is the government of Gabriel Terra, who in the early 1930s took advantage of bipartisan dissatisfaction with politics-as-usual to implant a "softly" dictatorial de facto regime with the collaboration of key Colorado and Nacionalista figures.[47]

To recap so far: strong party loyalties tracing back to the nineteenth century and passed down through families embedded large numbers of Uruguayans in dense political networks, but those patronage-based affinities had never been rigidly ideological in content, even if they did imbue their adherents with a certain partisan worldview. The emerging philosophical and class cleavages of the twentieth century interacted and combined with those prior party affiliations in ways that could either stack multiple motives for political hatred on top of one another or could cross-cut.[48] Some of the most intense interpersonal clashes in this era occurred when *batllistas*, as reform-oriented Colorados, fought with socially conservative Blancos, or when young radicalized *nacionalistas* faced off against traditional, old-guard Colorados. But nothing precluded bitter conflicts within the parties as well, particularly among Colorados.

The Montevideo press tended to amplify, significantly, both inter-party and intra-party conflict. Through the late nineteenth and early twentieth centuries, there was no *New York Times*–like paper of record. Newspaper business models did nothing to incentivize reliable objectivity and nonpartisanship. Nor was there any single newspaper that became dominant, as was the case with Bartolomé Mitre's *La Nación* in Buenos Aires, the Edwards family's *El Mercurio* in Chile, or the Miró Quesadas' *El Comercio* in Peru. The vast majority of papers were identifiably Blanco or Colorado, and most were associated with a specific party faction or an individual politician. Many came and went as their directors' political fortunes rose or fell.[49] Among those that managed to last for decades, *El Día* was always *batllista*, while *La Mañana* was Colorado but fiercely anti-Batlle. *El País* and *Diario del Plata* were two of the most important Blanco papers. Although virtually all papers were political in one way or another, some crossed Blanco-Colorado lines or reflected other interests. *La Razón* and *El Siglo* in the late nineteenth and early twentieth centuries were associated with *principismo*. *El Bien Público* was self-consciously Catholic, socialists published several papers, and there were periodicals that spoke specifically for and to the Spanish, Italian, French, and English immigrant colonies. And there were a few papers, such as *La Tribuna Popular*, that appear to have been a bit more attuned to the profit motive and sought a diverse readership, occasionally resorting to "extra-extra-read-all-about-it" sensationalism, but that did not stop its editors from engaging politically.

Chapter 4 brings this rough sketch of Uruguayan political history forward into the second half of the twentieth century and provides more detail on the eventual rise of the political left as a third electoral force. Ideological alternatives to the two dominant parties certainly existed in the early decades of the twentieth century, the two most notable being the Socialist Party of Emilio Frugoni and the Unión Cívica led by Catholic activist Joaquín Secco Illa, and both had been influential enough to send a tiny number of members to Congress. Frugoni in particular had earned respect for his independence and erudition, but neither party posed any challenge to Uruguay's dominant two-party order. Only in the 1960s did rising opposition to a string of ultraconservative Colorado administrations lead radicalized young people to abandon the parties they had been born into and join the left. The result was the founding, for the 1971 presidential elections, of the Frente Amplio (Broad Front), whose first presidential candidate, Líber Seregni, was a retired former Colorado general and, as mentioned earlier, a protagonist in Uruguay's last-ever duel.

Dueling in nineteenth- and twentieth-century Uruguay is by no means fully explained by the patterns of partisanship I have sketched here, but those patterns provide essential context. The duel was primarily the domain of the party doctors, though not exclusively so. It appears to be no coincidence that the rise of dueling in the late nineteenth and early twentieth centuries accompanied the growing power of educated men of letters within the Blanco and Colorado parties, as Uruguay evolved from endemic caudillo warfare to a liberal democracy with its own unique configuration of political conflict. The lion's share of duels and challenges found a Blanco on one side and a Colorado on the other, with each relying on their closest party companions as seconds. But duels between members of opposing factions within the two major parties were not at all rare. It is easy to see how duels might arise from the sense of betrayal engendered whenever internal discord fragmented the traditional parties, or whenever self-styled independents broke with those colleagues who insisted on party loyalty, come what may. Moments of rising political tension tended to see an increase in duels, but there is no ironclad correlation, and duels might well decline when things crossed the threshold into open warfare. The correlation that appears clearest is between the frequency of dueling and the level of vitriol in the public sphere, on the floor of Congress and in the daily press. The next two chapters explore why.

I

The Laws of Honor

The Code of Honor is the code of supreme law; of law that underpins dignity, respect, nobility, and personal and social respect among civilized peoples.

Pedro Federico Coral Luzzi, *Código de honor* (1950)[1]

When he picked up the paper and read the words "Coward! Coward! Coward!" in boldface, David Buchelli realized that his week-long argument with Salvatore Nicosía had spiraled out of control, with potentially serious consequences.[2] No longer could he respond as he had to Nicosía's previous columns, brushing off the editor of *L'Indipendente* as a nobody, an arrogant parvenu, a recently arrived adventurer whose claim to speak for Uruguay's Italian community was preposterous. Now people were following the escalating insults in the press, and the early spring air of September 1883 had become charged with anticipation: would there be a duel? Would it be Buchelli who finally challenged Nicosía, or would the representative for the Department of Florida keep stalling until Nicosía forced the issue and sent seconds of his own?

Nicosía wanted a duel: that was obvious. Ever since Buchelli had ill-advisedly insulted the memory of Giuseppe Garibaldi in a speech on Independence Day, Salvatore "Totó" Nicosía had been ratcheting up the invective, clearly hoping to incite Buchelli to challenge him.[3] At the age of twenty-eight, the Italian journalist had already fought a dozen duels in at least four different countries across Southern Europe and the Balkans, a record he wore as a badge of honor. Practically upon his arrival in South America, Nicosía had fought a duel in Buenos Aires, and now in Montevideo he prepared for another, ostensibly to defend the memory of Garibaldi.[4] He believed that any insult to "*il cavaliere dell'umanità*," the hero of the Risorgimento, was an insult to Italy and to all true Italians. And given that Nicosía's own travels, both intellectual and geographical, followed Garibaldi's with uncanny precision, small surprise that he took Buchelli's criticism of Garibaldi personally. More cynical observers suspected that Nicosía mostly wanted to make a quick name for himself in the New World, having frittered away what little remained of his family fortune in the Old, or at very least that he sought to boost the circulation of his forty-days-young newspaper.[5]

Buchelli, for his part, had no interest in giving the Italian hothead the satisfaction he sought, for a number of reasons. Unlike his adversary, Buchelli was untrained in arms and had never fought a duel or received a challenge. One reporter described him as a "*bon bourgeois*, who, though firm in his opinions, tolerates those of his adversaries and would rather live in peace and work for the good of his country and his family than provoke disagreeable incidents."[6] Not only was he the devoted father of eleven children but he was also devoutly Catholic, and the church had unrelentingly condemned dueling for some six hundred years, give or take a century. The Montevideo clergy and Catholic press had campaigned against the duel on several prior occasions, invoking not only moral arguments but also legal ones. As long as Uruguay lacked a post-Independence criminal code of its own, the old Spanish laws remained in force, and the 1805 Novísima Recopilación de las Leyes treated dueling as a serious crime.[7]

Convincing as all these factors were, Buchelli had yet another powerful reason for refusing to duel with Nicosía: he simply did not see why he should have to answer for his words. He believed, and many Uruguayans agreed, that he had every right to debate the historical merit of a man who had been controversial on both sides of the Atlantic.[8] The idea that an unfavorable opinion of Garibaldi was an insult to all Italians was ludicrous to him. Buchelli was himself the proud son of an Italian father, but as both a Catholic and a Blanco he had every reason to oppose the posthumous apotheosis of the anticlerical freemason who, during his years in Uruguayan exile, had commanded forces fighting for the Colorado enemy in the Guerra Grande. No wonder Buchelli had argued passionately in the House of Representatives (Cámara de Representantes) against commissioning a statue to Garibaldi, and no wonder he had repeated those words on Independence Day.

Buchelli could scarcely be more dismayed, therefore, by the dark turn of events. The argument had grown so ugly that all of Montevideo was now watching, and verbal barbs were no longer appropriate. Nicosía was openly accusing him of cowardice, of "insulting the dead but lacking the courage to measure himself against the living."[9] Now only two solutions were open to him: a legal denunciation for alleged defamation, or a duel. Mindful that Nicosía wanted to goad him into the latter, Buchelli chose the former, latching onto the fact that the editor of *L'Indipendente* had described him in print as the kind of villain whose only tools were "an assassin's knife and a hundred pesos to pay a *sicario*" (hit man).[10] Such a charge surely had to be a crime. Buchelli knew, however, that he might still be forced to accept a duel. As he told one interviewer: "I am not prepared to allow the staining of my honor, and my children will never be able one day to say about me, 'Having been challenged, he ran from the fight.'"[11]

Totó Nicosía received news of the criminal accusation with indignation. In his mind – and many agreed – true gentlemen did not appeal to the courts when honor was at stake. Such offenses had only one remedy, and that remedy lay in the "gentlemanly laws" as set down in the dueling codes. Only a man without valor would do otherwise. Believing now that no insult, no matter how brutal, could convince the congressman to do the right thing, Nicosía felt he had no choice but to force the issue himself, so he sent his seconds, Felipe Polleri and Salvador Ingenieros, to present Buchelli with the traditional ultimatum: either "explain" his offense or provide "reparation through arms."

Buchelli's position was difficult but not yet impossible: he hoped he might still avoid a duel without dishonoring himself. According to colleagues who understood the fine points of the honor code, the *diputado* (House member) still held one card: the fact that his criminal accusation against Nicosía was now pending in the courts. Depending on the outcome of that defamation case, either Nicosía was a slanderer and hence lacking the requisite honor to challenge anyone to a duel, or else Buchelli was an employer of assassins, and thus a man with whom Nicosía could not accept a duel. In short, Buchelli was led to believe that no duel was possible as long as the criminal accusation remained unresolved.

Thus appraised of his rights under the "laws of honor," Buchelli set into motion the preliminaries required by dueling protocol, thereby avoiding the appearance of cowardice, while at the same time his spirit remained buoyed by the thought that he quite possibly would never have to confront the swordsman from Messina. He named as his seconds Abdón Aróstegui and José Cándido Bustamante, both veteran politicians well acquainted with the duel.[12] Buchelli instructed his seconds to accept a duel only under one condition: that Nicosía formally and publicly retract the charge that he, Buchelli, was an employer of assassins. He surely assumed Nicosía would never accede to such a demand – after all, in the unwritten code of Uruguayan journalism, retraction was capitulation.

Before hearing the outcome of the negotiations between his seconds and those of Nicosía, Buchelli received an urgent visit from his priest, Monsignor Isaza, who implored him to reject the duel as immoral, illegal, barbarous, and anti-Christian. Buchelli may well have been moved by the monsignor's impassioned entreaty or convinced that to defy his church – not to mention the law – would invite dire consequences. Alternatively, he may have remained confident that his seconds, following his instructions and in accordance with their reading of the code of honor, were not about to agree to any duel. Whatever the reason, Buchelli made a promise to Father Isaza that he would not duel with Nicosía.[13] Later that day, however, Arósteguy and Bustamante reported on their negotiations, and despite Buchelli's instructions, they had in fact consented to a duel. As directed, they had refused at first, citing their interpretation of the honor code and insisting that no duel was permitted until Nicosía retracted the offensive words. Nicosía's seconds, however, countered with equally convincing arguments, similarly justified by the honor codes. They contended that by the very fact of having challenged Buchelli, Nicosía implicitly retracted the charge of "employer of assassins." After all, they reasoned, to agree to a duel is by definition to accept one's adversary as a worthy and honorable man, and no one would ever so consider an employer of *sicarios*. By the same token, they argued that Buchelli, by naming his seconds and allowing them to enter into gentlemanly negotiations, had also implicitly conceded that Nicosía was a man of honor and therefore could not be a slanderer. In other words, the challenge itself and its acceptance removed all impediments to a duel. By that reasoning, any continued refusal on Buchelli's part could only be motivated by one thing: cowardice.[14] Ultimately, Bustamante and Arósteguy came to the conclusion that as men of honor they could not refute Ingenieros and Polleri's reasoning, which they themselves found compelling. Nicosía's seconds had called Buchelli's apparent bluff, leaving Bustamante and Arósteguy little choice but to proceed with the duel or dishonor themselves. That Buchelli had not authorized them to accept a duel was irrelevant: by naming them as his seconds, he had entrusted himself to their judgment. Buchelli was now faced with a terrible dilemma: on the one hand, few violations of the honor code were more odious than backing out of a duel once agreed upon. On the other hand, how could he possibly break his promise to Monsignor Isaza? Forced to choose between his faith and his honor, Buchelli chose faith, a decision that may have saved his soul and his skin, but at an enormous cost.

The fallout from Buchelli's refusal to duel was swift and devastating. On the morning of 10 September 1883, following a couple of days of rumor and speculation, the Montevideo papers treated their readers to the details everyone had been waiting for. They published the formal record of negotiations between the seconds, the exchange of letters between Buchelli and his representatives, and the somewhat embarrassed letter in which Bustamante and Aróstegui announced Buchelli's refusal to duel and offered to take to the dueling ground in his place, as the "gentlemanly laws" demanded.[15] Nicosía respectfully declined their offer. Now in full damage-control mode, Buchelli tried to defend his decision. First he reiterated his original position, that he had in fact wanted to duel but refused to set foot on the field of honor until Nicosía took back the "employer of assassins" charge. In effect, he accused his seconds of overstepping their mandate by agreeing to a duel without the prior retraction.[16] This argument did not convince anyone. His own seconds, after all, had accepted the idea that Nicosía's challenge amounted to a de facto retraction. More importantly, the dueling codes made it crystal clear that Bustamante and Aróstegui had every authority to negotiate on Buchelli's behalf, and that he was honor bound to abide by their decisions, duel or no duel. Indeed, this principle of the seconds' absolute authority was a cornerstone of the entire superstructure of dueling. By criticizing his seconds, Buchelli only succeeded in insulting and angering them more than he already had.[17]

Buchelli then belatedly turned to the more reasonable argument, that he simply could not violate his Catholic faith and his promise to Monsignor Isaza. "Is a father," he wrote, "who owes his life to his country and to his family, allowed to hand over that life to the first swashbuckler who happens to come by and ask him for it?"[18] By finally standing on principle rather than attempting to finesse the honor code, Buchelli succeeded in enlisting some influential supporters. Father Isaza sent a letter to the papers corroborating that he had indeed called upon Buchelli at his home and had insisted that he promise not to duel. Isaza contended that by defying social convention and holding to a higher moral standard, Buchelli had demonstrated more courage than any duelist: "Today more than ever I consider you worthy of my friendship and of my highest esteem, and you can count on having risen greatly in the opinion of good and thinking people. That you are not an assassin, that you are a valiant man and a gentleman, is clear to everyone."[19]

Unfortunately for Buchelli, this profession of faith and invocation of law and morality came too late to convince those who believed him a coward. After all, he could have turned the other cheek instead of matching Nicosía insult for insult for over a week. He could have cited his religious convictions and refused to duel from the outset rather than naming seconds and later reneging on their agreement, and he could have been consistent in his explanations. Having done none of these things, he failed to convince most people that his scruples were sincere, leaving only one other explanation. As *El Hilo Eléctrico* caustically remarked: "No blood was spilled, but there have been victims … of ridicule."[20]

But no matter how egregious Buchell's transgression of the laws of honor, few could have predicted what would happen next. In a move that surprised nearly everyone, the Cámara de Representantes named an ad hoc commission to approach Buchelli informally and ask him to resign his seat. When Buchelli predictably refused, the Cámara met in secret session and voted to expel him, justifying their action by accusing him of having demanded a payoff of 2,500 gold pesos as the price of his resignation. This demand, according to the other Congress members, justified his removal on the grounds of "physical or moral incapacity," in accordance with Article 52 of the Constitution.[21] Abdón Arósteguy, who only days earlier had taken on what he now called the "thankless job" of representing Buchelli as his second, supported the expulsion and left no doubt the reason why. "I believe," he wrote in a letter to the House a few days later, "that the religion I profess is not in conflict with the duel. In order to be a Catholic gentleman, one must be a gentleman first and foremost, and the coward is no gentleman."[22]

Debate on the Buchelli matter exploded in the wake of his expulsion. A few papers applauded the action: *La Nación* advised Buchelli to "go home, work honorably, and stop thinking about ever again being a representative of the people."[23] But independent and opposition papers were highly critical, and many were appalled at how trumped up the charges against Buchelli were.[24] Few believed he had solicited money; Buchelli himself reported that it was the other representatives, not he, who had broached the idea of a payoff, that the figure of 2,500 gold pesos corresponded to the outstanding salary rightly due him, and that he had rejected the offer.[25] But even if Buchelli had agreed to resign for a price, argued *El Siglo*, he had done so in a confidential conversation with a group of congressmen acting as private citizens with no official status or authority. To invoke this private conversation to formulate a public charge against him was therefore an illegal and immoral act of betrayal.[26] *El Telégrafo Marítimo* went so far as to call the Cámara's action "nauseating."[27]

So the stated reasons for Buchelli's expulsion were clearly spurious.[28] But how legitimate was the *real* reason, his alleged cowardice? That the House of Representatives had felt the need to fabricate bogus charges against him appeared to be an admission that lack of valor was not, legally, a disqualification for public office. If it were, Buchelli joked, he would hardly be the only one expelled.[29] He and his supporters went even further, wondering out loud how it was possible, given that dueling was a crime, to find "moral incapacity" in a refusal to violate the law. As *El Bien Público* had argued a few days earlier, "It seems that there are those who are leveling charges against Buchelli and even considering him dishonored. Why? Because he committed the crime of accepting a duel? No! Because he rejected the duel, a crime that is expressly, categorically and severely punished by the laws of the Republic. This is the height of absurdity!"[30] In the end, neither Buchelli's entreaties nor the strongly worded objections of the independent press made any difference. The decision had been made. Buchelli was out, deprived of his seat and stripped of his parliamentary immunity.

And here is where the story took its final and most bizarre turn. At the very moment that the gentlemen of the Cámara de Representantes were considering whether or not to expel Buchelli for backing out of the duel, Judge Narciso del Castillo issued an order for the arrest of Nicosía and his seconds on charges of dueling, and sent to the House a request that Buchelli, Bustamante, and Aróstegui be stripped of their parliamentary immunity so that they, too, could face justice. For the judge, it did not matter that no duel had actually been fought, because Spanish criminal statutes, which still retained the force of law in Uruguay, equally punished the act of issuing or accepting a challenge. The *fiscal*[31] Carlos Muñoz Anaya made this intention clear: "The provocation and acceptance of a duel constitutes, according to the law, a public crime, in fact one of the crimes that social justice should repress most aggressively. The duel is a custom in conflict with the progress of our age ... and with the collective interest of all civilized societies."[32] So as soon as Buchelli ceased to be a member of Congress and lost his immunity, he was arrested for the very crime he had paid such a high price to avoid committing. On the afternoon of 17 September 1883, he was detained as he walked out of the Confitería Liguria and taken to a collective holding cell in the Central Police Station.[33]

Buchelli was treated with respect, allowed to meet with friends, family, and the press, and could easily have walked out had he agreed to pay bail. But this he refused to do, believing that it would be tantamount to accepting his expulsion from the Cámara and the removal of his parliamentary immunity. "What has been done to me," he lamented, "is an infamy without a name."[34] Bustamante and Aróstegui asked their colleagues to adhere to the judge's request and take away their own immunity as well, but the gentlemen of the

Fig. 1.1 Statue of Giuseppe Garibaldi, Montevideo, 1933. Centro de Fotografía de Montevideo.

House predictably turned them down.[35] Meanwhile the ever-critical *La Nación* gleefully cheered Buchelli's fate as a "prisoner for cowardice."[36]

A few days later, after giving his statement to police investigators, Buchelli broke down and permitted his passionate defender Dr Zorrilla de San Martín, publisher of *El Bien Público*, to pay his bail. In the end the judge and *fiscal* dropped all charges against the erstwhile duelists – one can assume that their intention from the beginning had only been to make a point rather than to send four or six highly respectable citizens to jail for any significant period of time. Nicosía, after a hero's welcome from the Círculo Napolitano, returned to his paper and his polemics, soon embroiling himself in yet more duels. Buchelli, for his part, fruitlessly petitioned the House and later the Senate to get his expulsion overturned; his requests were filed away without the courtesy of a response.[37] He returned to private life on his estate, his career in national politics over, while the Garibaldi statue got the government's go-ahead.[38]

The story of David Buchelli introduces many of the themes of this book. The first question is why a parliamentary debate over commissioning a statue could end up having such a strange and disastrous outcome. Why did Nicosía seek to force a duel with Buchelli over such a trivial matter? Why did Nicosía first wait for Buchelli to challenge *him*, and how did he justify turning around and sending his seconds after it became clear that Buchelli would not take the bait? Why did Buchelli pay such a high price for his refusal to duel, despite the fact that so many people recognized Nicosía's provocations for the self-serving bullying that they were? Why were Bustamante and Aróstegui so enraged when Buchelli reneged on their agreement to duel, even though that agreement clearly went against their previous understanding with him? Why did Monsignor Isaza's passionate and reasoned defense of Buchelli count for so little? How could the House of Representatives take the rash and extreme action of expelling Buchelli from their institution when their flimsy legal justification was so transparently contrived?

To comprehend these actions and the thinking behind them requires that we reconstruct the mental universe that late nineteenth-century Uruguayans brought to their debates about the duel. It is necessary to understand the motivations of duelists, to understand not only when and why they fought duels but also when and why they did not, why some duels were deemed inevitable while others were criticized as frivolous and irresponsible. It is equally necessary to recapture the worldview of the duel's opponents and to understand the responses that they gave when asked how one might conduct public affairs *without* the duel. It is an error to assume that all or even most of the answers lie in some deep-rooted medieval Spanish conception of honor; far more salient were the specific conditions created by the rise of a free press and the competitive politics of the nineteenth and early twentieth centuries.

One of this book's arguments is that the code of honor – the formal rules and regulations set down in the dueling manuals – constituted a virtual code of law, with all of the complexities and much of the compulsive force of genuine, state-sanctioned law. These "gentlemanly laws" or "laws of honor" governed far more than the act of confronting another man with a deadly weapon; they provided a detailed, coherent, comprehensive guide to social intercourse for men who lived and worked in the public eye. The "laws" did not demand that everyone become a swordsman; they allowed space for conscientious objectors who could refuse on principle to participate in the culture of the duel. But conscientious objectors, like everyone else, still had to conduct their public lives in accordance with those laws: there were acceptable and unacceptable ways to engage in political debate, acceptable and unacceptable ways to end a heated argument, acceptable and unacceptable justifications for declining a duel.

The second major issue raised by the Buchelli affair is the contradictory yet strangely symbiotic relationship between dueling "law" and Uruguay's written laws and statutes. An obvious question raised by the Buchelli case was how anyone could consider the refusal to duel a moral disqualification for public office when dueling was in fact a criminal offense. How could the gentlemen of the House on the one hand, and the judge and *fiscal* on the other, have such enormously divergent perspectives on dueling? How did the congressmen – many of whom were themselves lawyers (and a few of them eminent scholars of jurisprudence) – justify what all of them recognized to be an unlawful activity? How could the judges seek to enforce the law and prevent the duel when the key shapers of public opinion were so clearly set against them? How was this gulf between law and practice ultimately bridged, if indeed it ever was?

But the contradiction between criminal law and "gentlemanly law" was nuanced by the way in which the two laws coexisted and interacted. Take, for example, Buchelli's decision to bring Nicosía to court for slander rather than answer his insults with a challenge to a duel. At one level, this was a perfect case of forum shopping. Nicosía hoped Buchelli would choose the informal if no less minutely regulated jurisdiction of the dueling codes, and was incensed when he chose instead to turn to the law courts and the defamation provisions of Uruguay's 1867 Code of Criminal Procedure (Código de Instrucción Criminal). Buchelli sought redress in the legal arena because he felt he had the advantage there. But even more interesting is that Buchelli's decision to push matters into the arena of formal legality had a concrete effect on the way in which his confrontation with Nicosía played out in the realm of the honor codes. According to Buchelli's reading of those codes, the legal charges pending against Nicosía temporarily disqualified him as a duelist. The response by Nicosía's seconds depended on a different reading of the dueling codes. As we will see, there was nothing unusual about this kind of interplay. Not only was forum shopping commonplace but legal strategies could influence dueling strategies and vice versa.

The disagreement between Nicosía and Buchelli over the interpretation of dueling law leads to a third theme of this book: the tension between the dueling ideal, as set out in the honor codes, and the actual behavior of specific duelists in concrete circumstances. Just like actual laws, the dueling codes envisioned proper norms of moral conduct and sought to prevent or punish actions that violated those norms. They were designed to create a mechanism to deter people from attacking one another's honor, and if that failed, to reconcile the antagonists through a ritualistic assertion of equality and mutual respect, a ritual that sometimes – but only sometimes – included a cleansing trial by ordeal. In this chapter we will see exactly how the ritual was designed to function, both as deterrent and as reconciliation. But the "laws of honor" enunciated in the dueling codes, just like other laws, were frequently tested, bent, pushed to the limits, and violated outright. Furthermore, Uruguayans debated how to interpret the honor codes as they applied general rules to unique cases. Did Nicosía really have the right to treat Buchelli's comments concerning Garibaldi as an offense of the type that merited a dueling challenge? Was it legitimate for Buchelli to demand that Nicosía retract the charge of "employer of assassins" before any duel could take place? These were issues on which reasonable people could and did disagree.

The next chapter looks at some of these typical disputes in matters of dueling "law." Wrapped up in these arguments were the most basic questions that could confront any liberal democracy, particularly a young democracy characterized by a high level of political conflict. How do you preserve a free press and yet still prevent libel, incitement to riot, or even treason? What are the limits to legitimate public debate? How do you distinguish between criticism of a man's public actions and defamation of the man himself? When does a challenge to a duel constitute intimidation? Who has the proper standing to demand "satisfaction" on behalf of a collectivity, such as a nation or a political party? Similar issues were taken up on many occasions by the framers of Uruguay's constitution, criminal code, press codes, and other laws and statutes, but historians cannot fully understand those political-legal debates unless they also factor in the ways that the "laws of honor" confronted identical questions. Uruguayans forged norms of democracy and public debate on two separate but intersecting planes: of course they wrote (and repeatedly rewrote) the laws dealing with press freedom, defamation, and legal responsibility. But they also debated the exact same issues every time two pairs of seconds wrangled over whether certain words gave just cause for a duel, or whether a public official charged with misconduct was required first to clear his name before he could be considered respectable enough to meet his accuser on the "field of honor." The assumptions and principles embodied in the honor codes deeply influenced the men who debated the formal legal codes, and in so doing helped shape the contours of modern Uruguayan democracy.[39]

The Origins of Dueling "Law"

As early as the sixteenth century, Italian authors began to commit to paper the principles that governed the so-called "point of honor." By the nineteenth century, similar treatises had appeared in many countries, but the code that became the model for nineteenth-century duelists worldwide was the Comte de Chateauvillard's *Essai sur le duel*, first published in Paris in 1836 and reprinted countless times in several languages, Spanish among them.[40] Chateauvillard brought two fundamental innovations to the genre: first was his explicit effort to civilize the practice, by discouraging duels under potentially deadly conditions and by emphasizing the seconds' role as mediators, whose first duty was to seek an honorable reconciliation. Second was his code's notable legalism, exemplified in the logic of its structure and the precision of its language. In his words, "If the code of the Duel is outside the law ... we should nonetheless give that name to the rules imposed by honor, because honor is no less sacred than governmental laws."[41] These two characteristics – the civilizing intention and the legalistic framework – were reproduced in the scores of dueling codes written throughout Europe and the Americas over the course of the subsequent century. These codes, each reflecting the idiosyncrasies of its author, might disagree on the preferred type of weapon or on which practices should be expressly prohibited, but all shared a common doctrinal base, rooted in clear and explicit principles that were amply disseminated and widely understood.[42]

To the untrained eye, the codes might be dismissed simply as books of dueling etiquette. They explained how a challenge should be made, how to choose seconds, the distinct grades of offense (mild, serious, grave), the rights that the offended party enjoyed depending on the seriousness of offense, how to choose arms and position the combatants on the dueling ground, and even the fine points of dress for a fencing or a pistol duel. But these dueling codes were not mere etiquette books; they were deliberately modeled after legal codes, precisely to prevent any "crime" from being perpetrated in the guise of a duel. "When is a duel legal?" asked the Argentine author of one code, answering, "When the procedures followed in its planning strictly adhere to the dictates of the Code of Honor and when the duel is carried out in rigid conformity with the conditions agreed to by the seconds."[43]

How could advocates call the duel legal when it most certainly was not? Following Chateauvillard's example, they did so by writing honor codes expressly in the form of laws. Some codes underwent a drafting process not unlike that of actual legal codes: their authors formed a "commission" of notables, including congressmen, top military officials, and other important public figures, to whom they submitted the draft for comment and criticism. The "report" of the commission then appeared as a foreword or appendix to the published version. Other codes, again following Chateauvillard, came accompanied by long lists of prominent individuals who had given it their "vote" of endorsement.[44] One Uruguayan honor code, written in 1950, was minutely tailored to conform to the provisions of Uruguayan and Argentine law dealing with the duel. Articles from the two countries' criminal codes were reproduced verbatim in the dueling code, interspersed with the latter's own provisions, underscoring the author's clear intention that the two very different kinds of law be given equal weight.[45] All the various different honor codes made clear that to violate dueling law was to exile oneself from the community of respectable public men; not only was the transgressor dishonored and barred from any future duels but if the violation was serious enough, he was to be treated as a criminal. Many codes used the word "felon" to describe an individual who sought unfair advantage in a duel and asked seconds to report disloyal duelists to the authorities as common assassins.[46]

So even if the honor codes were in truth nothing more than the individual creations of their authors, approved by no legislature and enforced by no government, they nevertheless carried much of the authority of actual law, at least among the community of duelists. That was the whole point. Legalistic protocol, moreover, guided each and every step in the dueling process. The honor codes not only established a set of principles to govern affairs of honor but also provided a clear and explicit procedural guide. Indeed, much of the ill will toward David Buchelli arose not so much from his refusal to duel per se as from his many serious violations of that protocol.

The Honor Code in Action: Manual for the Compleat Duelist

Dueling codes had two primary functions: first, to deter or punish those who would commit offenses against another's honor, and second, to provide a ritual leading to eventual reconciliation. For that reason, no dueling code started off with a discussion of the actual duel. Instead, the codes began by defining what was meant by an offense against honor. Physical contact of any sort constituted the most serious affront; to touch another man in anger, however slightly, was to commit an offense *por vías de hecho*, the highest level of infraction envisioned in the codes. Verbal insults were graded according to their severity and their circumstances – all else being equal, an unprovoked insult was worse than an insult given in the heat of an escalating discussion, and an insult vented in public, either through the press or in front of witnesses, was worse than an insult given in private.[47] Offenses against the honor of a woman – be it an improper pass, a crude comment, or a cheeky glance – were taken seriously indeed, and the responsibility for responding to such offenses fell to the husband or father or brother who exercised authority over the woman involved.

When one individual believed that he had been offended by another, his first course of action was to ask two trusted friends to act as his seconds. This was done by means of a *carta-poder*, the dueling equivalent of a power of attorney, whereby he formally authorized the seconds to issue a challenge on his behalf and to act as his representatives in any negotiations that might follow. A typical *carta-poder* looked something like this:

> Esteemed friends,
> My honor having been offended by _____ in his editorial entitled _____ published in _____ on the day of _____, I bid you present yourself before said gentleman and request a full and complete explanation, or, in its absence, reparation by arms.
>   Allow this letter to serve as authorization toward that end, and accept my highest appreciation.

Although the *carta-poder* was the initial step toward a duel, the honor codes emphasized the seconds' duty to seek an honorable and preferably nonviolent resolution. Therefore, when they first approached the offending party, their mission was to respectfully demand "explanations." Upon receipt of the seconds' demand, the antagonist had two options: he could apologize, typically by

MONTEVIDEO, a 12 de Marzo de 1953.-

Sres. Dr. Alberto Abdala y Washington Fernández.-

Mis estimados amigos:
Habiendo sido retado a duelo por el Señor Héctor Álvarez Cina, les ruego que asuman mi representación ante los Sres. Dr. Antonio G. Fusco y Orestes Lanza, designados por aquél en calidad de padrinos.
A este efecto les otorgo amplios poderes.

Los saluda afectuosamente.

Fdo.- Luis Batlle Berres.-

Fig. 1.2 *Carta-poder*, or dueling "power of attorney," dated 12 March 1953. The author of the letter had just received a visit from the seconds of his adversary and was now authorizing seconds of his own to enter into negotiations with them. Archivo General de la Nación, Archivo Histórico, Montevideo, Colección Luis Batlle Berres. Photo by author.

issuing a standard formulaic statement that he recognized his adversary as a gentleman and that his intention had never been to offend. Alternatively, he could refuse to retract, and thus push the process to the next stage – negotiations for a duel.

Whenever "explanations" were given, the seconds communicated the message in writing to their *ahijado* (literally, "godson"), and sometimes also sent the *carta-poder* and their report to the newspapers, to let the world know that honor had now been redeemed. Most of the time, at least on the surface, retractions appear to have been sincerely given. After being challenged to a duel by Alberto Costa Podestá, dentist José Guerra's seconds reported that he "declared himself most surprised that offensive statements about you had been attributed to him, adding that he had never expressed himself in any such manner, that he would denounce anyone who said otherwise, and that he had the highest opinion of your character as a gentleman."[48] But that is not to say there were no exceptions to the rule. Assuming that this 1872 newspaper account was not apocryphal (which it very well might have been), a congressman in some unidentified country headed off an anticipated demand for explanations by sending his adversary the following letter:

> My Esteemed and Appreciated Sir:
> In the heat of improvisation in my speech, I said various things that were offensive to you, and that now, more serene, I lament having said. Although we are political adversaries, that does not mean that you should not be treated with the courtesy and consideration that you deserve; but my character is such that when I hear someone say barbarities and bull-headed stupidities like the ones you uttered in your simplistic oration, I simply cannot contain myself, and my response oversteps the bounds of propriety. Please forgive me.[49]

Public reaction to the giving of explanations varied from case to case. A man too willing to take back his words might be presumed a coward, particularly if the antecedents were sufficiently nasty and protracted that the retraction was interpreted as submission. If a politician or journalist gained a reputation for avoiding duels, he was perceived as weak and could expect more insults to follow.[50] But just as often, the giving of explanations brought no dishonor, for two reasons. First, the formulaic assertion that "there had been no intention to offend" fell short of a total apology, and people appreciated that a gentleman might say or do something in the heat of the moment that on sober reflection he could regret. But, more than that, the giving of explanations was not dishonorable because the dueling codes compelled the seconds to seek precisely that kind of reconciliation. A challenge that ended in a retraction was, by the logic of the dueling codes, a success: the offense was repaired and honor restored. Indeed, one honor code advised against even mentioning in the original *carta-poder* the eventual possibility of "reparation by arms." The initial discussion, the author argued, should be strictly limited to the request for explanations, and only if satisfaction was refused should anyone initiate talk about a duel.[51]

Buchelli could have answered Nicosía's seconds by giving the explanations demanded, and in retrospect he should have. He could have cited his Catholic convictions for not dueling and he could have argued that his thoughts on

Garibaldi were not intended to offend either the Italian community in general or Nicosía personally. Some would have read his retraction as cowardice, and the honor codes did not compel Nicosía to accept his explanation. But had Buchelli acted this way, in accordance with the laws of the duel, it would have been almost unthinkable for the House of Representatives to expel him as they did.

That the giving of explanations could be viewed either as a sign of weakness or as a magnamimous and gentlemanly act is well illustrated by a case that occurred in Montevideo in 1905. The Blanco intellectual Carlos Roxlo had written an article that two military officers took to impugn the valor of the Uruguayan army. When asked for explanations, Roxlo made it clear that he had intended to say no such thing: that he praised equally the bravery of the Uruguayan regular army and of the Blanco militias that had fought against it in prior civil wars. According to reports of the meeting, "From that instant the conversation ... took on a tone of gentlemanly cordiality." Nevertheless, Roxlo asked the officials to declare in writing that they did not attribute to weakness his giving of explanations, and that they accepted his explanation that he recognized as a gentleman that the laws of honor did not permit him to offend without just motive. The officials gave Roxlo their assent.[52]

If a man who was challenged refused to give explanations, he now needed to choose *his* seconds, issuing a *carta-poder* of his own empowering them to act as his representatives and to negotiate on his behalf. The four seconds met soon thereafter, first exchanging their respective *cartas-poder* to ritually verify their authority as delegates of the principals. They then sat down and studied the origins of the case, in order to determine the seriousness of the offense, to see if some reconciliation was possible or, if necessary, to decide the precise conditions under which the duel would be fought. At this stage of negotiations, a duel could often still be avoided, and many were. Sometimes the seconds collectively determined that the alleged offense that sparked the challenge was insufficient cause for a duel. Sometimes they declared that offenses were mutual and called on both sides to offer explanations.[53] Other times they consented to a duel.

Whatever the seconds' agreement, duel or no duel, the principals were honor bound to abide by that decision without hesitation or recrimination. Absent this principle of the seconds' total authority, the honor code could not function, because the seconds would be deprived of their all-important power to mediate. In theory, this power was absolute: indeed, the codes prohibited any direct contact whatsoever between the two principals while the seconds' negotiations were in progress.[54] In practice, seconds were often accused of abdicating that responsibility and deferring overmuch to the wishes of the men they represented.[55] Ultimately the point may be moot: a man hell-bent on a duel could always seek out seconds known for partisanship and bellicosity, just as a man hoping to avert combat would choose seconds known for their peacemaking skills. Still, every once in a while, duelists and seconds had a falling-out. David Buchelli ran afoul of his representatives when he declined a duel to which they had agreed. The opposite – that someone intent upon fighting a duel refused to accept his seconds' reconciliation – was more common.[56] In some cases, frustrated duelists in this situation enlisted two new seconds to deliver a fresh ultimatum, ostensibly in response to a new and different offense. None of these exceptions, however, disproves the general rule that seconds were supposed to exercise complete authority and their judgment was to be honored without question.

The seconds' negotiations were serious matters, not to be entrusted to amateurs. More often than not, they could all agree when a duel was in order. But when disputes did arise, they could be serious, and talks might go on for hours or even require several meetings over a day or two. Occasionally the failure to come to an agreement aborted a duel altogether.[57] Most disagreements revolved around whether or not an action that one party interpreted as an offense against his honor could objectively be so considered. If the insult was more imaginary than real, the seconds for the man who had been wrongly accused of offending had every right to reject a duel, and if the challenger continued to press the issue, the honor codes declared that *he* now became the offender and forfeited some of his rights.[58] But seconds could disagree on many things: the seriousness of an offense, who had offended first, whether an individual was sufficiently honorable to issue a challenge, whether a duelist previously injured on the right arm could be compelled to fence with his left, who was required to travel when the antagonists lived in different places. The possibilities were nearly endless.

The honor codes established several principles to guide seconds in their discussions. The most basic rule was that the victim of the perceived offense, the man who felt his honor had been impugned – in other words, the man who had first enlisted seconds to demand explanations – had the right to request a duel under conditions that *he* specified, be it pistols or sabers, two shots or three at twenty paces or thirty, how many fencing rounds of what duration, and so on.[59] In actuality, it was a little more complicated: the severity of the affront determined whether the offended party got to impose the conditions of the duel

Fig. 1.3 Duel between Enrique Areco and Luis Batlle Berres, 14 March 1922. Archivo General de la Nación, Archivo Histórico, Montevideo, Colección Luis Batlle Berres.

in their entirety, or whether he was limited to choosing the type of weapons to be used. The important point is that the *challenger* usually determined the conditions of the duel.[60]

That right was not absolute, however. Even if seconds accepted that their man was the offender, they remained free to reject dueling conditions that they considered unfair or inappropriate, because an equally important rule required that the details of the duel be calibrated to the original offense. The more egregious the affront, the more dangerous the duel was allowed and expected to be, and the stronger the presumption that the offended party could impose conditions unilaterally. The milder the offense, the more the seconds were expected to avoid a duel, or at least to ensure that the rules of combat made serious bloodshed unlikely. A third principle guiding the seconds was the concept of equality: they were to make every effort to remove any advantage one duelist might have over the other. So if one duelist had superior fencing skills, the seconds for the other had the legitimate right to request a pistol duel instead.[61] Finally, both pairs of seconds were expected to act with

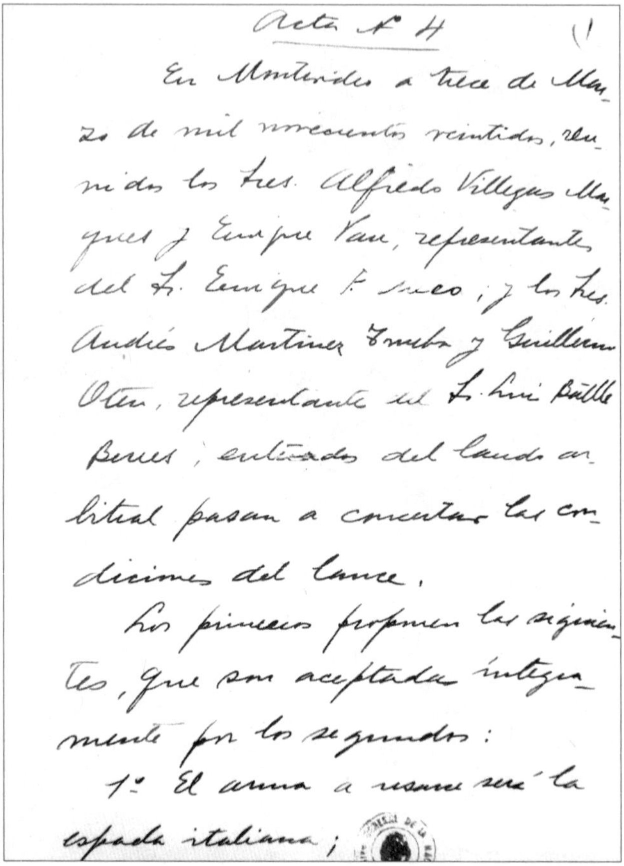
Acta N° 4 (1

En Montevideo a trece de Marzo de mil novecientos veintidos, reunidos los Sres. Alfredo Villegas Marques y Enrique Vaz, representantes del Sr. Enrique F. Areco, y los Sres. Andrés Martinez Trueba y Guillermo Otero, representantes del Sr. Luis Batlle Berres; enterados del laudo arbitral pasan a concertar las condiciones del lance.

Los primeros proponen las siguientes, que son aceptadas integramente por los segundos:

1º El arma a usarse será la espada italiana;

Fig. 1.4 *Acta previa* of the Areco-Batlle Berres duel, dated 13 March 1922. The conditions proposed by the seconds for challenger Enrique Areco were accepted by the seconds for offender Luis Batlle Berres: "1. That the weapon to be used will be the Italian epee (*espada italiana*); 2. The fencing rounds will last two minutes with one minute of rest; 3. The duel will end when in the judgment of the physicians one of the duelists is found to be in inferiority of conditions; 4. The duelists shall wear fine short-sleeved shirts, fencing gloves, shoes "de paseo" and if they wear a belt the buckle shall be on the left side; 5. The duel will take place tomorrow at 11." Archivo General de la Nación, Archivo Histórico, Montevideo, Colección Luis Batlle Berres. Photos by the author.

2º. Los asaltos serán de dos minutos con uno de descanso;

3º. El lance terminará cuando uno de los duelistas se encuentre en inferioridad de condiciones a juicio de los médicos;

4º. Los duelistas llevarán camiseta fina de manga corta, y guante corto de esgrima, y zapatos de paso ~~ambos~~ y en caso de usarse cinturón llevará la hebilla del lado izquierdo;

5º. El lance se realizará mañana a las 11 horas.

Los representantes del S. Batlle Berres proponen como director del encuentro al Coronel Domingo Mendívil, lo que es aceptado.

Como médicos han sido designados: por la parte del S. Arco, el Dr. Luis M. Otero; y por la del S. Batlle Berres el Dr. Francisco Ghigliani.

Se firman dos actas del mismo tenor.

A. Villegas Vargas   Guillermo Otero
Enrique Paive
R. Martínez Fonteli

magnanimity, defending the interests of their respective principals but not seeking an advantage.[62] To appear less than generous in dueling negotiations was itself a cause for dishonor.

Upon reaching agreement, the seconds collectively drafted a document known as the "first *acta*," a sort of cross between the minutes of a meeting and a contractual agreement.[63] At minimum, two identical copies were made, one for each party. If the seconds had concluded that there was no cause for a duel, the writing of the *acta* put the matter to rest, generally for good, and the ruling was free to be publicized if the principals so desired. If the seconds agreed to a duel, however, they held this first *acta* (now called the *acta previa*) in reserve, only for the eyes of those taking some part in the duel, until after it was fought. The *acta previa* usually declared who the offending party was, described the general type and degree of offense, and reported that all efforts at reconciliation had failed. The *acta* then went on to specify in detail the conditions that had been agreed upon for the duel (for example, "two pistol shots at twenty-five paces, turning and firing between the counts of two and three," or "ten fencing rounds with sabers of such-and-such a type, each round lasting two minutes with one minute of rest in between, ending when injuries leave one of the combatants in a position of inferiority"). It is here that the contractual nature of the *acta previa* is clearest: when the time came for the duel, both principals were honor bound to follow the stipulated conditions precisely, with the seconds serving as guarantors of the contract. The seconds had the responsibility to make sure that the man they represented did not back out of the duel: if he did, as in the Buchelli case, the seconds were themselves expected to fulfill that contractual commitment. Much like cosigners of a delinquent loan, they were to pay the "debt" of honor by offering to duel in their *ahijado's* stead. By the same logic, the seconds had the right and responsibility to seek vengeance if the opponent violated the contractual stipulations in a way that gave him an unfair advantage on the dueling ground – if he fired his pistol prior to the signal, for example, or thrust his sword after the end of a round.[64]

The duel was required to take place within forty-eight hours of the *acta previa* and often occurred the following morning. Both men came to the appointed spot accompanied by their seconds, and each brought a physician. If the duel was with swords or sabers, the doctors were charged with disinfecting the blades to prevent infection and with deciding whether an injury sustained was sufficient cause to suspend combat.[65] Pistol duels, of course, raised the specter of even more serious injury. In addition to seconds and doctors, each duel had a "director of combat," typically a fencing master, military officer,

Fig. 1.5 The director of combat issuing instructions in a fencing duel (Batlle Pacheco and de Castro). Archivo Fotográfico de *El País*.

or someone else universally respected for his expertise in weapons and in the protocol of honor. The director of combat gave the signal to fire in pistol duels, or timed and refereed fencing duels. His authority was absolute, and it was his responsibility to ensure strict adherence to the dueling codes, faithful fulfillment of all that had been agreed to in the *acta previa*, and perfect equality in the conditions of combat.

Once the duel was over, barring serious injury to one of the duelists, the seconds got together immediately afterward (often on-site) to draft the final *acta*. This document, known in Spanish as the *acta de combate* or *acta del terreno*, described what had happened, sometimes in great detail. Its purpose was to record the duel for posterity and/or for the inquiring public, showing that both men had comported themselves with bravery and honor, but most importantly, to document that the combatants had scrupulously upheld the terms of their contract, adhering to the stipulated conditions in every detail.[66] Copies of the *acta previa* and the *acta del terreno* were given to both combatants, and sometimes copies went to the seconds and director of combat as well; in Uruguay, additional copies were often sent to the newspapers and published verbatim. When a fencing duel was suspended at the physicians' behest, their decision became part of the *acta* as well, expressed in scientific terminology designed to invest the duel with the proper gravitas.[67]

The normal duel was thus a carefully scripted procedure that followed a set of laws designed to promote conciliation, to minimize the influence of violent passion by separating the antagonists and deferring to the seconds' objective wisdom, and to ensure a scrupulous equality between the combatants so that no one could claim that the duel masked a criminal or murderous intent. But the emphasis on legality by no means ended there. The honor codes also established quasi-judicial procedures to settle conflicts that might arise between the seconds, most commonly regarding the nature of the offense and/or who had the right to impose the conditions of the duel. Disagreements of this kind most often arose in two situations: either when both parties had insulted each other repeatedly and it was unclear who first crossed the line separating argument from offense, or when a public figure faced an attack on matters of policy and it was unclear whether the criticism overstepped the bounds of legitimate debate. When such disputes arose, some dueling codes called for the creation of "honor tribunals" or "honor juries," ad hoc bodies that usually comprised three members, one chosen by each side's seconds and the third chosen by the first two. The tribunal would study all the antecedents and issue an opinion that could not be appealed.[68]

The procedural legalism of these tribunals is illustrated in a 1913 controversy between two naval officers. Lieutenant Arturo Dubra, having been criticized in an enquiry into the sinking of a ship, mailed insulting letters to several of his fellow officers. He sent the letters individually rather than issuing a public statement in his defense, in order to avoid criticizing the military as an institution. The recipients of the letters were all severely offended, and several challenged Dubra in response. He fought a duel with at least one of them and ended up wounded, so when it came time for the next challenger, Ramiro Jouan, Dubra was in no condition to accept the duel that Jouan demanded. A tribunal was convened to decide what should be done, since Jouan's self-evident right to stipulate the conditions of the duel – because Dubra was clearly the offender – ran head-on against Dubra's physical incapacity. In the end, the tribunal decided that Dubra had no choice but to give Jouan satisfaction in the form of a retraction. In a long written statement that reads exactly like a judge's opinion, the tribunal justified its verdict (*fallo*) by detailing the facts of the case and analyzing those antecedents in the light of the "law," as set out in two dueling codes, *L'art du duel* by Adolphe Tavernier and *Codice cavalleresco italiano* by Iacopo Gelli. The tribunal's ruling was, as usual, published in the papers.[69] Even in the absence of an honor tribunal, seconds could be just as legalistic. In a 1916 incident between Alejo Idiartegaray and Manuel Solsona y Flores, the former's seconds invoked precisely enumerated articles of the Chateauvillard, Saint-Thomas, and Bruneau de Laborie codes to make their point.[70] In 1921, seconds arguing over where a duel should be fought cited Barbasetti's *Codice cavalleresco*.[71]

But not only did seconds and honor tribunals look to the dueling codes in search of guidance in difficult cases; they also consulted "precedents." In Argentina, for example, Carlos Moreno challenged Horacio Giménez Zapiola to a duel after Giménez opposed his application for membership in the exclusive Círculo de Armas social club. Giménez's seconds argued that such blackballing could not serve as cause for a duel, because Giménez was exercising a legitimate right that all club members enjoyed. The arbiter in the case agreed, "keeping in mind analogous situations that have occurred in Argentina's gentlemanly life."[72] In another dispute involving two doctors at odds over the internal politics of the Association of Municipal Physicians of the Federal Capital, an arbiter also ruled that no duel was justified, and was even more specific in support of his opinion, which he based both on the text of honor codes by Iacopo Gelli and the Marqués de Cabriñana, and on Argentina's earlier Massini-Martínez, Canilo-de la Torre, and Damas-Costa Paz incidents.[73] What we see at work here is a kind of dueling case law, or what one author, himself a judge, called "gentlemanly jurisprudence" (*jurisprudencia caballeresca*).

So the dueling world had its own laws, courts, and jurisprudence. But how could this parallel legal system possibly function, given that the duel itself was an express violation of criminal statute? Chapter 3 explores that issue in detail, but the simple answer is that society's most powerful men made the choice to treat dueling law as the moral equivalent of genuine law, and for decades no one successfully challenged them. The authors of the dueling codes were fully aware of this ambiguous position. On the one hand, some codes openly described the circumstances under which duelists were expected to guard silence when questioned by the police or court officials. On the other hand, the codes made a substantial effort to keep the duel's illegality to the necessary minimum and counseled cooperation with the authorities if one of the duelists violated the honor code in any significant way.[74] The laws of honor thus inhabited a twilight space between legality and criminality, between custom and statute, where duelists committed an intentional and premeditated crime but did so in strict accordance with a parallel law that had no nation-state's approval but operated in almost every way as if it did.

Forum Shopping: Dueling "Law" and Defamation Law Compared

Why did so many people turn to the parallel law and jurisprudence of the dueling codes? At first glance, it might appear that I am asking why people fought duels. But as we will see in chapter 2, "why people fought duels" is a more complex issue than the related but more limited query posed here: why did people, having been insulted, choose the remedy of the honor codes in preference to remedies provided by criminal law? The question is not an idle one. After all, when an individual believed that his honor had been attacked, he had two possible courses of action: to make a criminal accusation for defamation or to send seconds, and people were aware that this was a choice they were free to make. Juan Belinzón, defending himself against charges that he ran Montevideo's Escuela de Artes y Oficios in a despotic manner, spoke openly of the "two paths" open to him "to detain the advances of the *miserables* and to unmask the cowards who attack traitorously, hiding in anonymity."[75] The "legal" path (*via legal*) was the justice system; the "gentlemanly" path (*via caballeresca*) was the duel.

David Buchelli chose the *via legal* and was roundly criticized for having done so. Nevertheless, the court system remained a viable option in some situations. A defamation trial could be expected when the aggrieved party refused to recognize his alleged slanderer as a gentleman; when one of the antagonists was unable to duel for reasons of age, gender, physical disability, or the requirements of public office; when for whatever reason one of the two refused to duel; or when the seconds failed to reach an agreement on the choice of weapons or other conditions.[76] That the legal arena served as a second-best alternative for cases that could not be resolved on the field of honor appears clearly in a defamation case brought in 1916 in Argentina. Dr Eliseo Cantón, accused of waste and possible fraud in the construction of the José de San Martín Clinic, sought prosecution of the author of the charges against him, the Socialist congressman Enrique Dickmann. In his sworn statement to the judge, Cantón revealed that the case was at least in part a response to the fact that Dickmann represented a political party whose statutes expressly prohibited dueling. In Cantón's words, "it was impossible to convince him that he should accept other means of private solution."[77]

To understand why Uruguayans, like Argentines, usually preferred the gentlemanly path, it is helpful to show how the logic of the honor code was uniquely suited to matters that the courts and statutory law dealt with poorly.

Duelists and dueling advocates identified several problems with official, state-sanctioned law in questions of honor. First, they argued that in highly sensitive cases, such as when accusations of a woman's infidelity were involved, the formal legal processes only served to publicize matters that were best kept private. Second, they argued that no trial could truly succeed in restoring lost honor, because the courts were limited in the kinds of restitution they could impose. Winning a monetary settlement, or even seeing one's enemy put in jail, was no solace for a man of honor, because, in the words of congressman Duvimioso Terra, "the sting that a slap produces on the cheek of an honest man cannot be removed by a few months in jail or a handful of gold."[78]

Both claims may have been correct, but neither goes to the heart of the difference between the two codes. It is certainly true that a trial might give a true scandal or a false accusation greater publicity, but the evidence suggests that most duels in Uruguay, as elsewhere, originated in political and journalistic polemics that were quite public to begin with. Moreover, the charge that true gentlemen had no interest in the kinds of restitution that state law could provide is contradicted by the fact that Uruguayans did continue to litigate insults and libel (*injurias* and *calumnias*) in the courts.[79] To understand the preference for the code of honor as an alternative to state law, we need to dig deeper, comparing how the two parallel codes each operated in practice. Let's use a hypothetical case of journalistic defamation, because most Uruguayan duels did in fact arise from insults or accusations vented in the press.

To prosecute a defamation case in the courts, the offended party first had to prove that he had in fact been defamed. This may sound simple but often was not. In nineteenth- and early twentieth-century journalism it was common, indeed routine, for insults to be thinly veiled. Nicknames and indirect allusions were the political journalist's stock in trade. Called up on charges, the journalist could claim that he had not been referring to the plaintiff, or that the allegedly offensive words did not actually mean what his accuser believed they did. Even if it was clear to everyone that the journalist was lying, the lie could be difficult to prove.[80] This problem did not exist, however, in the codes of honor. Dueling rules recognized the right of an individual to issue a challenge whenever he believed himself offended, even if he was not mentioned by name, even if the slight was highly indirect. It sufficed that he recognized an insulting reference to himself (*darse por aludido*). If he truly was not the person the journalist had in mind, or if he had misinterpreted the allusion, the journalist merely had to say so publicly, and the matter ended with the individual's honor restored.

Second, to prosecute a case of defamation, the offended party had to prove who was actually responsible for the insult. This was also easier said than done, because journalists so often wrote anonymously or under pseudonyms.[81] When prosecutors came knocking at the door, the director of a paper would report that the author of the offending piece no longer worked there and could not be located. And again, it was very hard to prove that he was lying. On several occasions the Argentine and Uruguayan legislatures debated ways to remedy the problem. Some sought to import French press laws requiring that all columns be signed by their authors.[82] Others proposed that the owners or publishers of newspapers, rather than individual authors, be forced to respond legally for everything that appeared on their pages.[83] Although such reforms sometimes made their way into law, they were generally short-lived, either repealed by subsequent legislatures or left unenforced. After all, many of the parliamentarians debating the press laws (and even a few of the judges interpreting them) wrote for, owned, or edited newspapers that championed political causes. The last thing they wanted to do was to increase their legal exposure for polemics that they promoted on a regular basis. Journalistic insults therefore persisted, protected by the anonymity that unsigned columns provided.

Again, the codes of honor had an answer to the problem. Most journalists considered themselves honor bound to shoulder the consequences of their words when those consequences came in the form of a dueling challenge rather than a legal challenge. A writer who evaded his responsibilities by refusing to acknowledge authorship could easily be accused of cowardice, and if for some reason the author refused or was unable to accept a challenge, the laws of honor explicitly called on the paper's director to respond on his behalf. Most importantly, journalists were willing to respond to gentlemanly challenges because they saw their duels as a badge of distinction, something that defamation trials were generally not.

Another problem that faced the prosecutor of a defamation case was the thorny matter of proof. Normally, the last thing an insulted party wanted to do was to turn a slander trial into an investigation of whether or not the charges hurled at him were in fact true. In the legal arena, however, that was always a possibility. Whether the "truth defense" was permissible in defamation cases was a constant subject of debate. The laws in force in nineteenth- and early twentieth-century Uruguay – to simplify a more complex and frequently changing reality – tended to adhere to the following principle: if the charges related to public life, to the activity of an employee or a professional in the exercise of his duties in the public or private sector, then the truth defense was valid.

When the charges crossed the line into private life, then the truth or falsehood of the imputation was irrelevant to the case and not open to discussion.[84] In practice, however, it was exceedingly difficult to know exactly where to draw the line between the public and private spheres. To say that functionary John Doe acted corruptly in the granting of a particular contract might allow for the truth defense, while simply saying "John Doe is corrupt" might not. In determining the validity of the truth defense in a defamation trial, the burden of proof fell upon the *accuser*, the man who had allegedly been defamed, who had to demonstrate that the charges leveled against him were not related to his public role. Moreover, the accuser often had to prove *animus injuriandi*, meaning that he had to show that the journalist intended to damage his reputation rather than simply being misguided in an honest effort to act as a public watchdog. Some judges went so far as to demand that the accuser prove that the defendant knew his charges were false. In Argentina, the authors of a 1906 project to rewrite the Criminal Code complained, all this could be proven and the slanderer might still face no consequences, if, after years of falsehoods and years of legal stalling, he offered an eleventh-hour retraction, no matter how transparently insincere.[85]

Identical debates took place under the auspices of the honor code, but again the rules were different. In numerous instances, journalists refused to accept duels and argued that they were only doing their jobs. The offended parties countered that attacks on personal honor always called for a challenge and that no journalist who crossed the line into personal insult should be allowed to hide behind the pretense that he was serving the public interest. The terms of the debate almost exactly paralleled the arguments used in the legal arena. But in the honor code, it was the alleged defamer who had to prove his innocence. If a journalist refused a challenge in the belief that he was only exercising the rights of a free press, *he* had to make the case that his words fell within the bounds of legitimate public debate. If the journalist failed to convince public opinion, he could be accused of cowardice. Chapter 2 examines several disputes that fall into this category.

Remember that according to the honor codes, the very fact that someone had taken offense and sent his seconds was considered prima facie evidence that an offense had indeed occurred. After all, if the journalist truly did not intend to insult or defame, all he had to do was give explanations, recognize his interlocutor as a gentleman, and deny his intention to offend. Such a retraction automatically removed the insult, and at the same time did not dishonor the journalist, so long as it appeared to be sincere. But to issue an insincere retraction when everyone knew that a slight had in fact been intended was tantamount to admitting cowardice. The only way that a journalist could refuse a duel without providing explanations was to prove that he was exercising a legitimate right, that he had not crossed the line into personal invective, that the challenge itself had been unwarranted and illegitimate, and that cowardice had played no part in his decision to refuse the duel. This case was easier to make if one had an established reputation for courage, but the point is that the honor codes placed the burden of proof on the journalist, while defamation trials placed the burden of proof on the accuser.

The truth of the accusations also played little role in the world of honor because duels were simply not about who was right and who was wrong. Here, ultimately, lay the fundamental distinction between criminal law and the laws of honor: the former sought to convict the guilty and vindicate the innocent, while the latter sought to reaffirm the honor of both parties. Both the law and the duel had their repressive face: both hoped to preserve a climate of civility and restraint in public debate by making it an offense to attack another man's honor. But defamation trials were at heart a mechanism of punishment, while the duel was a mechanism of conciliation. Duels did not have winners or losers. If a man died on the dueling ground, his was the most honorable of deaths. If a man killed his adversary, he was in no way a victor – he was not proven right. Critics often pointed out this fact to underscore the idiocy and futility of the duel.[86] In the eyes of the duel's advocates, the critics entirely missed the point. The laws of honor offered a ritual of restoration, a cleansing of the stain caused by the original offense. A gentlemanly challenge was really a demand for reparations ("satisfaction" in the argot of honor), and that satisfaction could be given either in the form of explanations or in the form of a duel.

But in what way, exactly, did a *duel*, as opposed to an apology, give satisfaction? How did an exchange of pistol shots restore lost honor and remove the blemish caused by the original affront? The answer is at once simple and contradictory. In theory, the dueling ritual gave the aggrieved party the opportunity to face death, thereby proving his honor and courage. The duel restored a damaged reputation because the duelist showed society through his actions that he valued his reputation more than life itself. At the same time, however, the duel also gave the aggrieved party a chance to punish the man who had offended him. Many duelists believed themselves entirely justified in violently assaulting any man who, having insulted or defamed them, refused to accept a duel or who gave patently insincere explanations.[87] An affront to a gentleman could not go without a response, and many men believed that honor demanded that the punishment be direct and personal, not delegated to the cumbersome and unsatisfactory machinery of state law.

But herein lay the paradox that was for advocates the duel's great virtue, and for opponents the feature that made the duel so ridiculously illogical. The code of honor recognized the human urge to punish one's adversary and subordinated that urge to laws that compelled both parties to accept the other as an absolute equal, that gave both the identical opportunity to face death and so demonstrate their honor, and that served, no matter what the outcome on the field of battle, to cleanse the stain and ritually cauterize the wound to honor that the original offense had caused. Again, the duel was a rite of conciliation with no winner and no loser, no one proved right and no one proved wrong. With that goal of reconciliation in mind, it was the duty of the seconds to ask the principals to shake hands and settle their differences at battle's end. Sometimes duelists did offer their hands in reconciliation, sometimes they did not, and this was one of the pieces of information that was ritually recorded in the *acta del terreno*. But a crucial principle of the honor code was that after the duel, even in the absence of reconciliation, both parties *committed to never reopen the specific polemic that their duel had now officially closed*. The men might remain bitter enemies, and future insults might spark future duels between them, but according to the rules of honor, once an offense had been cleansed with blood, it forevermore ceased to exist.[88] The debt was paid, the contract fulfilled, reparations given, honor satisfied.

Comparing in this way the logic of criminal law versus the logic of the laws of honor, we can see why the latter so often trumped the former in the insult-filled world of politics and journalism. The duel and its code of conduct filled a void precisely where the laws to prevent *injurias, calumnias,* and *difamación* were arguably least effective. It is not hard to imagine that the ritualistic conciliation embodied in the duel – a process that settled matters within the space of a few days – offered a far better solution for matters of honor and reputation than did the long, drawn-out, punishment-driven approach of the formal justice system. The one drawback, of course, was that the honor code could not function without the duel; this ritual of conciliation demanded that the two parties go at one another with swords or pistols in open violation of the law and in blatant disregard for their own lives and bodies. Duelists fully recognized that this was a problem but believed that the alternative – not having the duel – was worse.

The Pen and the Sword: Press Freedom and "Responsibility"

Uruguayan public men, like their counterparts in France, Italy, Argentina, and other countries, thus came to the conclusion that dueling law, not defamation law, constituted the only effective means to protect honor in the rough-and-tumble world of politics and the press.[89] By extension, dueling law, not defamation law, became the everyday regulator of public discourse in Uruguay's young democracy. Whenever journalists or politicians considered whether or not to sign an editorial, whether or not to publicize an accusation for which they lacked proof, whether or not to use an inflammatory turn of phrase, their decisions were guided by an anticipation of how their adversary would respond in the gentlemanly arena, not the legal arena. Dueling law, as written in the honor codes and as established by gentlemanly precedent, made the rules by which the public sphere operated.

It is worth expanding a bit more on the implications of the duel coming to function as the essential institution that governed the norms of journalistic and political discourse in Uruguay. Uruguay's 1830 Constitution expressly prohibited prior censorship of the press. According to the text of Article 141, "The communication of thought, by means of the spoken word, private writings or published in any type of press, is entirely free, with no need for prior censorship; the author or publisher takes responsibility for any abuses that might be committed, in accordance with the law."[90] Given that dueling was exceptionally rare in Uruguay in 1830, we can assume that when the authors of the constitution referred to an author or publisher's "responsibility for any abuses that might be committed," they meant legal responsibility in accordance with the applicable laws on libel, defamation, and possibly sedition, incitement, and the like. But as we have already seen, laws regulating the press, and procedures for enforcing those regulations, were among the most hotly debated issues in Uruguay, as close to a political third rail as there was. Anger at the repeated tightening of press restrictions contributed to the outbreak of the 1886 Quebracho Revolution against General Máximo Santos, the subsequent attempt on his life, and the mutiny of Santos's own ministers that brought an end to his government. A central pillar of the November national conciliation and transfer of power to General Máximo Tajes was the repeal of those laws.[91] Similarly, Blanco opposition to proposed press restrictions during José Batlle y Ordóñez's second administration, denounced over months in the Blanco papers as the Ley Mordaza (gag law), ensured that no new government initiative would succeed in domesticating Uruguayan journalists.[92]

Over time, therefore, given the common belief that the statutory provisions against defamation were inadequate, impossible to enforce, and incapable of providing restorative justice to the victim, the meaning of "responsibility" as a bedrock constitutional principle gradually transformed. Politicians and journalists came to embrace an alternative concept they called "gentlemanly responsibility" and defined as the willingness to answer for one's words and actions in accordance with the dictates of the honor codes, and on the dueling ground when necessary. "Irresponsibility," the converse, explicitly described the man who hurled insults or engaged in heated polemics without being prepared to "guarantee" his words at sword point or gunpoint if challenged.

The doctrine of gentlemanly responsibility by no means demanded that everyone become a duelist. It did, however, call upon those who would not or could not duel to avoid the kinds of situations that might incite gentlemanly incidents. There was a clear idea that if you could not stand the heat, you needed to stay out of the kitchen, and the kitchen in this case meant the world of politics and the political press. The implications of this idea of responsibility were clear and profound. First of all, it meant that in order to participate in public debate, one had to accept and live by the dictates of the code of honor, notwithstanding the duel's illegality. Second, it meant that all those who were not allowed to participate in the culture of the duel found themselves excluded a priori from full participation in public debate. That is not to say that excluded persons could not write for a newspaper or hold a political post, but it did mean that most of their peers refused to recognize their right to engage in the kinds of heated exchanges that so often constituted the daily bread of politics. In other words, the idea of responsibility rendered intense public controversy off-limits to women, the elderly or infirm, and most of the lower classes.[93]

Some used gender-laden terms to stigmatize those who allegedly lacked "responsibility." If a man was unwilling to duel and refused to accept a challenge, his antagonist might dismiss his words as *insultos de mujer* or *ofensas de mujer* (insults or offenses of a woman). The implication was that a woman's insults had no authority, did not pose a challenge to a gentleman's honor, and did not need to be answered in any forum, legal or gentlemanly.[94] By publicly describing a rival's words as *insultos de mujer*, the man of honor was at one level making the obvious point that a refusal to duel betrayed a lack of masculinity. Some duelists spoke in almost biological terms about the manly qualities that compelled them to punish every affront to their honor, and implied that those who rejected the duel must be deficient in that regard.[95] Indeed, the most effective way to goad a reluctant adversary into a duel was to call his manhood into question, as Nicosía clearly tried to do with Buchelli.⁹⁶ But there was more to it than that. The idea of gentlemanly responsibility and its opposite, *ofensas de mujer*, held that the words spoken by a woman – the words themselves – did not and could not carry the same weight as the "guaranteed" words of a man who was willing and able to duel. This was not meant as a moral condemnation of women but as a statement of self-evident fact. Few believed that women were less likely than men to tell the truth or were more likely to offend. Uruguayans simply pointed out what they believed to be obvious: that women were neither free nor able to defend their words with their lives, and as a result their words did not and could not command the same authority. By extension, women could not help but be marginalized from the public sphere so long as the dueling codes were the de facto legal system regulating that sphere.

Insultos de mujer was not the only metaphor employed to stigmatize the words of the "irresponsible." On one occasion in 1886, José Batlle y Ordóñez dismissed in *El Día* the writings of one of his opponents as "the insults of the drunkard you come across along the road."⁹⁷ The extent to which the idea of gentlemanly responsibility imposed educational or class restrictions on access to the public forum remains to some degree an open question, varying also from place to place. In Buenos Aires in 1907, photographer Miguel di Santi sent his seconds to César M. Roldán, because Roldán had commented in public that it was "unfortunate that a girl of distinguished social position should be entertained by a photographer."⁹⁸ Di Santi demanded either a retraction of this offense or satisfaction in the form of a duel. Roldán answered with outwardly courteous words, appearing to issue the traditional, formulaic assertion that his intention had never been to insult Mr Di Santi personally. But as the ending of his "retraction" made clear, the true intention was not to apologize but to humiliate a social inferior: "With this statement I believe that I have provided ample satisfaction ... as regards the 'person' of Mr. Di Santi, as I have explained, he has never been the object of my attention, perhaps because I have other more agreeable, interesting, or important things to think about."⁹⁹ The example lends support to historian Sandra Gayol's perception that the universe of people empowered to demand or to give satisfaction offers a window onto the "criteria of belonging and mechanisms of exclusion" in any given society, because the duel was predicated on "the recognized condition of equality between adversaries."¹⁰⁰

But Gayol ultimately makes the case that Roldán's putting on of airs was highly unusual for Argentina, and in Uruguay, my research for this book did not uncover a single instance in which the challenger's occupation or social status was invoked as a cause or pretext for refusing a duel. There were a small handful of cases in which a man refused to accept a challenge on the grounds that his adversary was "not a gentleman," but when a reason was specified, it was always the opponent's conduct, not his class, that justified the rejection.[101] The closest thing to an exception I have found is a 1924 allegation in *La Tribuna Popular* that the ex-president, Baltasar Brum, refused to duel with a certain Lieutenant Goñi because he "believed himself to be of superior caste."[102] But Brum vehemently rejected that this was the case, and the accusation and denial together show that class-based exclusions were generally considered illegitimate.[103]

Of course the community of duelists was socially restricted. Anyone could engage in one-on-one combat with some sort of weapon, and Argentine and Uruguayan literature, folklore, newspaper crime pages, and police and court records were filled with stirring accounts of *duelos criollos*, the ubiquitous knife duels between rural gauchos or urban ruffians;[104] but by-the-honor-code dueling was something altogether different. It required knowledge of fencing and/or firearms (though the most rudimentary training could suffice), and an understanding of dueling protocol. To be a duelist, one had to be connected socially to individuals capable of acting as seconds, and duelists were expected to cover everyone's expenses. Nevertheless, even if these requirements tended to exclude the lower classes, we are not describing a world with excessively high entry barriers. Emergency fencing instruction was not a rarity, nor were seconds hard to find in a city-state like Montevideo where everybody knew somebody and partisan connections tracing back generations created dense webs of patronage. And while traveling to Buenos Aires to avoid police interference might incur significant expense, the cost of a locally fought duel was not much more than an honorarium for one's physician, a gratuity for the director of combat, and maybe a meal afterward. Pursuit or performance of aristocratic distinction was simply not the duel's raison d'être.

Instead, the norms of responsible debate created a community of duelists defined by *function*, by profession, with the lion's share of duels occurring in the world of politics and the press, and secondarily within the military officer corps. A journalist of middle- or lower-class origins was far more likely to find himself on the field of honor than a millionaire merchant uninvolved in politics. In another case from 1924, for example, Police Chief General Juan A. Pintos sent seconds to challenge the editor of *El País* for an unsigned hit piece that had appeared in the paper. When the editor directed them to the column's author, Pintos refused to accept a duel with a junior writer and accused the paper's editor-in-chief of cowardice. Citing the dueling codes by Gelli and Bruneau de Laborie, Pintos argued that the editor or publisher of a newspaper was responsible for all unsigned articles, whether or not the true author came forward. But *La Tribuna Popular*, which had no stake in the original dispute, publicly took issue with Pintos's claim, insisting that in Uruguay it was established practice for each and every writer to take responsibility for his own words. Criticizing the police chief's invocation of Italian and French dueling codes, the editorialist argued that "the majority of those codes were written in countries where the people are divided into castes – one noble, the other plebeian – while we live the democratic life, where all citizens are equal, with identical rights and concomitant duties."[105] An honor tribunal agreed, and Pintos ended up having to duel with both men.

Once we realize that Uruguayans viewed the duel as the only effective guarantor of responsibility in journalistic and political debate, and that the overwhelming majority of civilian duels arose from that world, we begin to see the practice in a different light. Although critics spoke often of the duel's medieval heritage and the duelist's aristocratic pretensions, Uruguayan dueling had a remarkably liberal-democratic pedigree. With the code of honor to enforce responsibility in the press, Uruguayan liberals believed they made a strong and convincing case against prior censorship and other restrictions on press freedom.[106] The logic went as follows: virtually everyone agreed that an unbridled press without some degree of responsibility was unacceptable; indeed, *El Heraldo* in 1881 called authorial responsibility "the indispensable precondition for all liberty."[107] Most people also agreed that the legal guarantees of responsibility, defamation laws in particular, were inadequate. Without the duel, therefore, the advocates of press freedom would have been left without a leg to stand on. With the duel, they stood strong.[108] Uruguayan press freedom was imperfect, to be sure, but compared to most other places in Latin America, far more often than not it was exemplary. We cannot and should not attribute this achievement to the duel, but absent the duel, it would have been much more difficult to imagine.

2

Dueling as Politics and the Politics of Dueling

Honor, like the gods, requires blood. We live off the opinion of others, and the public is cruel; it demands circus spectacles: gladiators.

    Rafael Barrett, "El duelo"[1]

Someone once said that the field of honor was the best possible place to build a hospital, because nobody ever died there.

    Víctor Soliño, *Crónica de los años locos*[2]

Many Uruguayans still know the story of the 1856 duel between Juan Carlos Gómez and the Argentine jurist/politician/journalist Nicolás Calvo. The rules for the duel were highly unorthodox: two pistols placed in a bag, one loaded, the other unloaded. Choosing their weapon by lot, the two men were to fire simultaneously on command at a range of only fifteen paces. Such unusual and dangerous conditions were not sanctioned by the most respected dueling codes, but Calvo, an experienced duelist and the superior marksman, had insisted on a duel whose outcome would be determined by fate, not by skill. After being handed their pistols, not knowing which was the loaded one, Gómez and Calvo took their places. At the agreed-upon signal, Calvo was the first to pull the trigger. Nothing happened. Gómez, realizing that his pistol was the loaded one, fired into the air with the famous words, "I came here to die, not to kill."[3] The story was told and retold until it gained mythic dimensions, symbolizing the courage and generosity of one of Uruguay's national heroes, a man who condemned the duel as a moral abomination but still put his life on the line "to prove," in his words, "that I am a man of courage and not a coward."[4]

    Calvo's very different version of events never made the history books. According to his telling, Gómez did not fire his weapon at the command

Fig. 2.1 Juan Carlos Gómez. *El Indiscreto* (Montevideo) no. 2 (8 June 1884). Digitized by Anáforas, Publicaciones Periódicas, Facultad de Información y Comunicación, Universidad de la República.

because he was immobilized by fear: Calvo described him standing like a statue, "like Lot's wife, transformed into a pillar of salt."[5] Only afterwards, once he knew that Calvo's pistol was the unloaded one and the danger had passed, was Gómez able to collect his wits and pronounce those so-quotable words. By that time, however, the seconds-long window during which he was permitted to fire had expired, so there was no generosity in Gómez's shot into the air. Indeed, to shoot now at Calvo would have been a violation of the laws of the duel, the equivalent of cold-blooded murder.[6] In no small part because Gómez's interpretation, not Calvo's, became the accepted version of what occurred during those few moments that morning in Buenos Aires's Palermo Park, Juan Carlos Gómez went on to enjoy an illustrious political career, while Calvo faded over time into semi-obscurity. Or was it the other way around: perhaps Gómez's subsequent political success permitted him to write his version of history and to silence Calvo's? Either way – and it surely

Fig. 2.2 Nicolás Calvo. Wikimedia Commons.

was some of both – Calvo had to have been thoroughly galled that Gómez succeeded in turning their duel into a badge of honor, when in Calvo's eyes his actions were patently cowardly and dishonest.

The story of Calvo and Gómez, now remembered as an epic confrontation between a bullying serial duelist and a principled opponent of the duel who nonetheless mustered the courage to face death, helps to introduce several of this chapter's key themes. If chapter 1 outlined how the code of honor was designed to function and why public men pledged themselves to the informal laws of the duel, the Gómez-Calvo affair underscores the gulf between design and reality. Neither man was motivated primarily by the defense of honor, nor was their duel about cleansing a genuine offense or restoring civility to public discourse. The two men had been political opponents for years, but the proximate cause of the confrontation was Gómez's open letter entitled "*El terror del florete*" (The terror of the fencing foil), in which he accused Calvo of abusing his abilities as a duelist in order to browbeat his political adversaries into silence. Wrote Gomez:

> There is nothing in the world more contemptible than the honor of the *espadachín* [swashbuckler], except perhaps the valor of the *espadachín* ... We revere the honor and courage of the hero or the martyr who faces all – persecution, ill-fortune, death – for a cause worthy of sacrifice, but there is neither honor nor valor in homicide, and the murderer who in cold blood seeks out victims using the duel as pretext, (relying on) his superior skill, is nothing more than a common criminal.[7]

Calvo's tendency toward both verbal and physical violence against his adversaries lends some credibility to Gómez's charges.[8] Yet when Gómez called him for his bullying abuse of the duel, Calvo realized that the accusation was serious and required an answer. That is why he insisted on the highly irregular condition of two pistols chosen by lot, one loaded, the other empty. By proposing a duel that would be decided entirely by chance, Calvo sought to prove that he was not an *espadachín*: that he, too, had come to die, not to kill.[9]

If dueling theoretically offered a means to safeguard decorum in public life, to prevent defamation and to provide a speedy conciliation when deterrence failed, the Gómez-Calvo duel proves that the real world of human motivation was not so tidy. When asked in general terms why dueling was necessary, Uruguayans might talk about gentlemanly responsibility and the need to ban personal attacks from politics, but when asked about specific duels and duelists, they recognized that people fought duels for all kinds of reasons, sometimes noble, sometimes venal. They admitted that some individuals offended deliberately and with premeditation, that many duels were frivolous, that some men were bullies, and that duelists were often motivated by cynicism.[10]

This chapter explores the ever-present tension between the exalted laws of honor and the sometimes base motives of those who invoked them. First, I look at why people actually fought duels. The forces that moved men to gamble with their lives varied widely, from a sincere preoccupation with honor to political damage control, from the quest for notoriety to a desire to intimidate, from fear of being accused of cowardice to partisan solidarity to sheer undiluted rage. Second, the chapter explores how clashing motives and strategies generated a strange form of public theater, performed for an avid audience of in-the-know observers. Duels were politics by other means, and actions on the dueling ground could make or break the career of an aspiring public man. The successful duelist projected himself to the world as fearless, committed to his ideals, incorruptible, generous, and loyal. The unsuccessful duelist, depending on how he was unsuccessful, might appear cowardly or bullying, arrogant or ridiculous, petty or criminal. Duels were a sort of text in action, read by contemporaries who sat in judgment of the participants' mind and mettle, just as Gómez's partisans read his shot into the air as a brave act of magnanimity and not as a cowardly violation of the honor codes.

Theory versus Practice: Duelists and Their Motives

Nineteenth- and early twentieth-century Uruguayans' general justifications for dueling rarely matched their analyses of particular duels. The specific explanations sometimes included quite candid appreciations of what influenced the duelist:

"Society only considers worthy of public acclaim the man who defends his moral courage by reacting *caballerescamente* [chivalrously] to an aggression or an insult. So firmly rooted is this belief in the minds of all, that even the most radical enemies of the duel ... recognize that those who cultivate this social formality grow in [public] opinion ... The duel, besides being a custom, is a social imposition."[11]

"An affront having been received, there arises instantly in the human spirit the need to avenge it. And when that sentiment is weak, when the desire to avenge does not emerge, society comes in and compels us to demand the reparation of the offense. The gospels teach us that we should turn the other cheek; but modern society, or, at least, Latin societies, demand reparation or vengeance."[12]

"So much pantomime! Why the duel? Ah, the ostentation! The names of duelists appear in embossed letters, the *actas* are published and the people say: 'so-and-so has honor; he's fought a duel.' And so-and-so can't contain his glee ... he's a respectable person!"[13]

"Consider ... the case of political thugs, who come onto the scene ready to provoke without cause, in order to gain notoriety and prestige."[14]

"There are people who fight duels for vainglory, for love of the commotion, to silence the gossip of the great anonymous mass, out of ambition, even for profit."[15]

"I have fought duels out of worry, not courage. If I had had the bravery necessary to confront 'what people will say' [*el qué dirán*], I would not have dueled. It is an act of moral cowardice."[16]

The common thread running through all of these answers is that defense of honor was but one of many motives that underpinned the duel, and probably not the most important. Concentrated among politicians and journalists,[17] duels generally served as a tactic to burnish one's image, and most arose from heated exchanges in public or in the press. As congressman Amador Sánchez attested, "If statistics had been kept of the duels that have happened among us, it would be clear that very few, the true exceptions, have taken place for inexorable causes or for true offenses that could not be resolved by other means."[18] While genuine anger certainly underpinned some duels (and absent the honor code, those conflicts might have degenerated into uncontrolled violence), the fact remains that behind most duels lay some admixture of political calculation, thirst for publicity, and fear of ridicule.

If the code of honor was designed to rein in the excesses of the political press, in practice the duel enabled those very strategies of attack journalism. To understand this point, we need to take a closer look at the norms of the press. As discussed in the introduction, nonpartisan journalism was the exception in Uruguay. Almost every paper had its party affiliation, not just Blanco or Colorado but down to the intra-party faction. Through the nineteenth century, most papers were sold by subscription to partisan supporters and other members of the political class. *El Día*, from 1886 the organ of José Batlle y Ordóñez, became the first successful major daily to sell on the newsstand by single issue, though that did not make the paper any less combative.[19] Batlle's innovation, followed by *La Tribuna Popular* and a few other dailies, simply brought more people of modest means into the circle of consumers of polemic. With journalism an extension of partisan struggle, staff writers were loyal soldiers whose faithful service to their editor was indistinguishable from their devotion to the party leader or factional caudillo. News and editorial content were inseparable, and the favored weapon of attack was the *suelto*, a short, usually unsigned, frequently sarcastic news item/commentary. A stint as a reporter was often the first stage of a political career, the place where a young man could demonstrate his abilities as a polemicist, the depth of his commitment to the cause, and his courage. It should come as no surprise, therefore, that the journalist's education included swordplay and marksmanship as well as grammar and rhetoric. Two famous Argentine papers offered fencing training on premises,[20] and while Uruguay lacked formal infrastructure on the same scale, the presumption was identical – that dueling was part of a young writer's job description.

Knowledge of arms was a prerequisite for a journalistic career because credibility was predicated on responsibility, and responsibility was defined by the will to accept a duel if challenged. But it was not merely a matter of being able to duel "just in case"; rather, the internal logic of political journalism fostered repeating cycles of brinksmanship, where each side tested the limits of responsible discourse and pushed into territory that might provoke a challenge. The political journalist's raison d'être was to defend his side and to attack the other, using all the verbal tools at his disposal. Antagonistic exchanges between newspapers took on the quality of battles and were so perceived by participants and spectators alike.[21] Some battles were fought exclusively with logic, argument, and fact, and most exchanges at least began that way. But time and time again, particularly in moments of heightened political tension, polemicists found themselves dipping further into their arsenals and pulling out any weapon they could use: imputations of motive, attacks on character, charges of hypocrisy or cowardice, and sometimes deliberate misrepresentations or outright libel. Each time a debate escalated into verbal warfare, politically aware readers watched to see what would happen next. Although the moderates might praise a journalist or politician for de-escalating the rhetoric and stepping back from the edge, hard-liners tended to view retreat as surrender. For most partisan journalists, forcing an opponent to back down was every bit as good as winning an argument on its merits.

In this climate, a skilled duelist who had a reputation for being easily offended and not averse to dangerous dueling conditions found himself at a clear advantage. If his adversaries were afraid of receiving a visit from his seconds, they would measure their words, while he was free to attack ad hominem, to push the boundaries of civilized debate, to insult, to slander. It was precisely this kind of intimidation that Juan Carlos Gómez accused Nicolás Calvo of cultivating; this was the "terror of the fencing foil." By the same logic, a man with a reputation for allowing insults to pass without taking offense could count on being insulted again and again. As Julio Herrera y Obes recalled advising dueling skeptic José Pedro Varela, who in 1870 was trying to decide whether or not to send seconds in response to an insult, "If they know you won't entertain challenges they will provoke you every day; once they see that you accept the duel, if you are lucky enough to come out the victor, nobody will bother you."[22] Domingo Arena, ally and later biographer of José Batlle y Ordóñez, recounted a story that illustrates a similar point. In the 1880s, Batlle got into a fierce exchange with a political opponent named Leopoldo López Vago. In *El Día*, Batlle called López Vago a *rastacuero* (uncultured nouveau riche). López Vago retorted pedantically that his dictionary did not include that particular word, so he could not respond.

Batlle answered back with a *suelto* that not only explained the insult but upped the ante with "a long paragraph of several centimeters filled with all the most denigrating epithets he could think of."[23] When instead of sending seconds López Vago backed down and went quiet, Batlle ended the polemic by commenting in print that Don Leopoldo had now revealed himself to be "Doña Leopoldina!"[24] This comeuppance, at least in Arena's telling, was enough to discredit López Vago entirely.[25]

To be fearless and feared by others was to enjoy the last word, while cowards were condemned to silence. The skilled and willing duelist was free to refuse ever to retract or apologize for his words, no matter how intemperate they might be. Some politicians embraced such intransigence as a badge of honor.[26] This was not the whole story, as we will see: the ideals of gentlemanly honor, enforced by public opinion, did place some limits on the duelist's latitude to intimidate. Nevertheless, press polemics tended to resemble games of chicken. Both participants escalated the invective incrementally, tit for tat, each hoping that the other would blink first and give them the moral victory of having the last word. If neither blinked, a duel or at least a challenge usually followed. Over time, the pattern became familiar and predictable. Spectators following an argument in the press could anticipate with fair precision when the rhetoric would cross over into dueling territory. When it did, they avidly awaited the resolution, presumably with mixed emotions of anticipation and relief – anticipation for what might occur on the field of honor, and relief that the public bickering would now end and everyone could go back to their normal business. Indeed, the duel's unique ability to stop an unpleasantly escalating exchange in its tracks was among its greatest selling points.[27]

This game of partisan brinkmanship explains the primary dynamic that generated dueling among journalists, but other motives came into play as well. For a politician or government official under attack, challenging a critic to a duel could be a highly effective damage-control strategy, because an agreement to duel was also an agreement to end, forever, the specific argument from whence the duel had originated. So imagine that an opposition politician accused a government minister of corruption in the granting of a contract. If the minister responded by sending his seconds, the opposition critic had two alternatives. If he refused the challenge, he could be accused of irresponsibility, of cowardice, of making charges that he was unwilling to guarantee on the field of honor. But according to the gentlemanly laws, if he agreed to a duel, he implicitly recognized the minister as an honorable man, and dueling protocol demanded that he never again raise the same issue. This Catch-22 gave the accused official a powerful means to avoid accountability without having to disprove the accusations against him. Indeed, years after his famous 1897 duel with Argentine Radical Party leader Hipólito Yrigoyen, party dissident Lisandro de la Torre lamented having agreed to fight, precisely because the rules of honor forced him to keep to himself the accusations that had occasioned their falling out.[28] Uruguayan Socialist Emilio Frugoni captured well this particularly noxious by-product of the honor code, writing, "Submitting to 'gentlemanly' imposition means renouncing the most precious rights that arise from [the legislator's] office, and constitutes an act of cowardice, muzzling necessary and useful truths whenever they might be disagreeable to those who live from privilege."[29]

Muckrakers and whistleblowers could sometimes overcome this logic by which duels were employed to thwart the investigation of improprieties. If the critic had an unimpeachable reputation for bravery or a scandal-plagued official was perceived to be abusing the duel, his demand for gentlemanly satisfaction might be rejected. But only a critic with overwhelming public support could put together those "ifs," and the exceptions mostly just proved the rule. Image, then as now, was legal tender in politics, and in a world yet to invent sound bites, spin doctors, focus groups, internet trolling, and the other modern marvels of political public relations, dueling was the tool of choice for the image-conscious.

Dueling could also promote careers and provide easy publicity. What was the best way for a new, unknown newspaper to sell subscriptions and gain a readership? One *could* slowly build credibility by providing unique information and well-crafted analysis, but why bother, when there was the surefire shortcut of taking on an established daily with a flurry of insults? Once you successfully goaded the more widely read paper into responding, a public thirsty for controversy would pick up your publication as well, to see for themselves what all the hullabaloo was about. If the polemic led to a duel, the publicity value went up even more. What was the best way for a young political unknown to capture public office? One *could* spend years earning qualifications, respect, and networks of like-minded supporters, but why bother, when you had the shortcut of making incendiary accusations against a well-known public figure? True or false, your charges would catapult your name into the public eye, and militants on your side would cheer you as a hero. If the object of your campaign challenged you to duel, all the better. You appeared before the world as a courageous defender of the cause, a loyal partisan with name recognition just in time for the next round of elections. Plus there was an extra bonus, particularly if your charges were without merit: because the duel put an end to all discussion of the accusations, you did not actually have to prove them to anyone. Your profile elevated, mission accomplished.

In all of these examples, we see that while "gentlemanly responsibility" rested on a hypothetical commitment *not* to offend, in practice the duel often had the opposite function: courage and dexterity with arms gave one a license *to* offend, and that license was essential to how the political and journalistic game was played. It was a game that put life and limb at risk, to be sure, but risk was an intrinsic part of Uruguayan politics. A typical Blanco or Colorado militant in, say, 1880 or 1900, would have taken part in at least one insurrection in his lifetime and would likely have experienced prison, exile, and moments of physical peril. Captured insurgents had been summarily executed on several occasions: the memory of Quinteros was all but encoded on the DNA of every Colorado, the memory of Paysandú on every Blanco.[30] Day-to-day politics and journalism also had their violent episodes, to the point that nineteenth-century Uruguayan Spanish developed its own specialized vocabulary. *Mazorcadas* were attacks by roving bands of partisans, or *mazorcas*, and when they sought to disable an opposition printing press, it was called an *empastelamiento*.[31] Journalists were used to being accosted by party thugs on the street, and assassination attempts, while rare, were not unknown.[32] Compared to this ever-present specter of violence, the dangers of dueling may have seemed manageable.

Later, as civilian rule triumphed in the early twentieth century, partisanship became less a business of citizen soldiers and more a business of citizen intellectuals. One might assume that a new generation of politicians who did not know civil war would increasingly fear the duel, yet the opposite occurred: duels increased in frequency. Several explanations are possible, the simplest and most cynical being that duels became more common as they became less perilous. The twentieth century saw a proliferation of first-blood saber duels and pistol duels where the type of weapon, rules, and distances minimized the likelihood that either man would take a bullet. Some duels continued of course to take place under dangerous conditions, and none was risk-free, but many contemporaries were firmly convinced that the duel's declining mortality and morbidity drove up its appeal.[33]

A case can also be made that belligerent partisan-attack journalism, and with it the cultivation of the duel, replaced armed insurrection as the preferred means of proving loyalty to one's party. As opportunities to offer life on the battlefield disappeared, young militants needed new ways to perform their readiness to sacrifice for the cause. The imagined continuity from nineteenth-century partisan warfare to twentieth-century dueling drew as well upon the near-mythic status that single combat enjoyed in Uruguayans' cultural memory of that earlier era. Some of the most famous, most mythologized battles in Blanco-Colorado warfare had been one-on-one confrontations between rival caudillos, either on horseback with lances or on the ground with the long gaucho knives known as *facones*, as their troops stood by and watched. Such had been the epic duels between Blanco caudillo Timoteo Aparicio and Colorado caudillo Gregorio Suárez at the battle of Pedernal in 1863, and between Blanco José Maria Pampillón and Colorado Gil Aguirre in 1870 during the Revolution of the Lances.[34] Twentieth-century political and journalistic duels bore little resemblance to those epic battles of history-made-folklore, and in many ways the laws of honor insisted on the deliberate distinction between proper duels and these violent contests of manhood, which still occupied the attention of local police in the Uruguayan countryside on a regular basis.[35] But the rhetoric of modern politics, filled with invocations of loyalty and sacrifice, sacred rights and vile usurpers, would still have sounded quite familiar to their nineteenth-century party forebears.[36] It is not at all far-fetched to visualize committed duelists in the 1910s or 1920s imagining that their actions in some way echoed the bravery and commitment of their heroes of old.

Similarly, it would be a mistake to assume that crass opportunism underpinned all or even most duels. Throughout the entire century under study, duels occasioned by genuine hatred and very real acts of verbal or physical violence continued to occur. An 1880 duel between Spanish-Argentine journalists Enrique Romero Giménez and José Paul y Angulo, discussed in detail below, began with a wad of spit to the face and ended in a death. A 1908 duel between two military officers in Paysandú, apparently the outgrowth of a barracks fight, stipulated repeated revolver shots with the adversaries advancing three paces after each shot until one of them fell.[37] Given the intensity of the emotions and the depth of the enmities involved, some duels could be deadly serious. That these were the exception does not negate their significance. Furthermore, even duels that seem trivial and cynical to us may well have appeared grave and inescapable to those involved. From a distance, we can see how the repeated cycles of tit-for-tat polemics in the press followed a predictable pattern of provocation and escalation, culminating either in retreat or in the sending of seconds. But if we put ourselves into the shoes of the editor who saw himself attacked by name or by implication in the pages of a competing paper, what would we feel? If we sincerely believed that the insult could damage our reputation, yet we also feared confronting a skilled swordsman, how would we respond? If, at the same time, we were terrified of public scorn as a coward, would that affect our decision? With a cynical and objective eye, we can see how convenient it would be for a corrupt public official, or even an innocent one, to shut down his accuser by challenging him to a duel. The naked instrumentality of the response seems self-evident. Yet if we were in that official's place, would we view our actions as cynical and instrumental, or would we genuinely feel aggrieved, angry, and desirous of a face-to-face confrontation? Even when we contemplate the editor of the fledgling newspaper or the aspiring young politician whose provocations appear the most blatantly self-promoting, can we truly penetrate the psychology? Maybe the pursuit of notoriety responds to some profound emotional need, a feeling that a life spent in obscurity is not a life worth living.

The point, I hope, is clear: we can discern the structural patterns in the cultural practices of Uruguayan politicians, but that does not negate the emotions and thoughts and fears that motivated those responses. At the same time, emotions and thoughts and fears are themselves shaped by culture and cannot be divorced from the structural patterns they follow or the practical ends they serve. So on the one hand, we must be skeptical of claims that the duelist was motivated by the defense of honor. As we have seen, contemporaries recognized that duels were just as often about character assassination, posturing, intimidation, damage control, and cheap self-promotion. But on the other hand, that does not mean that the individual duelist, when he issued or accepted a challenge, was consciously plotting strategy rather than thinking about honor. Humans have a boundless capacity to rationalize, to invoke high-sounding principle, to believe in their soul that the path of self-interest is also the path of righteousness. For public men in late nineteenth- and early twentieth-century Uruguay, the idea that honor was a possession more cherished than life itself, and that an insult in public constituted a theft of honor, made possible that rationalization of self-interest. To this extent, but to this extent only, the duel *was* about honor.

The Reluctant Hero: Dueling as Political Theater

As an ideal, honor also shaped the duelist's world by defining a cultural code that public men had to appear to follow, no matter what their actual motives and goals might be. After all, a duelist guaranteed his word with his blood, and despite all the posturing and trite gamesmanship, this guarantee was real. It invested the duelist with the authority of a man publicly willing to die for his ideals, for his party, for his paper, for his name. Yet at the same time, Uruguayans remained highly ambivalent about the duel itself, despite broad support for the idea of gentlemanly responsibility. Most saw dueling as a necessary evil; few saw it as a shining ideal. The public might praise the man who risked all to defend his honor and ostracize the man who ran from a duel, but society did not look kindly upon those who seemed too eager to pick up arms, too quick to take offense, too unwilling to give or accept an apology when reasonable people agreed that an apology was called for. The idealized duelist was supposed to embody masculine courage and sang-froid, responsibility for his actions, and loyalty to his cause, but also generosity: the duelist, after all, voluntarily gave his antagonist a chance to kill him. The idealized duelist was not a man of unbridled ambition; if he was willing to die on principle, he could not be a man who coveted worldly goods. At the same time, the idealized duelist showed civility and self-control; he was passionate, but capable of dominating his passions and subordinating them to the polite protocol of the honor codes. This ideal is well exemplified in a biography of José Batlle y Ordóñez, in which the author went over the top in extolling Batlle's qualities as a duelist: "Batlle never made display of his valor; if anything, he seemed to want to hide it, as if it were a vice, or at least a somewhat perverse inclination. But when the insult burned, he offered his life with heroic serenity. And unlike most people, this superior man, who disdained his own life, felt a profound, deeply rooted respect for that of others. Willing to give his own life without vacillation, he balked, horrified, at any act that might compromise the life of another."[38] A reluctant warrior, steadfast but conciliatory, prepared to defend his honor by arms but not eager to do so, trained in weapons but not excessively skilled, prepared to die but never wishing harm upon another: such were the imagined qualities of the perfect duelist.

These ideals created expectations of every duelist and placed certain limits on the duel's abuse. No matter how many duels were born of cynical calculation, the ideal of honor compelled the duelist to pretend, at least, that his motives were beyond reproach. Keeping up the pretense depended upon acting in a way that communicated the proper message – the readiness to die for an ideal – while veiling the less noble messages. No one, for example, would openly admit to issuing a challenge in order to silence an opponent, notwithstanding the number of duels that were about exactly that. The same ambivalent ideal made dexterity with weapons a tainted advantage. On the one hand, every public man was expected to defend himself adequately with saber or pistol; on the other, unusual skill with arms gave a duelist such an unfair advantage that it could undermine the purpose of the duel. As the Gómez-Calvo affair illustrated, a man who knew in advance that he was the better swordsman or the superior marksman did not run the same risk as his adversary. Was he therefore really a man willing to die for his ideals, or was he just a bully?[39]

One assumes that most duelists hoped to walk off the dueling ground in better physical shape than their adversary. Even if dueling was not supposed to be about who won and who lost, the price of losing might turn out to be higher than a man would hope to pay, so duelists and their seconds had to play a careful game, balancing self-preservation against the requirement that they appear magnanimous and concerned more with honor than with life itself. It was no easy task. This kind of careful calculation came into play at the moment the seconds met to negotiate the conditions of a duel (so many pistol shots at a certain distance, or so many fencing rounds of a certain duration). Seconds were charged with protecting the interests of the men they represented, preventing a duel if possible but also ensuring that their charge not be put at a disadvantage if a duel could not be avoided. The trick was that they were not to appear to be seeking advantage, and certainly not unfair advantage.

The verbal and mental gymnastics involved in seeking favorable dueling conditions without appearing to do so were sometimes comic. In November 1883, for example, Salvatore "Totó" Nicosía sent his seconds to the offices of the newspaper *El Nacional*, demanding that the editors, Duvimioso Terra and Manuel Herrero y Espinosa, retract a *suelto* he found insulting. Terra informed Nicosía's envoys that he was not responsible for the article, which had appeared under the pseudonym "Un Nacionalista," but that the author would be happy to answer for his words. Only two months earlier, the same Nicosía had permanently destroyed David Buchelli's career and reputation, as we saw in chapter 1, but this time things went differently. "Un Nacionalista" turned out to be a young Blanco militant named Juan Smith, who coincidentally just happened to a fencing champion.[40] It is reasonable to surmise that the editors of *El Nacional*, knowing that the offending piece might provoke a duel, had taken some care in choosing its putative author. When Nicosía learned the identity of the man he was expected to duel, he understood the trap that had been set for him. Incensed, he continued to demand that one of the editors, not the writer, answer his challenge, and loudly raised the possibility (not at all far-fetched) that Smith was nothing but a front man, a *testaferro*, who had affixed his name to an article written by others.[41] But Terra and Herrero y Espinosa resolutely refused to accept a duel, and pointed out that journalists in Uruguay always answered individually for their writings. If Nicosía wanted to make a *legal* claim against the paper, they would happily put themselves at his disposition, but satisfaction in the gentlemanly arena could only come from Smith.[42] Ultimately Nicosía resigned himself to his fate, and the six men (two duelists and four seconds) set sail for Buenos Aires in order to avoid meddling by the authorities.

Uruguayan police apparently tipped off their Argentine counterparts, because on arrival in Buenos Aires the party was intercepted by an official who made them swear an oath not to duel in the city.[43] They did so, but that was the least of their concerns, because the seconds had yet to agree on weapons and rules for the duel, and the negotiations were unusually conflicted. Nicosía's seconds sought to counter Smith's fencing skill by demanding a duel with pistols. In defense of that position, they reminded Smith's seconds that Nicosía had the right to choose the parameters of the duel, and that he would be at an unfair disadvantage with sabers because of an injury sustained in a previous affair of honor.[44] But Smith's seconds would have none of it. First, they challenged Nicosía's right to declare himself the offended party, charging that "El Nacionalista" had only written in response to an earlier article of Nicosía's, which had allegedly insulted all the women of Uruguay.[45] They further argued that Nicosía's arrogance in calling Smith a *testaferro* and demanding a duel with *El Nacional*'s editors instead constituted the gravest possible insult to Smith's honor as a gentleman. And Smith's seconds also provided a medical excuse, attesting that their charge had a bad right eye and was incapable of aiming a pistol.[46]

The seconds met several times over the course of two days, but nothing could break the impasse. As the preliminaries dragged on without a duel, both parties began to worry how this might reflect on their images. Neither man had an interest in dueling under conditions imposed by the other, but neither could appear to be running from his gentlemanly responsibilities. Nicosía used his paper to carry on in public the argument that his seconds were making in private. Posturing masterfully, he painted himself as a generous man of honor, willing to face his adversary in any place, at any time, under any conditions, despite the seriousness of the injury he had sustained in a previous duel (his thirteenth). Caring not for his life, which, as he told it, he was almost certain to lose, all that mattered was his honor.[47] For all the bombast, it is only fair to recognize that Nicosía did keep his word, although his seconds, as it turned out, were not about to let their *ahijado* sacrifice much of anything, least of all his life. The duel took place with sabers, as Smith had insisted; in short order, the young fencing master dealt Nicosía a gash on the index finger; the doctors intervened to declare the Italian "in a condition of inferiority"; the seconds agreed to stop the duel; Nicosía offered no complaint; and it was all over, much to the relief or disappointment of the many spectators on hand.[48]

In the aftermath, some papers tried to present the duel as a noble event that restored the honor of both parties, but others ridiculed what they described as a farce. *El Hilo Eléctrico* was among the most uncharitable. In an editorial entitled "É finita la commedia" (the title in Italian to mock Nicosía), the paper criticized both men: Smith for insisting on dueling only with the weapon with which he was skilled, Nicosía for allowing doctors to stop the duel at first blood, and the whole affair for its melodramatic buildup and anticlimactic denouement. "As we see it," the article concluded, "both adversaries come out reduced to their exact proportions, which are certainly small indeed. My God! How about something more serious!"[49] In this case, the duel became a farce because neither antagonist, for all the rhetoric about dying for honor, showed much willingness to die for honor. Both seemed primarily concerned with saving their skins while putting on a show of valor and conviction. Nicosía paid a somewhat higher price than Smith for that show: he alone was detained by Argentine authorities after the duel, and *L'Indipendente* ended up surviving only another year and a half.[50] He eventually took up diplomatic postings in Peru and later Chile, where he served for years.[51]

The Nicosía-Smith case may be an outlier, but it seems clear that most Uruguayan duelists were not particularly interested in dying, or killing, for that matter. Nevertheless, the legitimacy of the duel as an institution rested on its seriousness of purpose, and the idea of responsibility presupposed the possibility of facing death. Still, everyone had heard the tales of well-meaning seconds, who, unbeknownst to the duelists, loaded their pistols with powder but no projectiles and took to the grave the secret that no one had actually been in any danger.[52] Worse than that, the proliferation of trivial duels, first-blood duels, and duels for show threatened to undermine the entire institution. This was a major concern because advocates had to combat stereotypes that portrayed the duel as a farcical ceremony in which two self-important twits went at each other with swords for five or ten minutes, declared honor satisfied, and went off to a banquet to celebrate their reconciliation. The Socialist paper *Justicia*, for example, lampooned the "dueling epidemic" of 1919:

> Two very serious, correct, and foppish gentlemen present themselves before two other gentlemen as serious, correct, and foppish as they. They contemplate each other seriously, and speak of offenses, of pistols, of sabers, of sword-points and edges. They talk of Honor Codes. They contemplate each other again, with dignity. Later they go out … they arrive at the "terreno." Each group salutes the other with chivalry. The duelists

Fig. 2.3 Salvatore "Totó" Nicosía, from his later years as a diplomat for Argentina. República Argentina, Archivo del Ministerio de Relaciones Exteriores. Courtesy of Guillermo Silva Grucci.

take a few swipes at each other with swords, with the same circumspection with which they tie their neckties or their bootlaces.

Both get cut and they go back to their homes. Seconds and friends run to the newspapers with the *actas* all written out, and the whole novel is recounted. Care is taken to emphasize that both men fulfilled their duty, demonstrating their valor in every way. And then, the comedy concluded, after having been the subject of every conversation and the object of every invective, the ephemeral glory of having been the "men of the hour" (the aspiration behind virtually all duels) slowly fades.[53]

True or not, these were clichés that Uruguayans knew all too well, and which had the potential to delegitimize the duel as the guarantor of honor and responsibility.

If the legitimacy of the duel was threatened by trivial duels where no one got hurt, it was equally threatened by duels whose danger seemed disproportionate to their cause. Another common cliché – perhaps nothing more than an urban legend – was that of the duel fought between two young men over the affections of a woman of dubious morals. Newspaper stories about such cases always came from other countries: presumably they were reprinted for their value as cautionary tales.[54] Far more serious were those duels in which the seconds agreed to severe and perilous conditions that the original offense simply did not warrant. Uruguay's first recorded dueling fatality in 1866 raised precisely those kinds of questions. The duel was fought between José Pedro Bustamante and Servando Martínez, former friends and political allies, whose momentary exchange of sharp words did not in retrospect merit the deadly exchange of pistol shots that ended Martínez's life. In a meeting to elect directors of the Club Libertad, Bustamante objected to comments made by Jacobo Varela, and an argument ensued. When Martínez interceded in support of Varela, Bustamante reportedly snapped back, "Shut your mouth, insolent!" A challenge followed, and the seconds agreed to severe conditions: pistols at fifteen paces.[55] The two men met on the field of honor, and Martínez fell with a bullet to the heart.[56] The tragic death of the young officer made a deep impression, and people immediately began to wonder how two former friends, who had fought side by side for the Colorado caudillo Venancio Flores and later in the Paraguayan War, could have agreed to a duel to the death.

Many blamed the seconds for ignoring their responsibilities as mediators and permitting a duel whose conditions were not calibrated to the offense. Press accounts began to emerge that José Pedro Ramírez, brother of one of Martínez's seconds and long-time enemy of Bustamante, possibly egged Martínez on. It was alleged that José Pedro coached Martínez before the duel and that the brother, who was supposed to put Martínez's interests above everything, had rejected a suggestion by Bustamante's seconds that they render the pistols harmless by loading them with gunpowder alone. Unable to convince skeptics that his actions were beyond reproach, José Pedro Ramírez published a pamphlet that portrayed Bustamante as the provocateur and Martínez as a man who would not be dissuaded from a dangerous pistol duel, no matter how hard his seconds had tried to convince him to duel with sabers instead. As for the charge that his brother Juan Augusto had thwarted the unloaded-pistol gambit, José Pedro argued that no second had the right to violate previously agreed-upon dueling conditions.[57]

The stakes of this debate could not have been clearer, or higher. José Cándido Bustamante himself was the man behind the accusations against the Ramírez brothers, and one suspects that his campaign may have been a cry for absolution after having killed a friend, perhaps a projection of his own feelings of guilt onto an enemy. The subtitle of his anti–José Pedro Ramírez screed, "the cry of an afflicted conscience," might lead the psychoanalytically inclined in that direction, and historians have tended to give greater credence to Ramírez's version of events. But if Ramírez did in fact goad Servando Martínez into a duel to the death with *his own* archenemy, if José Pedro connived with his brother Juan Augusto to sabotage any chance of a pre-duel conciliation, if Juan Augusto rebuffed Bustamante's seconds' plot to render the pistols harmless and insisted on loading them himself, then he was at least an accessory to murder, if not worse. If the accusations were true, the Bustamante-Martínez duel was a conspiracy, not an affair of honor, a crime rather than a tragedy, and Servando Martínez was both the unwitting instrument and the victim of his own second's nefarious plan. That the duel could potentially provide cover for premeditated murder was one of its most unsettling qualities, a point often made in legal debates about its appropriate penalization.[58]

The point is that duelists routinely had to negotiate a precarious path between the Scylla of ridicule for duels in which no one faced genuine danger, and the Charybdis of tragedy or even criminality. Seconds, doctors, and the director of combat shared a profound responsibility. In saber duels, it was important to know when to call an end to combat: too late and someone might really get hurt, too soon and the duelists could come out looking silly. Luckily, the intervention of medical professionals aided in that task. Normally fencing duels were stopped by the seconds on the basis of the physicians' expert evaluation, dutifully recorded in the *actas* in appropriately technical scientific terminology. It is sometimes hard not to see a bit of face-saving exaggeration in the medical mumbo-jumbo. "First-blood" duels, frowned upon as unserious, supposedly never happened in valiant Uruguay, but it was hardly unusual to read physicians' reports like the following: "During the second round, Espalter presented a laceration of the skin and subcutaneous cellular tissue of the dorsal region of the right hand, which placed him in a condition of manifest inferiority."[59] Decoded version: combat was stopped when José Luis Espalter got a cut on the back of the hand. Only when spectators were involved did it become more difficult to cook the *actas* in a way that emphasized the participants' bravery and put them in the best possible light.

Pistol duels presented a thornier problem. Although most pistol duels ended with all shots missing, because smooth-barreled dueling pistols were imprecise by design, a hit could easily cause death or serious injury. How carefully, then, did one aim? At first glance, the magnanimous act would seem to be to aim at the ground or shoot into the air, as Juan Carlos Gómez had. Things were not that simple, however, for two reasons. First, the man who missed on purpose had no guarantee that his adversary would do likewise, and thus never knew whether his generosity would turn out to be a reckless act of unilateral disarmament. But far more importantly, a man who made a spectacle of *not* firing at his opponent was in effect delivering an insult. By not aiming and not shooting, he robbed his adversary of the chance to confront death in defense of honor, denying him the opportunity to demonstrate his valor, demeaning him as a gentleman and as a man. Many believed that such "generosity" was anything but, and most dueling codes agreed. This helps to explain why Francisco Bauzá was so bitterly enraged when Carlos Maria Ramírez twice fired at the ground in their 1871 duel. "I didn't come here so that you could spare me my life," he reportedly shouted. "And I didn't come here to assassinate anybody," Ramírez is said to have retorted.[60]

A man who deliberately spared his opponent was also, arguably, trivializing the whole enterprise. By the logic of the honor codes, either an affront was serious enough to merit a duel or it was not. If one or both of the participants believed it appropriate to hold their fire on the field of honor, then they should not have gone to that field in the first place. In reality, however, when the time came in a pistol duel to choose whether or not to take aim at a congressman or a journalist with whom one had sparred for years, Uruguayans often did deliberately miss. Despite what the honor codes said, seconds conventionally read such an action as evidence of a desire for reconciliation, not as an insult. Take, for example, a 1914 duel between Eduardo Castro and Mario Ferreira Martínez, two "well-known young men of our society," following an unspecified but apparently serious altercation at a local nightspot. The *acta previa* negotiated by the seconds called for three shots at twenty-five paces. On the first shot, Castro (who an honor tribunal had ruled responsible for the original affront) aimed at the ground, while Ferreira's bullet barely missed. On the second shot, Ferreira reciprocated Castro's gesture in the first exchange by firing into the air. Seeing the two men's attitudes, the seconds stepped in and asked if they were willing to stop the duel rather than take their third shots, and both agreed.[61]

But on other occasions, duelists could face criticism for averting their fire, particularly if they were suspected of communicating in advance their intention to do so. In February 1916, the minister of interior, Baltasar Brum, read the

Executive's message (signed by the president and his cabinet) before a joint session of both houses of Congress. In the speech, he railed against the "notorious irresponsibility" of opposition newspapers such as *La Tribuna Popular* and *Diario del Plata*, which "daily insert in their columns the most gratuitous diatribes against the Public Powers, going so far with their abusive language as to incite violence against the current situation."[62] Juan Andrés Ramírez, editor of *Diario del Plata*, considered the speech an offense against his honor and sent seconds to demand explanations of Dr Brum. The seconds agreed to a pistol duel, two shots at fifteen paces – a shorter distance than usual for these kinds of political affairs. After a sudden appearance by the police frustrated one attempt to carry out the duel, Brum and Ramírez met at dawn the next day, at which time Ramírez shot into the air and the seconds intervened to reconcile the duelists, which they did, shaking hands.[63] Ramírez's decision to fire in the air was understandable, given the circumstances surrounding the duel. Brum, after all, had only been the messenger: the phrases to which Ramírez took offense were part of an official presidential address, written collectively, with the president ultimately responsible for its content. Ramírez therefore had no real issue with Brum as an individual, yet it was Brum he was obliged to challenge because Brum was the man who had uttered the offending words, and also because challenging a sitting president was problematic.

The day after the duel, however, reports got out that Ramírez had planned from the outset to avert his fire, and that he had communicated this intent to his seconds, confiding that he did not believe Brum had offended him personally. Ramírez immediately took to the press to clarify and defend his actions, because as an expert on the duel and matters of honor, he realized how bad this looked. If Brum had not really offended him, the original challenge was frivolous by definition. If he never intended to aim and fire, he was, at least arguably, violating the honor codes and making the duel a farce. If he directly or indirectly communicated his intention to Brum in advance, this was the most serious transgression, because it rid the encounter of any valor, it insulted Brum by depriving him of the chance to confront death, and worst of all, it forced upon Brum a certain moral pressure to reciprocate by also missing deliberately. After all, if Brum knew he was in no danger, to persist in his intention to fire was tantamount to murder. For any duelist to force such a choice on his opponent would have been an act of cowardice, not magnanimity. In his defense, Ramírez emphasized that his choice to avert his fire was spontaneous, not premeditated; that he had come to his decision on the field of honor the day before, when their first attempt at a duel was thwarted by police; and that he had divulged his intention to his seconds only in the strictest confidence. He also emphasized that Brum's offense against him was both real and legitimate cause for a duel, yet he made a distinction between his need to punish an affront and his lack of personal animosity toward Dr Brum: "I accept the duel as a necessity and I accept its fundamental laws," he wrote, "but when dealing with a man's life I believe one should follow the impulses of the heart."[64] What actually happened is probably impossible to know, but Ramírez's defensive framing of events demonstrates how important he believed it was to restore a master narrative of generosity, integrity, and seriousness that the flurry of post-duel rumors had threatened to undermine. The narrative mattered.

"Reading" a Fatal Duel: Romero Giménez and Paul y Angulo

Every duel had an audience that sat in judgment of the participants. Fatal duels greatly elevated the stakes of that verdict: any deviation from the letter or spirit of the honor code, the slightest hint of advantage seeking, dishonesty, or lack of magnanimity, might open up the question of whether a duelist could be held morally and/or legally responsible for the death. An 1880 duel fought in Montevideo between two Spanish-born Argentine journalists provides a tragic but illuminating example. José Paul y Angulo, editor of *La España Moderna*, had become violently estranged from Enrique Romero Jiménez, editor of *El Correo Español*, a more established rival paper. Their disagreements were in part political, in part personal, and likely exacerbated by competition for the same Spanish immigrant readership. Whatever the cause, the last straw for Paul y Angulo was a satirical piece in *El Correo Español* that he believed ridiculed him personally. Incensed, he accosted Romero Jiménez in the Centro Gallego of Buenos Aires in front of numerous witnesses and demanded to know whether he was in fact the person to whom the insulting article alluded. Romero Jiménez refused to answer. Paul y Angulo insisted, and after a heated exchange of words he committed the unspeakable outrage of spitting in Romero Jiménez's face. According to the press reports, Romero Jiménez reached for his revolver, but cooler heads prevailed upon him to settle the matter in proper gentlemanly fashion.[65]

The next day, the two enemies and their four seconds sailed across the Río de la Plata to Montevideo to consummate the duel. On their arrival in Uruguay, they spent the night in separate hotels; the following day, 13 August 1880, the seconds bought a pair of pistols and all set off for the outskirts of the city. Given the severity of the offense, the conditions of the duel were equally severe: the two men were to exchange up to five shots at twenty-five paces, and if neither of the duelists was yet incapacitated, they would advance and continue exchanging bullets at ever-closer range until one of them could proceed no longer.[66] The weapons chosen, at Romero Jiménez's insistence (and over Paul y Angulo's objections), were modern and precise Remington pistols, as opposed to the muzzle-loaded dueling pistols of tradition.[67] At the signal, Paul y Angulo (at least by his own account) fired deliberately at the ground; immediately he felt Romero Jiménez's bullet whiz by his head, missing by centimeters. On the next shot he took aim and this time hit Romero Jiménez squarely in the chest. When the Montevideo police arrived, Paul y Angulo and his seconds had fled the scene and were soon on their way back to Argentina, while Romero Jiménez was rushed to the home of Dr Herrero y Salas, who had attended the duel as his physician, for treatment of his wounds.[68]

Over the next nine days, Romero Jiménez lay incapacitated in Montevideo as a team of doctors tried and failed to extract the bullet. Initial reports that his wounds were not critical gave way to increasingly pessimistic assessments, and at 5 a.m. on the morning of 22 August 1880, he died.[69] All the while both the Montevideo and Buenos Aires papers covered the news in a media frenzy. The story was all the more tragic and melodramatic because at the very moment that Romero Jiménez agonized in Montevideo, his wife in Buenos Aires (a blind poetess known popularly as La ciega del Guadalquivir) was giving birth to their first child.[70] When news of his death reached the Argentine capital, it sparked an outpouring of grief. In Montevideo, as many as fifteen hundred well-wishers, mostly freemasons, Spaniards, and journalists, accompanied Romero Jiménez's remains to the steamship docks for the trip back to Buenos Aires. An even larger crowd – estimates range from two thousand to five thousand – awaited the ship's arrival on the other shore.[71] After a procession to La Recoleta cemetery, the mourners listened to eulogies from such luminaries as Bartolomé Mitre.

In the days and weeks following the funeral, the writers of *El Correo Español* published a flood of telegrams and letters of condolence, and they began a collection on behalf of Romero Jiménez's widow and orphaned newborn daughter.[72] Accompanying the grief and praise for the fallen journalist came a rising undercurrent of hatred for the man responsible for his tragic end. *El Correo Español* described Romero Jiménez as having been "brought down by the arm of Cain," and published a letter that called Paul y Angulo an assassin: "Damn them once and a thousand times, damned be the vile assassins of the patriot among patriots, the father of the poor, the honorable, frank, noble and loyal friend! Be damned, men without honor and without conscience!"[73]

Another letter spoke of Romero Jiménez's enemies as Judas Iscariots and asked rhetorically whether they were "satisfied with their work."[74] A third was more explicit still: "What heart, no matter how cold, does not rise up to protest the evil and infamous action of a man who does not deserve to be called by any other name than traitor, traitor even to his own ideas? ... Let it be known that we protest once and a thousand times against the evil conduct of that *vile* Paul y Angulo and his henchmen, who seek to destroy truth, reason, and morality ... Glory, a thousand times eternal glory to him who has been the victim of an infamous villainy."[75]

It was by no means inevitable that Paul y Angulo should be treated so badly. Fatal duels always brought praise for the valor of the fallen, but only occasionally did they lead to outrage against the man left standing. The grieving writers of *El Correo Español* deliberately whipped up the climate of indignation, but that does not explain why so many Argentines shared their opinion, so much so that Paul y Angulo felt compelled to exile himself to Paraguay.[76] Instead, the denunciation of the journalist as an "assassin" arose from a particular interpretation of the duel, of its origins, and of Paul y Angulo's apparent motives and intentions. The events provided a kind of text in action, filled with deeper meanings into which people read their own prejudices and preconceptions. No one, for example, accused Paul y Angulo of treachery or disloyalty in the combat itself. *El Correo Español* wrote that the "majority of Spaniards consider the death of unfortunate Romero Jiménez an assassination not because of any violation *on the Field of Honor* of the rules that pertain in such acts, but on account of the circumstances that made their presence on that field inevitable."[77]

Three themes ran through the anti-Paul y Angulo reading of those "circumstances":

1) *Paul y Angulo's ambition, ingratitude, and betrayal of a friend and benefactor.* When Paul y Angulo first arrived from Spain to Buenos Aires, Romero Jiménez gave him a job writing for *El Correo Español*. The way some people told the story, Romero Jiménez had been more than simply an employer; he had been a generous protector and a friend who helped Paul y Angulo get established in his new home. Yet Paul y Angulo had showed his ingratitude by soon leaving *El Correo Español* to found his own rival paper, which he then used as a vehicle to contradict, criticize, and slander his former benefactor. So even before the duel, according to his enemies, Paul y Angulo had proved himself a Judas, and this interpretation profoundly colored many people's interpretation of what happened subsequently. Given their prior relationship, critics believed, Paul y Angulo had no right to confront Romero Jiménez in the Centro Gallego, and

no right to demand "explanations" from the editor of *El Correo Español*, any more than a man had the right to demand gentlemanly explanations from a father or older brother.[78]

2) *The egregious, deliberate, and unprovoked nature of Paul y Angulo's offense.* Spitting in a man's face, particularly in front of witnesses, constituted about as grave an insult as one could imagine. The dueling codes made clear that any physical contact in anger constituted the most serious category of offense, and in such cases the offended party had the right to demand a duel under the most dangerous conditions. Romero Jiménez's supporters failed to see anything in the journalist's satirical barbs against Paul y Angulo that could justify such a rash and violent reaction. Many press polemics led to duels, but Paul y Angulo's ugly offense seemed (to his critics) totally lacking in any sense of proportion. Small surprise, then, that some of Romero Jiménez's supporters began to wonder out loud whether the insult had been a deliberate provocation. These suspicions were nourished by allegations that Paul y Angulo had once said, when facing a possible duel with a man named Moncayo some time earlier, "If I die, *La España Moderna* will get more subscribers; and if Moncayo dies, the same will happen for identical reasons."[79] The clear implication was that his actions as a duelist had nothing at all to do with honor.

3) *Paul y Angulo's murderous intent.* If the incident in the Centro Gallego *had* been a premeditated provocation, then Paul y Angulo's intentions became suspect. Was this a case of a man attempting to precipitate a duel in order to eliminate a rival? In the majority of fatal duels, this was a question that no one dared ask out loud. But the writers of *El Correo Español* began making just this accusation in the aftermath of Romero's funeral. They alleged that about a year and a half previously, Romero Jiménez's political enemies had hatched a plot whereby they insulted him in the press with such violence that a duel should have been inevitable. They then planned to tip off the authorities, who would arrest and convict him for dueling. Romero Jiménez, however, supposedly got wind of the plot and refused to take the bait.[80] And this, *El Correo Español* charged, was only one of several sinister plans that his opponents had cooked up. Given such antecedents, it only stood to reason that those same unnamed enemies had put Paul y Angulo up to the job, bankrolling his *España Moderna* precisely in the hope "that the two men would kill each other."[81] Whether Paul y Angulo was the intellectual author of an assassination or just the instrument of others did not particularly interest his critics: his guilt was the same either way.

Paul y Angulo found it nearly impossible to answer these accusations, especially in light of the genuine outpouring of grief and concern for his adversary's blind widow and orphaned infant. He obviously could not challenge his critics to a duel – that would only prove them right – so he had his attorney petition the correctional judge to bring libel charges against *El Correo Español*.[82] The case was thrown out, and as public opinion turned ever more hostile, Paul y Angulo had little choice but to remain in Asunción, stewing in his juices.

He did not remain silent for long, however. Starting in early October 1880, the Buenos Aires paper *El Nacional* agreed to publish a series of unbearably polemical letters, under the headline "Intereses españoles," in which Paul y Angulo tried to vindicate himself.[83] To counter the impression that he was an ambitious adventurer, he talked about his importance in Spain, where he had spent his considerable personal fortune on behalf of the Republican cause, had been director of two papers (*La Igualdad* and *El Combate*), had served as *diputado constituyente* in a country "where one does not rise to public office by mere luck,"[84] and had been in every way a respected public man of unassailable character, who only left Spain because he was forced into political exile.[85] In light of those noble and gentlemanly antecedents, it was impossible, then, to conclude that he was some nobody who owed his career in Buenos Aires to the generosity of Romero Jiménez. To make that argument even more forcefully, Paul y Angulo went on in great detail about his late rival, whom he portrayed as a failure in Spain, a man with no career, no abilities, no ideals, and no political followers.[86] The subtitle of Paul y Angulo's series of articles, "El envidioso y el envidiado" (The envious and the envied), made clear his contention that if anyone was guilty of acting out of envy, it was Romero Jiménez. Romero Jiménez's envy of *him* led *El Correo Español* to wage all-out war against *La España Moderna*. Envy led Romero Jiménez to insist on dueling with the deadly Remington pistols. Envy led Romero Jiménez to aim carefully for his head, even as he, Paul y Angulo, directed his first shot toward the ground.[87]

Unfortunately for Paul y Angulo, as self-vindication degenerated into diatribe, he only succeeded in digging a deeper hole for himself. P.J. Rosselló, who had been one of his accusers throughout August and September, was so angered by "Intereses españoles" that he published a fulminating, insult-filled response in *El Correo Español* and then appointed seconds to deliver a new challenge.[88] But a far worse blow for Paul y Angulo came when *La Nación* publicly denounced his letters as repugnant and criticized *El Nacional* for having agreed to publish them.[89] *La Nación* was among the most powerful and respected papers in Buenos Aires, and even though it was by no means impartial (its publisher Bartolomé Mitre had been a political ally of Romero Jiménez and had spoken at his funeral), its opinion mattered. Several other papers with no obvious partisan axes to grind, including those published for

Buenos Aires's French and German colonies, joined in the condemnation. Their criticism was double: first, they argued that "insulting the dead" was as cowardly as it was undignified. Second – and this critique was made forcefully by *L'Union Française* – it was also an explicit violation of the dueling codes, which forbade revisiting the polemic that had given rise to a duel once that duel had been fought.[90] At one level, this second criticism was truly unjust: no one could deny that writers for *El Correo Español* had been the first to break the silence, and yet almost no one had criticized them for doing so, or at least not in print.[91] But in the end, justice mattered less than opinion, and there was nothing Paul y Angulo could do to win opinion over to his side, nothing to overcome the images of a blind widow and a newborn child who would never meet her father.

In a heart-wrenching letter born of desperation, Paul y Angulo published his parting shot, entitled "No puedo más."

> I can't go on any longer! Not because of remorse; I know very well that I have acted humbly and with unassailable morality, but I am amazed at so much injustice and iniquity. What kind of society is this? ... I am insulted once, twice, thrice, a hundred times ... I protest once, twice, thrice, a hundred times before demanding explanations ... once again I am clearly insulted, so finally I confront the provocateur face to face ... and ask for verbal explanations in public, and in public I am again denied any apology; and then, only then, do I offend ... so I am challenged [to a duel] ... and I fight, allowing my adversary the choice of weapons and conditions; and I shoot the first bullet pointing at the ground; and he aims at me, at my head; and so [on the second shot] I defend my life by firing at the man who tried to kill me; and then, out of respect for the pain (either feigned, or true, or exaggerated) of the friends of the wounded man (who finally dies), I even leave the country; and then in the press they call me assassin, infamous, evil, disloyal, I am called (my God!) just about everything in the dictionary that could possibly offend an honor, a soul, a heart that feels; and all those who were my friends remain silent ... and the press says not a single word of rebuke against so much injustice, so much barbarous cruelty; and then, only then, do I go to defend myself and my friends so atrociously defamed ... and then, on the pretext, just the pretext ... that I insult the dead, I am once again condemned by serious and important newspapers, whose editors forget how silent they were and are in the face of the infamies committed against me and many others ...

> *Yo no puedo más.* If society en masse abandons me, I'll shut up and let men be unjust. As for what will happen to me, I will carry out my duty as a gentleman with the one man ... who I believed noble out of all of those who have defamed me [i.e., Rosselló]. God willing may he have the good fortune to kill me.[92]

In the end, God was not willing to mercifully end Paul y Angulo's life. The seconds decided that a new duel was not justified, and both sides vowed to put an end to the polemic.[93] Paul y Angulo was left to deal with life as a pariah: at some point he abandoned South America and ended his days alone and poor in a Paris hotel.[94]

It is hard to say whose story was more tragic, but the fates of Romero Jiménez and Paul y Angulo attest to the power of public opinion to give meaning to a duel, no matter how imperfectly that meaning might fit the facts. Public opinion made the winner of a duel the loser, turning dead man into hero and victor into villain. In this case, actual events on the field of honor were not particularly important; what mattered were circumstances, antecedents, and above all, personalities. Much the same could be said for the Gómez-Calvo, Bustamante-Martínez, Smith-Nicosía, and Ramírez-Brum duels. The tension between the imagined values of chivalry and the varied and conflicted motives of actual duelists played out as spectacle, performed for a select audience of insiders. Duelists ostensibly paid tribute to man's highest ideals – courage, integrity, responsibility, generosity, and sacrifice – even when their goals might be as mundane as silencing a critic, winning an argument, scoring political points, or boosting the circulation of a newspaper. Success or failure was measured by how well the duelist convinced his audience that he embodied the values of the reluctant warrior, the man who did everything for honor and principle, even when that meant disdaining life itself. On the one hand, it was a game of posing and dissembling, but on the other, playing one's part convincingly demanded at least some genuine courage, integrity, responsibility, generosity, and sacrifice.

Dueling, the Press, and the Norms of Public Debate

On 5 July 1880, two army officers arrived at the home of Washington Bermúdez, editor and principal writer of a satirical weekly called *El Negro Timoteo*. They were delivering a challenge from another officer, Alberto Schilemberg, who for some time had been fed up with the paper's constant attacks on the government and the military. Days earlier, Schilemberg had placed in the pro-government *La Nación* an anonymous recurring message (*permanente*) that opened with the words "Washington Bermúdez is a coward and a scoundrel" and escalated from there.[95] Though unsigned, the word "guaranteed" appeared at the bottom, sending the message that its author would willingly come forward if challenged to a duel. Bermúdez, however, would not be provoked. He answered with an editorial denouncing the regime's *testaferros*, whom he compared to the *condottieri* of medieval Italy and described as "modern-day Jews," *espadachines* without shame who sold their services to the highest bidder.[96] "Is it worth it," Bermúdez asked rhetorically, "to allow oneself to be killed by such a man in a duel?" His answer: "If it were a decent individual, sure, as men we were born to die. But to gamble one's life with a *testaferro*, who trusts not in valor but in his skill with weapons, now that would be lunacy if it weren't stupidity."[97] Unable to contain himself at this new insult, Schilemberg asked officers José Gómez and Mariano Sábat (the latter a renowned fencing master) to act as seconds and communicate his challenge to the editor of *El Negro Timoteo*.[98] Once again, Bermúdez refused to play their game. He invited the seconds into his office, where he promptly reached for a revolver, pointed it at the flabbergasted officials, and ordered them out of his house.[99]

On the surface of things, one could hardly imagine a more direct assault on the laws of honor. To pull a gun on two unarmed seconds in the exercise of their gentlemanly mission was unheard of, and in most circumstances would have discredited Bermúdez as an irresponsible coward, unwilling to answer for his words. Certainly that was the interpretation that Schilemberg, his seconds, and all the pro-government papers presented.[100] But Bermúdez succeeded in painting himself as the victim of aggression, and his version of events ended up being repeated by all the opposition papers, from the Catholic *El Bien Público* to the liberal *La Razón*. What is interesting is that Bermúdez's version of the facts diverged from that of Schilemberg's seconds in only one small but pivotal detail. As the journalist told it, when Sábat and Gómez arrived at his house, they did not immediately announce the purpose of their visit but instead stammered and beat around the bush. So when Bermúdez pulled out his revolver, he ostensibly did so in self-defense, not knowing if the strangers had peaceful intentions. The pro-Bermúdez accounts faithfully reported this version, no matter how unlikely it sounded, because it was the only possible explanation that validated his actions.[101] Still, although that one detail was indeed crucial, how people read that detail hinged upon a series of other considerations that set the context. First, did the dueling laws give

Schilemberg any right to challenge Bermúdez in the first place? Had the satirist actually committed an offense against his honor? Schilemberg said yes: for months, *El Negro Timoteo* had been in the business of insulting and ridiculing the Uruguayan military. As a loyal officer, he had felt those attacks deeply, and he had published the *permanente* in response. When Bermúdez answered the *permanente* by calling its author a *testaferro* and *espadachín*, the insult was no longer collective but individual, thus giving Schilemberg the right to demand satisfaction.[102]

Bermúdez, however, asked how it was possible to attack the honor of a man he had never mentioned by name – indeed, a man he did not even know. And if Schilemberg was responding to a collective insult to the military rather than to any personal affront, many questioned the presumption that he was authorized to do so. Though an officer in the 5th Chasseurs Battalion, Schilemberg was of Swiss nationality. If the whole Uruguayan armed forces had been insulted, why was the only challenger to come forward a foreign-born middle-level officer whose sole qualification appeared to be his skill at fencing and marksmanship?[103] And finally, Bermúdez clearly had a point in noting that *El Negro Timoteo*'s worst insults never remotely approached the language used by Schilemberg in his *permanente*. By what logic, then, did the officer now claim the right to act as if he were the offended party, issuing a challenge in the name of *his* supposedly damaged honor?[104]

The second and more complicated question that divided Bermúdez's supporters and opponents was the motive behind Schilemberg's actions. If we believe the officer and his seconds, this was a transparent affair of honor, in strict accordance with the dueling codes. After being insulted indirectly in Bermúdez's columns, Schilemberg deliberately attacked the journalist in print in the hope of obtaining a proper gentlemanly response. When Bermúdez refused to act like a gentleman and answered instead with more insults, Schilemberg had no choice left but to take offense and to name seconds.[105] If, in the pre-duel negotiations, the seconds determined that Schilemberg's provocation had been more egregious than Bermúdez's, then they had every right to award Bermúdez the choice of weapons. But in no way did Schilemberg's offense give Bermúdez the right to refuse a duel, and certainly not the right to chase away two seconds at gunpoint.

Bermudez's supporters, however, rejected the idea that this erstwhile duel had anything whatsoever to do with honor. In their view, the minister of war, Máximo Santos, acting as the true power behind figurehead President Vidal, had handpicked Schilemberg to write the *permanente*. By choosing a skilled duelist to intentionally provoke an incident, Santos hoped to leave his opponent only two options – either fight a duel he was guaranteed to lose, or go silent to save his skin at the cost of being proven a coward. When Bermúdez failed to be provoked but also refused to shut up, Schilemberg stepped up the intimidation on Santos's behalf. Inventing a trumped-up offense to honor where none existed, they set the dueling ritual in motion to force Bermúdez to choose either submission or suicide.[106] Understood in this broader context, the self-defense argument becomes much easier to believe. It still strains credulity to imagine that at the moment Bermúdez pulled his gun on Gómez and Sábat he did not know who they were or the reason for their call. But this necessary lie pointed to a deeper truth. On the surface the seconds' visit may have conformed to the gentlemanly procedures set down in the dueling codes, but Bermúdez's supporters saw in those formalities of honor a paper-thin mask to conceal a more sinister purpose: the elimination of an opposition journalist by intimidation or, if necessary, by murder in the guise of a duel.[107] It was surely because they were convinced of this deeper truth that so many opposition papers proved willing to accept Bermúdez's far-fetched telling of what happened that day in his home.

In the end, Bermúdez paid no significant price for what should have been an unspeakable violation of the dueling codes. In the aftermath of the encounter, he fired off an open letter to the minister of foreign relations, demanding to be told whether or not freedom of the press still existed in Uruguay. The minister replied that writers remained free to say whatever they wished, as long as they took responsibility for the consequences (legal or otherwise) of their words.[108] But despite the clear message that the authorities would not protect journalists from dueling challenges, neither Schilemberg nor Santos chose to press the matter further. Nor could they have, given the outpouring of support for the editor of *El Negro Timoteo*. Bermúdez had escaped a duel by chasing away his adversary's seconds at gunpoint, and yet he won the contest of public opinion or at least fought to a draw. He had avoided society's condemnation because a sufficient number of influential Uruguayans, closely reading the events of early July 1880, agreed that this was not a case of cowardice but of a dictatorial government's aggression against the press.

At one level, the Bermúdez-Schilemberg incident was unusual, even extraordinary. But the tensions it illustrates between the code of honor, the abuse of government power, and the rights and responsibilities of a free press were not only common but typical. Given the distance between gentlemanly ideals and ignoble realities, we should not be surprised by the frequency with which

No ha tenido jamás Montevideo,
un hombre *de color* mas guapo y listo
que el *Negro* de Bermudez, segun creo.

Fig. 2.4 Washington Bermúdez, editor of the satirical weekly *El Negro Timoteo* (hence the racial caricature). *Caras y Caretas* (Montevideo) 1, no. 12 (5 October 1890). Digitized by Anáforas, Publicaciones Periódicas, Facultad de Información y Comunicación, Universidad de la República.

duelists and seconds disputed gentlemanly law, and few questions cropped up more often than the limits of press freedom and the boundaries of acceptable discourse. If a journalist accused the chief of police of corruption, for example, was he committing an offense against the honor of a public servant, or was he exercising his rightful duty as watchdog and defender of the public good? If the police chief challenged that journalist to a duel, was he legitimately defending his name and the reputation of his family, or was he holding a gun to the journalist's head in order to silence him, all as part of a cynical cover-up? Time and time again, decade after decade, opposition journalists would charge that corrupt governments and venal public officials abused the duel in order to intimidate and censor. This pushback by the press sparked ongoing debate about the proper line between defense of honor and free democratic discourse. And just as judges in libel trials had to determine where legitimate criticism crossed over into defamation, so, too, did those called to respond on the field of honor to challenges they believed unjustified. Though aired in the arena of dueling codes, seconds, and honor tribunals, these were conflicts about the rights and responsibilities of a free press.

Public officials sincerely believed that they had a right to their reputation, and many were convinced that the duel was the only effective protection against the *prensa brava*, the slash-and-burn political press that would stop at nothing to tear its adversaries down. Many in the press were willing to admit that journalistic malpractice was a problem, to the point that they tried several times to craft voluntary codes of professional conduct. In 1881, for example, Julio Herrera y Obes, editor of *El Heraldo* and later president of the republic, brought together the editors of all but two of the Montevideo papers to draft a set of rules designed to abolish "all personal insults, provocative and defamatory expressions, and anything that could be construed as diatribe." The draft document actually enumerated the prohibited words: "*crápula, canalla, chusma, bribón, pillo, corrompido, estúpido, cretino, animal, sinvergüenza, sucio, cornudo, tramposo, mulato, bastardo, libertino, embrollón, embustero*, and other terms of a similar nature."[109]

Attempts at collective self-regulation may have been motivated in part by a desire for greater professionalism within the industry, but they almost always came as preemptive strikes against proposed censorship laws. Rarely did journalistic practices change much, or at least not for very long. After all, political debate *was* heated, and for every journalist who decried the *prensa brava*, another argued that the indelicate realities of the world sometimes had to be expressed indelicately. Wrote Carlos Maria Ramírez's *La Paz* in 1870:

> It is more polite, without a doubt, to say "*mismanagement*" – rather than robbery – to characterize the sacking of the public treasury that we have been witnessing for some time; but it is not as exact, not as clear. It would be more measured to say that the government "*fails to comply with the laws*"; but more truthful to say that it runs roughshod over them, that it consistently mangles the Constitution, that it prostitutes its mission on a daily basis ... It would be more politic to say that "*the Minister of Government lacks the necessary qualities to be a good leader*," but clearer and more concise to say that he is a hustler and an ignoramus.[110]

José Batlle y Ordóñez made virtually the identical argument in 1886:

> There are certain moments ... when the events that occur are so monstrous that in all the Spanish dictionary there are only words that express clearly, albeit faintly, the enormity of the offense. For example, an assassination is committed by the political authorities, or public monies are stolen by those in power. How do we describe these events? Do we say that "a lamentable act" has been committed (as *El Siglo* did)? No, that is immoral and cowardly. The man protected by the public post he occupies, who in treachery strikes against the life of another, is called an *assassin*, just as the man who takes the property of others, be it public or private, is called a *thief* ... To use other words would be to falsify the truth, sacrificing the noble independence of thought at the altar of supposed decorum in language.[111]

Both Ramírez and Batlle, like Washington Bermúdez, lamented the misuse of the honor codes by those bent on stifling what they believed to be legitimate critique on matters of national interest. A generation later, after Batlle had himself served two terms in office, nothing had changed, the complaints were the same, and the tension between the honor of government officials and the duties of a free press continued to occupy the attention of duelists and seconds on a regular basis.

In 1921, for example, *La Tribuna Popular* published a news story that English authorities had boarded and searched the Uruguayan steamship *Rio Negro*, docked in Limerick, Ireland. According to the report, sailors had invited some local girls aboard the ship, gotten them drunk, and allegedly raped three of them. Commenting on the story, the paper wrote: "Granted that the rape of three Irish girls is an unspeakable outrage, it is a national disgrace that one of our fleet has been boarded by force."[112] The ship's second commander, Juan Sanmartín, either read or heard about the article upon returning to Montevideo and sent his seconds to demand explanations. Vicente Lápido assumed the duty of responding for *La Tribuna Popular*. When the four seconds met, Lápido's representatives refused to recognize Sanmartín's right to consider himself offended. If anyone should have to give explanations, they argued, it should be the persons accused of wrongdoing, not the journalists who brought that wrongdoing to light.[113] Lápido fumed at the idea that accused rapists, whose alleged actions had brought shame upon the nation, believed they had any right to invoke their honor. His anger went beyond the case at hand to a more fundamental principle. In Europe, he argued, no one would consider "solving questions of public accountability through private duels": "The sending of seconds to a journalist, who in the name of the public interest demands the clarification of a matter that affects the moral, social, or administrative credit of the nation, is as ridiculous as it would be to demand gentlemanly explanations of a prosecutor for the accusations that he might formulate."[114]

A few years later, the same newspaper took on the police chief of Montevideo in a very similar case. The paper had published a series of articles accusing him of corruption. The chief, General Juan A. Pintos, sent his seconds to demand either a retraction or a duel. But editor Juan Pedro Suárez refused to accept the police chief's challenge. Instead he handed the seconds a note declaring that he refused to consider General Pintos a gentleman "by virtue of the reprehensible deeds attributed to him, charges he has never refuted and which diminish his moral stature." Suárez declared himself willing to duel with one of the seconds instead.[115] *La Tribuna Popular*'s publisher José Lápido justified this attitude in a public letter ostensibly addressed to his editor-in-chief Suárez but in reality directed back at Pintos:

> Dear Friend, the Chief of Police of the Capital is attempting to offend me gratuitously, on account of this daily's campaign against a police force that has become the laughingstock not only of decent people but of the thieves and pimps as well, so horrible is its disorganization. In responding to this Mr. General who's never fought a battle, I say that in order to offend me, one must not only want to, one must be able to. And [Pintos's] actions in defense of pimps and low-life scum – charges that have been made against him publicly and which he has not yet refuted – render me immune from all provocation on his part.
>
> Let him resign his post and prove that he is not guilty of the accusations, and then he can talk about honor and have moral authority ...

> As long as General Pintos does not prove that the accusation against him is false, his words will have the same effect on me as the mud that gets splashed around on rainy days as the cars go by, which only dirties you for a moment, because no one is safe from all the crap in the street.[116]

As opposition journalists had done for decades, Suárez and Lápido denounced Pintos's abusive attempt to employ the duel as a means of suppressing critical reporting. Yet again, arguments about press freedom played out in the arena of the duel and followed its conventions. The only new twist here was the imputation that the legal and ethical clouds hanging over Pintos disqualified him as a gentleman and thus deprived him of the authority to go around challenging people to duels in the first place.

Paradoxically, though understandably, only persons well trained in the protocol of honor, whose "gentlemanly responsibility" was not in doubt, could so easily get away with refusing a duel while employing the kind of insulting language that Vicente Lápido had used in writing about the *Río Negro* incident, or that Suárez and José Lápido had wielded against Police Chief Pintos. It surely helped that Vicente was an accomplished fencer who had excelled in top European competitions: no one was likely to view his refusal to duel with Captain Sanmartín as a sign of cowardice.[117] Similarly, José Batlle y Ordóñez – according to friend and biographer Domingo Arena – "was never an advocate of the duel; he reluctantly accepted the practice as a barbarous necessity imposed by custom."[118] While he was president, Batlle had often ordered the police to intervene and stop duels before they occurred, yet he fought at least five duels, one fatal for his opponent, as we will see in chapter 3, and was involved in countless gentlemanly incidents.

For the Lápidos to enjoy the freedom to censure public officials that they believed corrupt, and for Batlle to defend his "noble independence of thought," these men had little alternative but to be duelists; this was the price of admission to the arena. Had they feared losing their lives in a duel, their license to engage in polemics would have been curtailed, their opponents would have insulted them freely, and their journalistic and political careers would have been far less successful. Such was the power of the code of honor in Uruguayan society and politics. Even those who most lamented its abuse were bound by its conventions, notwithstanding the duel's illegality prior to 1920. It is to these legal questions that we now turn.

Fig. 2.5 José Batlle y Ordóñez. Detail from a photo taken with visiting officers of the USS *Pittsburgh*, 1917. Museo Histórico Nacional, Montevideo.

3

Impunity to Legality: Dueling and the Law, 1860s–1930s

We take the opportunity to once more protest most earnestly against this wretched custom of illegal but licensed murder.

Uruguay News, 29 October 1893[1]

Periodically our judges remember that the law against the duel exists. They make one, two, three attempts to enforce it and later they give up, comprehending that it is absolutely impossible to make these laws effective.

Juan Andrés Ramírez, 23 May 1919[2]

Virgilio Sampognaro, Montevideo's chief of police, was a trusted public servant, loyal to the Colorado Party and his president, José Batlle y Ordóñez. When Batlle charged him with the duty of clamping down on a recent epidemic of duels, Sampognaro spared no effort in pursuing duelists, seconds, and even doctors, putting officers on their tail in the hope of frustrating duels before they happened. The goal was prevention, not punishment. Sometimes the chief succeeded, but determined duelists went to great lengths to escape detection, rushing all over town in their automobiles, using fake seconds as decoys to lead the police on wild-goose chases while duelists and the real seconds slipped off to some undisclosed location, or publishing phony *actas* in the papers to announce the peaceful resolution of conflicts that were in fact hours away from a duel.[3] The next day's news recounted these cat-and-mouse stories in vivid detail. In one often-retold anecdote, police officers ushered Sampognaro's friend Pablo Minelli into the police chief's office having caught him in flagranti delicto, pistol in hand after a duel with Alfredo García Morales. But Sampognaro let him go, unable to shake Minelli's insistence that he and his companions had only been out "target shooting." According to one version of the story, Minelli, also a Colorado, later confessed to Sampognaro with a play on words: "For the record I didn't lie to you. I *was* target shooting [*tirando al blanco*] ... [I was shooting] at the Blanco García Morales."[4]

One day in 1914, Sampognaro's agents arrived just moments after two duelists had exchanged their first shots. The policemen brought everyone to the station house, among them congressman Washington Paullier, who as one of the seconds was found with a recently fired pistol in his possession. Legally, the arrest of a sitting legislator was permitted by the constitution if and only if he was caught red-handed in the commission of a crime; in such cases it was the responsibility of the police to inform Congress immediately, so that the institution could decide whether or not to revoke parliamentary immunity. Paullier, however, was indignant that any policeman would have the audacity to arrest him. He marched out of the station, carrying under his arm the case with the two dueling pistols, and went home without anyone daring to stop him. When Sampognaro found out what had happened, he reasonably interpreted Paullier's action as a demonstration of contempt and ordered one of his men to stand guard at the congressman's home and detain him the moment he walked out the door.[5]

That made Paullier even angrier: he called on the Cámara de Representantes to censure this alleged abuse of police power, and he criticized Sampognaro personally, in deliberately harsh and indelicate terms.[6] Paullier's letter to Congress, published in all the newspapers, did not please the chief of police, who responded as he believed any public man would act in the face of blatant defiance of his authority. He resigned his public office in order to place himself "in gentlemanly conditions" – in other words, to be free to demand a duel if Paullier did not retract his words.[7] Remarkable as this turn of events may have been, just as remarkable was the public reaction. *El Siglo* was certainly struck by a "sui generis" police chief, "energetic pursuer of criminals, who resigns his post when he wishes to commit an infraction himself, only to return to work once the deed is done."[8] But *Diario del Plata* had the opposite response, seeing Sampognaro's turnabout as unremarkable, even logical:

> The functionary who is compelled by duty to intervene in the name of public authority to prevent the realization of a duel, divests himself of his official authority in order to be able to challenge to a duel one of the men that he himself had detained for the offense of dueling. This individual conduct appears illogical, but it is not so when examined in light of the contradiction that exists between law and custom; between the

articles of the [Criminal] Code, which impose specific obligations on the representatives of authority, and social conventions that impose certain duties for the defense of personal honor.[9]

In the end, Paullier's seconds chose the path of conciliation, politely urging him to retract the words that Sampognaro considered offensive and declaring that both men had been justified in their own way, Paullier in defending his parliamentary immunity, and Sampognaro in defending his authority as chief of police.[10] The crisis over, Sampognaro returned to his post and to his duties enforcing the law, including enforcing the laws against dueling.

This would not be the last time that the chief of police triggered the preliminaries of a duel while in office. Five years later, he sent seconds to Socialist Emilio Frugoni in response to a blistering two-part editorial that accused the police force of excessive violence against workers and accused Sampognaro of corruptly turning a blind eye to gambling and prostitution.[11] Refusing to have anything to do with Sampognaro's challenge, Frugoni pointedly called out the criminality of the chief's actions:

> It's hard to believe that a chief of police sees no path to obtain the reparations that his honor demands other than the path of the violation of the very laws whose compliance it is his job to enforce. Because the sending of seconds is a crime. Look at Article 438 of the Criminal Code … In any reasonably organized country where the government has a sense of public morality and a clear notion of implicit duty, Mr Sampognaro would not be able to return [after the duel] and take charge of the police. In our country he "can," because such is the determination of those who exercise the authority to do so, even though it defies logic, tramples morality, decrees open disregard for the law, and ignores the most elemental principles of good government. Because at this moment either Mr Sampognaro has a debt pending with Justice, or there is no Justice in my country.[12]

Law against Custom

Sampognaro's dilemma, and Frugoni's irrefutable criticism, encapsulated a problem that Uruguayans in public life had faced for decades: their own behavior routinely violated laws that they themselves had written and sworn to uphold. Colonial Spanish Americans, confronting the often contradictory dictates of quarreling royal and ecclesiastical authorities in competing power centers, had long been accustomed to a certain mental separation between one's loyalty to the monarch and one's strict adherence to every latest edict from faraway Madrid or Seville. The civil conflicts of the early independence years impeded the emergence of a legal framework to replace what had been overthrown. Indeed, as we saw in the David Buchelli case in chapter 1, for several decades Spanish legal codes from the turn of the nineteenth century remained in force. But from the 1860s onward, those conditions were changing in Uruguay: new legal codes were all being written, with a Civil Code adopted in 1868, a Code of Criminal Procedure (Código de Instrucción Criminal) in 1879, a Military Code in 1884, and a comprehensive Criminal Code (Código Penal) in 1889.[13] Uruguayan jurists saw legal codification as a crucial pathway to modernity and stability, the goal to secure at last the supremacy of statute over man.

Yet this new era of codification coincided with the explosion of press freedom, hyperpartisan politics, and dueling. Liberalism underpinned the quest for law's dominion but also its negation, because public men so often chose to resolve their conflicts in private on the field of honor. Dueling advocates, as we have seen, tried to paper over that contradiction by treating the various codes of honor as if they were legal codes, and at some level the codes served that practical function, however imperfectly. But opponents' critique of the duel as fundamentally lawless never entirely went away, and that critique put the duel's advocates on the defensive.

The clamor for more effective repression of the duel rose and fell periodically, typically peaking in the aftermath of some tragedy or outrage. Because Uruguayan duels only occasionally resulted in death or grave injury, the public shock when they did could be intense, and shock led to debate about why the authorities did not crack down on a practice that was clearly illegal. One such moment of national reflection followed a fatal 1893 duel between two military officers, lieutenants Guillermo Ruprecht and Joaquín Tejera, former Colegio Militar classmates. Although the dispute arose from a trivial barracks taunt, the two men, apparently long-time enemies, insisted upon dueling conditions that one newspaper described as nearly unprecedented in their severity: highly accurate Remington pistols at ten paces. The duelists – or by most accounts, Tejera in particular – set out with the intention of dueling to the death and refused to consider honor satisfied after their first exchange of shots. On the second exchange, Tejera received a fatal bullet to the head. A talented twenty-one-year-old with a bright future, he had lost his parents less than a year before and was the sole provider for four younger siblings.[14]

The *Uruguay News* voiced the following lament:

> On several occasions lately we have had to refer to duels that have taken place here, for trifling causes, the sequel of which has been rather amusing than otherwise, and calculated to be useful, rather than otherwise, by turning the absurd custom of dueling into ridicule. The aggrieved parties have met, vowing eternal vengeance, have exchanged shots or sword thrusts without doing any harm to anybody, and have then declared honour satisfied, embraced one another, breakfasted together like the most devoted of friends, and finally published lengthy minutes of their proceedings warmly eulogizing one another and posing before the public as heroes of the first water. To-day, however, it is our painful task to chronicle a duel, which has anything but a playful termination, and while we do so, we take the opportunity, to once more, protest most earnestly, against this wretched custom of illegal but licensed murder.[15]

Noting that Ruprecht, the seconds, and the two doctors had all been arrested by the authorities, the paper nonetheless predicted their rapid release: "Perhaps they will be detained in custody a month or so and then dismissed, branded not as assassins but as 'men of honour.'"[16]

Eulogies for Tejera spoke of his honor and valor,[17] which only made critics of the duel more determined in their denunciation. The English-language *Montevideo Times* led the way:

> Bad as the duel and its consequences have been, the expressions and sentiments to which it has given rise are still worse, and only illustrate how barbarous and ghastly are the false "laws of honor" which still dominate a large section of society here, and especially in military circles. On all sides we hear of the death of this duellist spoken of as deplorable, but scarcely ever as reprehensible – yet that is far the more appropriate word. He has been converted into a hero, and tributes have been paid at his tomb as great as if he had fallen in some heroic action in defense of liberty or country. For our part, we fail to see anything heroic or noble in the fate of an individual whose passions cannot be satisfied without blood, and who unnecessarily exposes a life which was not his own to throw away, and falls in the act of breaking the law of religion, of civilization, of the country, and the code of the service to which he was bound. Such an end seems to us ignominious rather than heroic … If such a

death be honorable, chaos is come again. He showed physical courage sufficient to face death boldly, a courage shared by many an animal and savage, but he showed himself entirely wanting in the far higher moral courage, solely the attribute of civilized man, which would have enabled him to dominate his passions and to defy a barbarous custom.

... Lieutenant Tejera has paid the penalty of his offense with his death; his punishment has passed out of human hands. But his accomplices remain, and it is to be hoped that no false sentiment will prevent them from receiving the punishment they deserve. On them there rests a very heavy responsibility, which should be brought home to them by the law and even more by public opinion. The Lieutenant Ruprecht has killed a man deliberately and in cold blood, for no reasonable cause whatsoever. He is a murderer in the first degree, and nothing else, and we ask that he may be treated as such.

... It is hoped that this fatal duel ... will cause a reaction in the false and foolish sentimentality which has hitherto condoned such acts. Duelling is already condemned by the law, but the law against it, like that against other forms of assassination, has never been properly enforced, to the detriment of Uruguayan civilisation.[18]

Uruguay's English newspapers were long-time critics of dueling, and the only thing different about their commentary in the wake of the Ruprecht-Tejera duel was a new intensity. But they were joined on this occasion by a broader than usual cross-section of public opinion. In *El Nacional*, the columnist "Hermias" denounced the "sad spectacle ... presented by a cultured and civilized people, marching in the vanguard of progress, when in order to cleanse an offense they allow a useful member of society to be left on the field of honor, soaked in his generous blood and lost for eternity to his friends and family ... This is the consequence of a barbarous custom! A person dead! ... Is honor satisfied? No! God is outraged, Christ denied, humanity insulted, and the Prince of Darkness has received new victims."[19] *El Telégrafo Marítimo* similarly focused on the contrast between dueling and civilization: "It seems impossible to believe, in this nineteenth century that has brought so much illumination to questions involving the order and progress of society, that there are those who still fail to see as a throwback to times of obscurantism the retrograde practice of the duel as a means to satisfy disordered passions or vengeful instincts."[20]

In the face of divided public opinion but in accordance with the law, Ruprecht was put on trial, with the prosecutor asking the military court

(Consejo de Guerra Permanente) for the mandatory minimum one-year prison sentence stipulated in Article 992 of Uruguay's 1884 Military Code.[21] Ruprecht's counsel mounted an oral defense that one newspaper described as "filled with social considerations concerning the duel, which made a powerful impression on the members of the Consejo."[22] The military judges declared Ruprecht guilty but with extenuating considerations that reduced his sentence to time served; the ruling called out the seconds as morally responsible for having permitted such a deadly duel but imposed no additional sanction. *La Tribuna Popular* and *El Siglo* both called the guilty-but-attenuated verdict an "absolution."[23] In the end, the *Uruguay News* had underestimated by about two months the time Ruprecht would spend in detention but correctly predicted that his conviction and punishment for dueling would in no way discredit him or derail his career. Ruprecht later rose to general and minister of war.

The details of the Ruprecht verdict are interesting in themselves, because they point out how the narrative of events, even in the case of a fatal duel, might be massaged in a way that made the case for leniency. The main technique was to emphasize Tejera's "firm resolution" to proceed with the duel and his unilateral and intransigent rejection of conciliatory overtures from the seconds and from Ruprecht.[24] The testimony of Ruprecht and all the seconds coincided that after the first exchange of shots, it was Tejera alone who insisted on continuing when all others expressed a willingness to declare honor satisfied. Furthermore, the witness-participants all agreed that Tejera's repeated insults of Ruprecht were responsible for the conflict in the first place, even though the *acta previa* of the duel did not in fact disclose who was the offender or which man was given the choice of weapons, as it absolutely should have.[25] "The unavoidable situation in which Tejera placed Ruprecht," wrote the judges, "made it impossible for him to avoid the duel, given that without doubt his moral standing in the army would have been diminished, and this, in a military man, would signify the loss of something more precious than his existence."[26] All of these factors, according to the judges, triggered the attenuating factors set out in Articles 750 and 752 of the Military Code, based on principles such as "irresistible force," "provocation or threat on the part of the other," "urgent necessity," and "prior good conduct and distinguished service."[27]

It is possible that Ruprecht *was* highly conciliatory and that Tejera was both the unilateral instigator and the intransigent "wall" upon which every effort at mediation "smashed to pieces."[28] None of the contemporary press reports makes a case otherwise. But given that Tejera was dead, that Ruprecht and the seconds had a compelling interest in portraying themselves as innocents, and that there were no witnesses who were not themselves implicated in the crime of dueling, we might be forgiven a skeptical suspicion that the agreed-upon narrative of events just happened to be conveniently exculpatory. Indeed, attributing intransigence solely to the man who got killed and emphasizing the survivors' futile peacemaking efforts seem to have been the boilerplate template for testimony whenever a duel ended in death or severe injury. Those implicated in other fatal encounters employed the identical formula.[29]

The Ruprecht-Tejera duel and its legal resolution left the duel's opponents deeply unsatisfied. The arguments against dueling, as we have seen, were many. Catholics had always opposed the duel on principle, in keeping with hundreds of years of church doctrine and based on the conviction that God alone was authorized to give and take life. In this respect, dueling and suicide fell into the same category of transgression.[30] Moralists of all stripes looked at the human tragedy of lives lost, children and widowed mothers abandoned to their fate without a protector, for motives that did not justify tragedy. The legally minded focused instead on how dueling usurped the powers of the state, rendering the courts irrelevant and generally trampling on the rule of law, converting the duelist into judge, jury, and executioner of his own cause.[31] Alfredo Vásquez Acevedo, in his 1893 *Concordancias y anotaciones del Código Penal*, bluntly challenged the duel's pretension to have anything really to do with honor:

> Honor is not vindicated by being killed or wounded by, or by killing or wounding, the person who has damaged it. If the offended person is a liar, if he is a thief, if he is an arbitrary or corrupt functionary, he will continue to be so in the eyes of public opinion, even if he has had the nefarious glory of leaving dead on the ground the man who, perhaps in performance of his duty, had the courage to publicly denounce his transgressions. Honor is vindicated by demonstrating the falsehood of the imputations, by proving rectitude or decency, with genuine proofs, with convincing actions.[32]

Underpinning all of these arguments was the idea that the duel was an atavistic artifact of an age of medieval barbarism, out of keeping with the modern progress of civilized and enlightened peoples.

But defenders of the duel were not without arguments of their own, as we have seen in the previous two chapters. Abdón Arósteguy, the man who had served as David Buchelli's second but subsequently supported his expulsion from Congress for cowardice, refused to recognize any contradiction between dueling and "the religion I profess."[33] Fear of ecclesiastical sanction carried less weight in liberal Uruguay than in just about any other Latin American country. At first glance, a 1912 incident might seem to contradict this assertion: in the aftermath of a duel in which he had served as one of the two attending physicians, Dr Rafael Schiaffino received a communication from the board of directors of the Catholic Workers' Circle, informing him that they no longer wished to contract his services. Citing "the incompatibility" between his legitimation of the duel and his service as physician for a Catholic mutual aid society, the directors intended to make a statement that might bring some moral persuasion in the face of a wave of high-profile political duels. But rather than giving in to this pressure, Schiaffino responded by asking the Montevideo papers to publish his response:

> It matters not whether the patient who suffers is virtuous or guilty, and the doctor should not ask him his nationality, his religion, or his political party ... The doctor attends the bed of the person of faith just as he cures the ulcers of sinners, just as he goes to the prison cell where the criminal is dying, he bandages the wounds of the suicide, he goes to the battlefields to kneel before the fallen, and he attends duels of honor where gentlemen settle their conflicts sword in hand ...
>
> The board sustains its resolution in I-don't-know-what dispositions of the church, which are beside the point ... It has always been – and this is as it should be – that among the doctors of the Circle there have been a great many of publicly recognized liberal ideas ... without anyone inquiring about their opinions, and reciprocally, liberal societies such as the Christopher Columbus [have employed Catholic doctors].[34]

It is not Schiaffino's predictable Hippocratic argument so much as the vehemence of his tone that hints at the debility of the church's anti-dueling stance in Uruguay. *El Siglo* was a liberal paper, to be sure, but it still says something that it saw the Catholic Workers' Circle directors as so out of line with public opinion that the item bore a screaming sarcastic headline: "Christian Charity: Duelists Should Die Like Dogs."

Nor did the duel's advocates accept the proposition that it was the enemy of civilization and progress. Quite the contrary: taking as a given that normal human intercourse would from time to time generate conflicts that might lead men down the path of violence, supporters praised the existence of gentlemanly laws that enlisted the "always beneficent" mediating role of seconds and assured "the prior determination of the conditions under which the duel would be carried out, completely freed from the force of passion and sentiments of rancor and vengeance."[35] As one editorialist put it in 1914, "Between the possibility of homicide and the duel, society has reasonably opted for the latter."[36]

The argument that dueling usurped the powers of the state and that its persistence undermined the rule of law was less easily refuted or dismissed, however. As long as the duel remained a crime, its critics could point to the hypocrisy with which dueling senators and representatives denounced violence committed by the lower classes. "If some poor devil steals in order to eat, he will not escape going to jail," wrote *El Socialista*, "but one can make an attempt on the life of another man with impunity, so long as one does so in acordance with the Code of Honor."[37] On the one hand, this was the anti-dueling argument that Uruguayan advocates of the culture of honor took most seriously and found most troubling. On the other hand, if the abyss between written law and accepted social practice was the agreed-upon problem, then there were two distinct solutions: more rigid and consistent enforcement of the law was one, but legalization was the other.

The Criminal Code and Evolution of the Legal Debate, 1880–1908

When a commission of notable jurists was convened in 1880 to write Uruguay's Criminal Code, dueling was among the most controversial questions debated. Various events complicated their deliberations, which drew extensively upon the writings of European legal theorists and took up most of a decade. The David Buchelli case remained a fresh memory, underscoring the enormous gap that existed between the old Spanish legislation's strict prohibition of the practice and a dominant moral climate that not only authorized the duel but sometimes all but demanded it. At the same time, just as fresh was the memory of the tragic 1880 duel that had cost the Spanish-Argentine journalist Romero Jiménez his life, not to mention another even higher-profile duel in Buenos Aires that same year in which General Lucio V. Mansilla had shot and killed the journalist and politician Pantaleón Gómez.[38]

In light of these contrasting antecedents, the commission entrusted with writing the draft Criminal Code sought to chart a middle path between repression and permissiveness. "Regarding the controversial crime of dueling," the report began, "the Commission believes it has placed itself in the most just and reasonable terrain. The draft code does not allow the impunity that is painfully established in practice, but neither does it accept the rigor of legislations that, forgetting the powerful pull of certain social sentiments and preoccupations, punish this offense with severe sanctions."[39]

The code, finally approved in 1889, resembled the Spanish (1870) and Italian (1889) criminal codes – but not the French – in treating the duel as its own unique category of crime. In this respect, the new Código Penal also followed the lead of the 1884 Military Code. It punished the issuing of a challenge with three to six months of prison, the acceptance of a challenge with a fine, a duel resulting in no injuries with nine to eighteen months of imprisonment, and a duel that resulted in death with two to four years. In Article 356, the code enumerated the elements that distinguished a duel from an ordinary act of violence, for which the far more severe punishments for homicide or battery (*lesiones corporales*) applied. Those qualities included the intervention of seconds, rigid adherence to the conditions pacted by those seconds, strict equality of weapons, and the prohibition of conditions so severe that they amounted to duels to the death.[40] By codifying in law the difference between duels that adhered to chivalric protocol as set out in the honor codes ("regular" duels) and those that did not ("irregular" duels), the code implicitly recognized the legitimacy of the dueling codes' gentlemanly values.[41] Indeed, this concession to duelists *in the very definition of the crime of dueling* underscored and cemented the honor codes' status as quasi-law, while enshrining the assertion that he who killed in a duel could not be considered a common assassin.

Notwithstanding this far from insignificant concession to the parallel laws of honor, Uruguay's 1889 Criminal Code did little to diminish the contradiction between law and practice. Despite the exceptional rigor of the judge and *fiscal* in the David Buchelli case, very few judges had made an effort to apply the severe penalties of the Spanish legislation previously in force, and just as few saw fit to apply the reduced penalties of the new code. Perhaps this was to be expected: How would one begin to repress a practice that up to that point had generally gone unpunished, when the new, milder penalties were an official recognition that the crime was not considered serious? It is more probable – though impossible to confirm because the Criminal Code was approved in toto without debate on specific articles – that the code's authors knew what they were doing and harbored little expectation that the new penalties would be enforced in the immediate short term. In other words, they could live with the gap between law and practice as the lesser of evils. A radical decriminalization, which had no precedent in the world, would have legitimized the actions of men like José Paul y Angulo and Enrique Romero Giménez. Retaining limited penalties at least kept alive the hope that some day it might be possible to apply the punishments and win respect for the law. In the meantime, the statutes would serve as a goal and an aspiration.

As the years following 1889 passed, duels continued, most of the time with impunity. Sometimes the police frustrated a duel in gestation, or fear of discovery obliged the combatants to travel to Buenos Aires, where they might still face surveillance if the incident was sufficiently high profile.[42] Nor was it unusual, when the authorities were on the lookout to foil a duel that all Montevideo knew to be imminent, for the participants to resort to deception in order to lose the men on their tail. In an 1893 duel between José Batlle y Ordóñez and Eugenio Garzón, for example, the four seconds put on a show of reaching conciliation by meeting at the Hotel Español, only to slip out the back and into two cars that drove them to the house where the duel was set to take place. At that same moment, Batlle strolled into a restaurant and out a back door to a car waiting for him, while Garzón went one better, clambering down a rope hung from the roof of his home to make his way into the restaurant next door and from there to yet another waiting automobile.[43] At the same time, however, Uruguayan duelists continued on a fairly regular basis to publish *actas* in the newspapers, an indication that the protagonists were mostly unworried about their legal exposure. As we saw, a military court freed Guillermo Ruprecht after he served only three months, despite the unjustified severity of his fatal duel with Lieutenant Tejera.[44] It was thus with some justification that jurist José Irureta Goyena could write in 1908: "In our country, in twenty years, not a single duel has been prosecuted, despite many having occurred, some with very tragic outcomes."[45]

Over the course of those twenty years between 1889 and 1908, duels were becoming more frequent, not less so, and the authorities were always, it seemed, a step behind. One paper recounted in novelistic detail a much-anticipated duel between rising young Blanco leader Luis Alberto de Herrera and Batlle y Ordóñez's stepson, Ruperto Michaelson, serving in effect as the president's proxy. While a large and growing crowd gathered outside the locked doors of the Club Rivera listening to the clash of sabers within, Instructional Judge Dr Pastor arrived and gave police the order to intervene. As he fruitlessly banged on the doors with the classic "Open up in the name of the law!" Herrera and Michaelson finished fourteen rounds inside and then opened the doors, innocently proclaiming that they "were there for pleasure, peacefully exercising the noble art of fencing" under the expert tutelage of two masters of arms. The judge appeared satisfied until he noticed the first aid equipment nearby, but on further questioning, one of the two physicians claimed to always carry these materials with him whenever he went out. Since no one appeared to be hurt, Judge Pastor let everyone go.[46]

But if neither popular nor official attitudes toward the duel were changing significantly, criticism of the gulf between the duel's rigorous penalization de jure and the climate of permissiveness de facto was very much on the rise. The voices of inconformity came from every direction. Anti-dueling leagues in Europe were leading a high-profile campaign for more effective repression of the duel, while also promoting the innovative idea of permanent honor courts that would solve gentlemanly conflicts in acordance with honor code principles and practices but without recourse to combat.[47] Duelists raised their voices against a criminal code that they did not obey but which inconvenienced them all the same, obliging them to duel clandestinely, to lie to authorities, and to violate the law in ways that many considered dishonorable.

People on both sides were arriving at the conclusion that the open conflict between the Criminal Code and the honor code should not continue. Among the political class, the prestige of written law and the desire for a regime of legality continued to grow, at least as a value in the abstract. These were, after all, the glory years of legal positivism and the quest for technical, legislative solutions to recurring crises of public health and social order. A new medical-legal establishment was at its apogee, and from the pages of their new scholarly journals to the offices of their new institutes, they sought as never before to confront criminality and deviance with the twin tools of science and law.[48] These were the culminating years, as José Pedro Barrán reminds us, of efforts to "discipline" the Uruguayan people, of no-quarter battles against laziness, vice, and disorder.[49] And these were also years when the political class was becoming ever more a class of professional attorneys, the great majority trained in the law school of the Universidad de la República.[50]

It should therefore come as little surprise that there would be a growing dissatisfaction with the law going unenforced – indeed, openly flouted – and that pressure would mount for the existing prohibitions against dueling to be applied more effectively. And it was in this climate that José Irureta Goyena took on the problem in a long-form treatise, published over two days in February 1908 in the influential daily *El Siglo*:

> Everyone or almost everyone repudiates the duel, yet no one or almost no one fails to duel if circumstances arise ... We are convinced that this contradiction in the psychology of the people would be much less

generalized if the laws designed to repress the duel were enforced ... What objective reason, apart from scruples of conscience, can a citizen invoke to refuse a duel, or to abstain from provoking one? Respect for the law? But what happens when the law is an abandoned rite, only known for the number of times it gets broken?[51]

Unlike many other critics of the duel, Irureta Goyena was no stranger to dueling culture. He understood well why men fought fuels, and he shared the opinion that the laws against defamation offered scant redress for the victims of slander and insult. So with all the good reasons *to* duel, what was needed was a reason *not* to duel, and for Irureta Goyena the only possible reason was the legal prohibition. But that legal prohibition could not be a mere dead letter: "One thing is the punishment according to the letter of the law and another very different thing is the punishment applied."[52] The best way to overcome society's strong and unfortunate inclination toward the duel was not to increase penalties but to enforce the existing ones with constancy and firmness: "A couple months of prison, no more, but certain and infallible."[53] He concluded, "A little energy from the magistrates is all that is necessary."[54]

There may be no way of confirming a direct connection, but it seems more than coincidental that in the weeks immediately following Irureta Goyena's treatise, judges in Montevideo started to persecute duelists with an "energy" not seen in some time. At the end of March, Correctional Judge Juan José Gomensoro opened an investigation into a saber duel that had occurred two weeks earlier between two well-known university activists, Baltasar Brum and Lorenzo Carnelli.[55] Taking advantage of the fact that neither of the duelists and only two of the four seconds enjoyed parliamentary immunity, Gomensoro brought the four men in for questioning, while sending the congressmen official letters requesting their cooperation in the investigation. Duelists, seconds, the director of combat, and the attending physicians all frustrated the investigation by declaring that they had no knowledge of this supposed duel, which they denied had taken place. The only thing they admitted to knowing about was "a simple fencing match, which was effectuated, as is natural, in friendship. As for the wounds that it is said Mr Carnelli and Mr Brum received, those were the result of pure chance, and have not been cause for any complaint."[56] The judge employed his own forensic physician to examine the scars on the two duelists' hands and arms, but the two policemen who had originally observed the men fleeing the scene of the duel failed on further questioning to identify them definitively.[57] Undeterred by this stonewalling, however, on 16 May, Gomensoro ordered the arrest of Brum, Carnelli, and the two non-immune seconds, Carlos Maria Sorín and Enrique Andreoli. He let the four men experience the rigors of Montevideo's correctional jail overnight, despite a release order from the *fiscal*, because it was delivered after 4:30 p.m. When lawyers bringing the papers for the judge's signature tracked him down at his club, the Círculo de Armas, he reportedly brushed them off, saying, "I've already left my office and justice is the same for everybody."[58]

Much of the Montevideo press criticized Judge Gomensoro severely, accusing him of having abused the legal rights of four distinguished young men.[59] One editorialist singled out the capricious, inconsistent enforcement of the law:

> Every day, continuously, the press provides news of duels that take place in Montevideo, and worse, sometimes tells us not only where the duel took place but the names of the duelists, the seconds, the doctor, even the exact time. Why do the authorities "not know anything" about these other notorious cases but have come to find out everything about this alleged duel between Messrs Brum and Carnelli? What explains the differences between judges and prosecutors? Why such hesitation, such negligence, such deference to "what people will say" in some cases, and such ruthless rigor in others?
>
> Dueling is a crime that is identified and punished by the Criminal Code. Agreed ... But you don't let something happen ten, twenty, fifty times without penalty, in order to punish one single instance ... This turns justice into a lottery.[60]

Judge Gomensoro, as if responding directly to this accusation that he was singling out certain duels while ignoring others, decided to dust off some cold-case files. He took a declaration from the minister of industry, identified as a witness to a 1906 duel between two congressmen.[61] A week later, this wavelet of investigation came to touch the most unexpected of victims. José Irureta Goyena, the jurist who had just called for more consistent repression of dueling, found himself jailed at the order of Correctional Judge Bocage for refusing to divulge details of a recent duel in which he had served as a second. He ended up being held for eight days, even over the objections of the *fiscal*, because he refused to talk rather than inventing some convenient lie.[62]

In response to Judge Gomensoro's demand for a Congressional vote on the parliamentary immunity of Brum and Carnelli's other two seconds, Diputado Juan Giribaldi Heguy presented to the Cámara a proposal to repeal the articles of the code that criminalized the duel. Explaining his bill, the legislator did not defend dueling but instead seconded all the recent criticism that it was unjust to have a law rigidly enforced for some and ignored for others:

> A law such as this is a law that perturbs society: it is a disruptive law, it is a law that, without repressing or preventing the duel, serves as a means by which the judges charged with punishing the duel make a farce of their august mission, choosing not to proceed in some instances, accepting as truth the most absurd declarations of innocence in other instances, refusing always to punish, as is notoriously public knowledge.
>
> Bringing no benefit, the worst aspect of such a law is the derision it brings upon the nation's institutions of justice, forcing them into tacit complicity with the duelists, aggravated by the odious exceptions, which foster in these functionaries a spirit of rebellion against the rectitude and impartiality that should be the unbreakable norm in all of their acts.[63]

It is likely that the "odious exceptions" bothered Giribaldi Heguy more than the habitual impunity, but all the same, pro- and anti-dueling forces coincided in their criticism of the distance between statute and practice, between criminal law and gentlemanly law.

Ultimately, though, the Giribaldi Heguy bill went nowhere. Passed to the Codes Commission of the Cámara de Representantes, it was rejected without ceremony, presumably because the committee continued to respect the views of the authors of the 1889 Criminal Code, that it was the lesser evil to keep dueling on the books as a crime in the hope that someday there might be a will to prosecute, rather than go to the extreme of declaring it licit. Furthermore, the cause for decriminalization took a major hit when news arrived of another fatal duel, fought in Paysandú between two officials of the First Chasseurs Batallion, Lieutenant Arturo Gomeza and Alférez Alfredo Giordano. It was a duel with revolvers, not dueling pistols, and called for the repeated interchange of shots, advancing three paces after each exchange "until one of the adversaries is left on the field."[64] Gomeza, the author of the fatal shot, enjoyed fame as a marksman and appeared to be the one who had initially provoked the incident. In this case, the press criticized the authorities for their apparent lack of energy in prosecuting Gomeza and the seconds who had allowed this unconscionable duel to the death to proceed. In the face of a duel that most considered an evident crime, made worse by the brazen absurdity of the cover story that the victim had shot himself accidentally,[65] even Giribaldi Heguy came to declare himself opposed to the full legalization that his own bill would have conceded.[66] The prohibition remained, and the practical impunity as well.

Toward the Ley de Duelos

For twelve more years, criminal law and gentlemanly law continued in open conflict while duels kept increasing in frequency, much to the consternation of critics on all sides.[67] At least sixteen gentlemanly incidents were negotiated between January and mid-June 1914, five on a single day in May, all despite an active police persecution that had Chief Sampognaro's men frustrating several duels and jailing duelists and seconds on more than one occasion.[68] No one was detained for long, but the repressive measures did underscore the law's inconvenience for the potential duelist. House members and senators were the least troubled, given their immunity, but for others the illegality of dueling was a genuine bother. Few years passed without seeing some government minister or high functionary resign his post, as Sampognaro had, in order to issue or accept a challenge.

José Batlle y Ordóñez, unable to resign the presidency, asked *his* several challengers to wait, promising that he would give them satisfaction as soon as his term concluded. This attitude disgusted his political opponents, who argued that his constitutional incapacity to duel rendered him "irresponsible" and that he should therefore stop writing editorials for *El Día*, refraining altogether from the attack journalism for which he was famous.[69] On several occasions Blanco leaders including Carlos Roxlo, Luis Alberto de Herrera, and Juan Andrés Ramírez had spoken out against the idea that Batlle might postpone his duels while continuing to insult his opponents (and presumably working on his fencing and marksmanship).[70] In their view, the norms of gentlemanly responsibility simply did not allow for a journalist-president, so Batlle needed to choose one public role or the other.

Batlle habitually responded that it was ridiculous and unfair to ask a person legally prohibited from dueling to unilaterally forfeit his right to express an opinion on crucial matters of state.[71] He also countercharged in Ramírez's case that the Blanco journalist and self-appointed expert on matters of honor engaged in a deliberate and cowardly campaign of defamation against the only man in the country who was barred from holding him to account on the field of honor. Batlle asked, in effect, "Who was the irresponsible one?"[72]

So public men in general recognized that the criminality of the duel was incompatible with their exercise of high government functions. But they kept on dueling all the same, and the authorities, albeit inconsistently, kept on trying to stop them beforehand or to send a message by investigating afterward.

Á Batlle desafía exasperado,
pretendiendo hacer blanco en colorado.

Fig. 3.1 1906 Caricature of Partido Nacional leader Luis Alberto de Herrera, complaining about President José Batlle y Ordóñez's "irresponsible" penchant for offending others in the press when as president he could not duel. Batlle promised to answer his challengers after his presidential term concluded. *Caras y Caretas* (Buenos Aires) 5 May 1906. Courtesy of Guillermo Silva Grucci.

After a particularly acrimonious session of the Cámara de Representantes in April 1918, Lorenzo Carnelli got into a war of words with not one but two Colorado congressmen, César Miranda and Roberto Mibelli. Among the epithets exchanged were *bellaco, indecente, miserable, desgraciado, canalla*, and *advenedizo*, any one of which would have been enough to spark a challenge, but which all together made a duel inevitable. That night, police surrounded the Círculo de Armas, tried to cut off access to the entire city block, occupied the upper floors of the building, and blocked the main doors, but they arrived too late and the saber duel between Carnelli and Mibelli took place inside without the police being able to do anything, given both men's parliamentary immunity. Over the two days that followed, police tried to break up Carnelli's next planned duel, this one with Miranda. They succeeded in frustrating two attempts and detained the men briefly three different times, but eventually the duelists were able to steal away to the nearby town of Pando, where Carnelli received a bullet to the chest. Only skillful intervention by doctor Alfonso Lamas prevented the wound from being life-threatening. Questioned afterward by police, "all the persons who intervened in the *lance* declared uniformly that the wound occurred by accident, when a pistol that was tied hanging from a tree fell to the ground and discharged."[73] So even though as a general rule no duelist was held for long, police persecution nonetheless obliged congressmen and cabinet members to skirt police vigilance, to give false testimony, to act like criminals. Congressman Duvimioso Terra described the "frightening dilemma" that confronted people like himself: "Required by the Judge to give a declaration about the events [of an alleged duel], either they tell the truth, and thereby violate their duty as gentlemen, or perhaps for the first time in their honest and upstanding lives they have to stop being cultivators of the truth, and consequently this is another immorality of the legislation of the duel."[74]

This was the general context in which Juan Andrés Ramírez introduced a bill on 15 March 1918, calling for decriminalization of the duel. His proposed law would punish duels only if they took place without seconds, with unequal weapons, or in such conditions that one or the other of the combatants was likely to be killed.[75] As in the case of the Giribaldi Heguy bill, Ramírez justified his reform not by defending the duel as an institution but by criticizing an unenforceable law. In the justificatory preamble (*Exposición de Motivos*), he was particularly blunt:

Setting aside the philosophical aspect of the duel and whether its criminal repression is legitimate or illegitimate, irrefutable practical considerations militate in support of the present bill.

Experience teaches that the law cannot repress the duel. [Because we are] dealing with a crime whose authors and witnesses tacitly swear on their honor to keep hidden, there is no possibility of obtaining the evidence that is indispensible for a conviction. So neither the police nor the courts can stop a duel except in extremely rare circumstances, and because duelists constantly flout both, the articles of the Criminal Code that sanction the duel only serve to discredit the justice system, the police, and the law itself.[76]

But as in 1908, the idea of total legalization faced resistance. The Codes Commission pronounced in majority against it, arguing that the duel was an anachronism out of step with the progress of civilization, that no country in the world had approved such a radical proposal, and that the decriminalization of the duel would create a new class privilege.[77] Commission spokesman José Salgado expressed his skepticism with a series of questions: "Will the police have to stand with arms crossed, after the Ramírez bill is passed, when they see two persons crossing swords just because there are two seconds and gentlemanly canons are followed? The police won't be able to do anything at all to avoid this? According to the Ramírez bill will it be possible to duel in the theaters, because it is a licit act, even if one of the duelists ends up dead?"[78]

Placed on the legislative calendar for early May 1919, debate on the bill dominated six full sessions of the House into early June, with more than a dozen legislators taking part, some speaking at great length, citing Italian, Spanish, and French legal experts and drawing on their own experiences as duelists, seconds, and recipients of challenges.[79] Discussion was wide ranging and included philosophical musings about the meaning of honor, what led people to issue or accept a challenge, how to deal with the more general problem of crimes that are difficult to prosecute, and why a duel that adhered to the code of honor should be treated differently than an unregulated *duelo criollo* between two ruffians. Salgado, citing the late nineteenth-century Italian penalist Giulio Crivellari, noted that modern criminology treated the blinding power of passion as a mitigating factor when assessing criminal responsibility, yet the Ramírez proposal would paradoxically free from criminal responsibility the man who "duels in cold blood, after having named his seconds who discuss the conditions of the duel in perfect tranquility."[80] Meanwhile, the plebeian who killed in a knife fight would be charged with homicide.

> Which of the two is more blinded? He who kills in passion, the gaucho who fights a *duelo criollo*, or those who duel in a fencing salon? For the latter, we will abolish all criminal responsibility; for ourselves, the fencers, even the current light penalties will not be applied …
>
> The authors [of the Codes Commission's report] point out the injustice that would signify exonerating the gentlemanly duel of all punishment while leaving in the Criminal Code the charge of murder for the duel of passion.[81]

Ramírez and Representative Duvimioso Terra countered that criticism by emphasizing the civilizing and disciplining role of the laws of honor. Terra brought up the example of a hacienda owner whose workers had been taught to play polo and now competed against professional teams. In just the same way, Terra maintained, if the Ramírez law was passed, the less cultured classes would "of course adopt civilized practices, and as a result duels without seconds will disappear."[82] The fact that the gentlemanly duel proceeded with cool-headed premeditation was its signal virtue, Ramírez argued, because the intervention of seconds and adherence to the code of honor were the best defenses against criminal or immoral intent:

> First, the gentlemanly duel banishes any question of self-interest; no one can or should duel for pecuniary interests … a debtor and a creditor are not allowed to duel or even to interevene as seconds in a duel. In the *duelo criollo*, all kinds of sentiments and motives are permitted, even the most base.
>
> Second, in the *duelo criollo* … nothing guarantees fair play or even comes close to ensuring equality of conditions: he who has a better weapon, uses it; he who is able to get the drop on his enemy does so. The objective of the *duelo criollo* is not, in reality, to vindicate honor: it is to kill the adversary, and that is why a *duelo criollo* will sometimes recur between the same persons, because they are always retaliating, seeking revenge, and sometimes the hatreds pass down from fathers to sons.
>
> … Representative Salgado was surely thinking of the revolutionary dictum "Liberté, Egalité, Fraternité," and in trying to make a point with the second of those three principles, said that passing special legislation

Fig. 3.2 Juan Andrés Ramírez, original author of the Ley de Duelos. From Daniel Pelúas, *José Batlle y Ordóñez: El hombre* (Montevideo: Editorial Fin de Siglo, 2001).

that concedes impunity to the *duelo caballeresco* [gentlemanly duel] is to act against the principle of equality and establish a privilege in favor of a social class. I absolutely refute this: the duel is open to all men. When a man climbs the social ladder, even if just in the refinement of his spirit, he can duel, he can look for seconds in the city, in the countryside, or wherever he may be.[83]

He concluded by noting that the real inequality was the fact that congressmen alone had the privilege of dueling without legal consequences, because of their parliamentary immunity. Meanwhile, violent catastrophies among plebeians might be avoided if they had the chance to resort to "the gentlemanly means of resolving conflicts of honor, the most civilized means, despite all its flaws and imperfections."[84]

The most notable fact about the debate in the House of Representatives, however, was not the distance between the two sides but how much they shared in common. There were almost as many duelists among the bill's opponents as among its champions, and with only a few exceptions there was something approaching a consensus that the duel was an unavoidable evil, at least at present. Fundamentally, the discussion revolved around a different and more profound question: the relationship between law and society. For Ramírez, the legislator had to recognize that with or without the legal prohibition, police and judges would always cross their arms and do nothing in the face of the duel, because society demanded that they do so: "There exists, in reality, this complicity of all of us with the duelists, because no one sincerely sees them as immoral or criminal men; no one refuses to shake the hand of a duelist, nor to open the door of his house to one, nor to sit one at his table. The social alarm regarding the duel is absolutely zero ... consequently, to maintain criminal punishment for dueling when society itself impels the crime and protects the criminal afterward, is purely and simply hypocrisy."[85]

When social norms make written law unenforceable, Ramírez continued, it undermines respect for justice in general: "Periodically our judges remember that the law against the duel exists. They make one, two, three attempts to enforce it and later they give up, comprehending that it is absolutely impossible to make these laws effective. Then, can one say that it fortifies the dignity of the administration of justice, that it favors public order, that it moralizes society, to maintain laws that compel judges either to place themselves in the eyes of the public as objects of derision and ridicule, or to fail to fulfill the duties that their office demands that they execute?"[86] National Party representative Washington Beltrán, another decriminalization advocate, encapsulated this position in just a few words: "What I believe is that there shouldn't be a law that the president, the chief of police, and the legislators all violate."[87]

Against this logic, Representative Ismael Cortinas turned to arguments very similar to those expressed by Alfredo Vázquez Acevedo and the other proponents of the Criminal Code thirty years earlier:

> One can accept that the duel is a necessary evil; but even accepting this, I believe that we cannot in any way give up the right to strive, by means of the law, to make sure that this ill (even admitting its necessity) has as few perturbing repercussions as possible, because this is the mission that the people entrusted to us when they elected us to represent them.

... The contrary, Mr President, would be to declare that humanity is incorrigible and there does not exist even the remote possibility of organizing humanity within a decent system of conduct. Fortunately, not everyone thinks this way, and there are those who believe that persistence in propaganda and action can lead to the moderation of the aggressive instincts that are inherent in human nature, subordinating them to the tranquil and serene dictates of reason and justice.[88]

In some ways, the distance between Ramírez and Cortinas was surprisingly small. Cortinas, too, was familiar with the field of honor and shared with Ramírez the opinion that it was impossible to repress the duel without a radical change in social mores. The disagreement between them had less to do with the duel itself than with their respective visions of the legislator's duty to society. According to Cortinas, "We come here as the people's representatives, not to legislate in deference to custom, prejudice and sentiment, but in order to elevate ourselves to a more serene plane, where the severe majesty of the law is absolutely beyond question."[89] For Ramírez, the legislator had to listen to the dictates of society and legislate according to values that society imposed. For Cortinas, the legislator must issue opinons in accordance with his conscience, acting with the certainty that that he knew better than society itself what was good for it. José Salgado expressed the same position: "If the legislator considers that public opinion is mistaken, it is not his duty to allow himself to be swayed by public opinion's error; he should put himself face to face with that error and try to correct it; that is precisely why he is a legislator."[90]

The champions of legalized dueling in many ways brandished ideas that more faithfully reflected early twentieth-century legal thought, including positivist criminology's conception of a flexible law that served the cause of social defense, while the enemies of the bill relied on a theory of law more firmly rooted in an older enlightenment ideal of the perfectability of man via inspired legislation. Of course one needs to be careful not to overstate the contrast: when Ramírez spoke of "society," he had in mind the society of people like him. But this fact does not negate the essentially modern principles underpinning his thought. Nevertheless, in face of such divided opinion among the legislators, divisions that crisscrossed party lines but with Colorados generally the more skeptical, the Ramírez bill did not win approval in its original form and ended up back in the Codes Commission for still further study. Several different revisions were given consideration, and the version that finally secured the committee's blessing in October was mostly the work of member Duvimioso Terra.[91] The innovations in the reworked bill are discussed below.

But as all this legal wrangling was going on in the background, the problems that the Ramírez bill sought to resolve had not gone away, and in short order they touched Ramírez himself. On 15 June 1919, Ramírez had sent seconds to José Batlle y Ordóñez, now out of office, in response to an insulting *suelto* Batlle had written in *El Día* entitled "Embuste" (Big lie). The next day the two men – who had a very long history, Batlle having postponed several challenges from Ramírez back when he was president – exchanged two shots at twenty-five paces without either being injured.[92] Police arrived in the aftermath and took account of what had occurred. A month later, Correctional Judge Dr Juan M. Minelli ordered the arrest of Batlle, the director of combat General Sebastián Buquet, and seconds Francisco Ghigliani, Alfonso Lamas, and Rafael Schiaffino, while also notifying Congress of his request for a vote to strip immunity from Ramírez and second Julio Maria Sosa. General Buquet avoided arrest because he was out of the country, but Batlle, Ghigliani, Lamas, and Schiaffino, after questioning at the central police station, were all arrested and taken to the Correctional Prison until their attorneys negotiated their conditional liberty.[93] As far as Ramírez was concerned, "lacking any coercive means to oblige him to declare, by virtue of his status as a legislator," the correctional judge gave up after taking an eight-page voluntary statement in which Ramírez eloquently defended the principle of parliamentary immunity but gave no other useful information.[94]

The revised dueling bill, despite the Codes Commission's blessing, might have languished forever without returning to the Cámara for debate, had it not been for one of those unique, unpredictable twists of fate that change the course of a nation's history.[95] In this case the catalyst was the fatal duel on 2 April 1920, in which José Batlle y Ordóñez killed Washington Beltrán, the thirty-five-year-old rising star in the Partido Nacional. The origin of the conflict was in no way trivial: it arose, as with most Uruguayan duels, out of partisanship in the press, but the polemic came at a moment of particularly acute political tension. *El País*, the paper for which Beltrán wrote, had accused the government of committing fraud in the previous elections of 30 November 1919, the first national vote carried out under the auspices of a new constitution that had enshrined a series of electoral guarantees, including the secret ballot. The opposition alleged that the Colorados had persisted in their old habits of using the police to coerce voters and falsify ballots, in spite of these electoral reforms.[96] The controversy had already resulted in one saber duel

Fig. 3.3 Washington Beltrán. Archivo Fotográfico de *El País*.

between Batlle and the paper's co-proprietor, Leonel Aguirre, in January 1920, in which Batlle had received minor wounds.[97] But Washington Beltrán, who had served as one of Aguirre's seconds in that first duel, was unwilling to let the matter rest. On the first of April, incensed at *El Día*'s counter-allegations of Blanco electoral wrongdoing, he penned an editorial entitled "*Qué Toupet!*" (What nerve!), in which he recapitulated in detail charges of electoral fraud going back several years. He attributed responsibility for those irregularities directly to Batlle, calling him the "champion of fraud" and comparing him to Guatemalan and Mexican dictators Manuel Estrada Cabrera and Porfirio Díaz.[98] Early the next morning, Good Friday, the two men met with pistols, and Batlle's second shot (the autopsy would reveal) fatally punctured Beltran's lungs and aorta.[99] Never before in Uruguay had a duel between such high-profile participants – the two-time president and decades-long leader of the dominant political party against an heir-apparent to leadership of the main opposition party – resulted in a death. The tragedy was a signal national event, and the shock reverberated internationally.[100]

Upon receiving word of the duel, Correctional Judge Juan José Gomensoro, one of the magistrates who had energetically tried but mostly failed to prosecute duelists in the past, sent Chief Detective Tácito Herrera to investigate, and Herrera found his way to the Club Nacional where Beltrán's body had been taken. Gomensoro immediately ordered Batlle's arrest and began interrogating the director of combat and one of the two intervening physicians. The former refused to make a statement, citing personal reasons, and the latter denied having anything to do with a duel, having just learned of it "by public rumors."[101] Beltrán's doctor and all of the seconds were congressmen, so they could not be compelled to testify in the absence of a vote to remove their immunity, something that was not going to happen. On the next day, 3 April 1920, Batlle himself, accompanied by his defense attorney Carlos Maria Sorín (who had his own history with Judge Gomensoro), declared that he did not know who Washington Beltrán was and that he would not make any further statement.[102] Sorín, who was also president of the House of Representatives, appealed for Batlle to be released on his own recognizance, a request that Gomensoro rejected but his colleague Judge Pedro Lago approved on appeal.[103]

Moving into July and early August of 1920, as Batlle stayed at home awaiting trial, his Colorado colleagues looked back upon the previous year's debate of the Ramírez proposal and realized that the revised decriminalization bill, endorsed by the Codes Commission the previous October, was their leader's best legal hope. They needed to act quickly because Batlle could not be a candidate for election to the National Council of Administration (the new Collegial executive) if felony charges were pending against him, and the deadline for publicly declaring his intention to run was drawing near.[104] Luckily for Batlle, key supporters of the duel's legalization, including Duvimioso Terra, Juan Andrés Ramírez, and Eduardo Rodríguez Larreta – Blancos all – had not abandoned that support just because their archenemy Batlle, the man who had shot and killed Washington Beltrán, would be the law's first and greatest benefactor. So in the legislative session of 4 August 1920, Batlle's compatriot Francisco Ghigliani moved that preferential consideration be given to the dueling bill, and the Cámara voted to take it up in debate. Ghigliani now made the case that it was "absolutely unjust" that certain citizens might be disqualified from holding office because of a dueling charge, "when in reality we are all convinced that the duel is not a crime that should be punished with the force that the law establishes."[105]

There were two good reasons why the revised dueling bill might have had an even harder path to passage in 1920 than it had the year before. First, the new 1920 legislature had gained three passionate and eloquent opponents of the duel who had not been in the House the year before. Socialist Emilio Frugoni had for many years been a principled voice against dueling, denouncing it as archaic, uncivilized, class-ridden, corrupt, and ridiculous. Frugoni had also lived his creed by refusing numerous challenges from government officials – most notably the police chiefs Pintos and Sampognaro – all in the name of freedom of expression and the citizen's right to investigate and denounce misdeeds by the powerful and connected.[106] His colleague Celestino Mibelli similarly denounced the gentlemanly protocol of seconds and challenges and honor tribunals, despite having been goaded into a duel himself a few years earlier.[107] And Joaquín Secco Illa of the Unión Cívica Nacional voiced the Catholic critique of the duel.[108] Second, it is worth recalling that both in the 1880s when the Criminal Code was first debated and in 1908 with the Giribaldi Heguy bill, the memory of recent fatal duels had given a strong impetus *against* decriminalization. It might be expected that a tragic death on the field of honor would reinvigorate the voices calling for more aggressive enforcement of the laws against the duel, and indeed, the eminent jurist Justino Jiménez de Aréchaga had recently given precisely such a speech on the Senate floor in the memorial session held in Washington Beltrán's honor.[109]

Defying those expectations, however, the impact of the Batlle-Beltrán duel was to advance the cause of decriminalization, for several reasons. As already alluded to, pro-Batlle Colorados' devotion to their larger-than-life leader played a crucial role, especially given that the bill's mostly Blanco sponsors did not abandon that support just because the law would now benefit Batlle. But several other considerations, beyond the vote-switching of Colorados who had opposed the Ramírez bill in the previous legislature, contributed as well. In 1908, the Gomeza-Giordano duel that scuttled the Giribaldi Hegui proposal had appeared in the eyes of many to be an act of criminality: it had been a duel to the death instigated by the superior marksman and carried out with highly accurate weapons not designed for dueling. No such accusations swirled around the Batlle-Beltrán duel, which at the time was perceived by virtually everyone as fair and legitimate, at least in its adherence to the laws of honor. The pacted conditions for the duel had not been unusually severe. The weapons were traditional dueling pistols, notoriously imprecise and shot at the reasonable distance of twenty paces. And because the combatants had been required to start with their backs to one another, to wheel around on the first of three handclaps, to point their weapons on the second clap, and to fire before the third, they had been afforded scant seconds to aim. Numerous pistol duels following similar rules had ended without injury.[110] As a result, the death of Beltrán was recognized by most as just a terrible stroke of bad luck. There was no indication that either duelist had arrived at the field of honor with the deliberate intention to kill or with an intransigent refusal to entertain the possibility of reconciliation once honor was satisfied, nor was there any hint of misconduct or negligence on the part of the seconds or the director of combat, who were all experienced veterans of previous encounters.[111]

Yet there was another reason why the revised bill was able to win in the House of Representatives, win in the Senate the following day, and take immediate effect on 6 August 1920 as Law no. 7253 or, as it was more commonly known, the Ley de Duelos. Duvimioso Terra's revised draft of the bill, endorsed by the Codes Commission back in October 1919, was different from the original Ramírez proposal in one essential way. Instead of abolishing outright the articles of the Criminal Code that dealt with the duel, it declared instead that the punishments the code contemplated would remain on the books but would not be applied if the duel took place with the prior authorization of an honor tribunal, composed of three citizens of forty or more years of age. The seconds for each duelist would designate one member of this honor tribunal, and those members would together choose the third. It was the honor tribunal's duty to examine the events leading up to the challenge and to determine if the offense was of sufficient gravity to merit a duel: only in the case of a ruling in favor would the resulting duel cease to be a crime.

This reform to the bill, which Juan Andrés Ramírez had originally opposed but came around to embracing, made honor tribunals obligatory and gave them uncontestable authority. An ad hoc institution borrowed from the dueling world, honor tribunals were an idea whose origins traced back to the late 1800s; they had been promoted by the European anti-dueling leagues that flourished at the turn of the twentieth century and had been debated in 1907–08 as a model for Spain.[112] In Uruguay, this innovation succeeded in winning over many of the skeptics, those who viewed the duel as a necessary evil but who also did not wish to promote or further legitimate it. More cynically, perhaps, it also served as intellectual cover for those Colorados who had opposed the original Ramírez bill but now prioritized Batlle's exculpation and habilitation as a candidate in the upcoming elections. The deal closer was Article 10 of the revised version, which grandfathered the decriminalization retroactively to duels in which no honor tribunal had intervened.[113] As tailor-made as this provision was for the precise legal situation in which Batlle y Ordóñez found himself, it had in fact appeared in the original October 1919 revision as approved by the

Codes Commission, justified by the idea that "nobody should be inculpated for omission of the honor tribunal at a time when the law did not demand it."[114]

Most of all, though, the honor tribunal formula appealed to the doubters because it held out the promise that dueling might decrease rather than increase as a result of the new law. In Ramírez's words,

> If the Honor Tribunals are constituted by men who possess moral authority, and if these men issue a verdict that clearly establishes the responsibilities that correspond to both parties to the incident – and if they don't systematically conclude that there is never cause for a duel, but instead leave the duel as it should be, only for those cases in which ... two persons truly cannot coexist simultaneously in the world – it is very possible that honor tribunals might result in the duel, if not disappearing absolutely, at the very least becoming more and more rare, more and more extraordinary.[115]

Others went further to imagine that with the progress of civilization and the modernization of attitudes, a future day might come when *no* duel received an honor tribunal's authorization. That at least was the implicit hope.[116]

Judging the Impact of Decriminalization

If those who voted for the 1920 Ley de Duelos were convinced – or at least convinced themselves – that the introduction of compulsory honor tribunals would reduce the frequency of duels, critics were just as convinced that the decriminalization of dueling would open the floodgates. The proposed law, Emilio Frugoni argued, "will not make this practice better or more humane; I believe, on the contrary, that it will spread and popularize even more, conferring legality onto an act that everyone rejects and condemns."[117]

In the beginning, Frugoni's prediction appeared to hold. Numerous duels did win the tribunals' approval, and decriminalization made it possible for certain categories of public officials to issue and accept challenges for the first time. Prior to the law, as we have seen, representatives and senators dueled routinely, secure in their parliamentary immunity, but officials in the executive and judicial branches, local government, and the police had no such protection. If they wanted to duel, they had to resign, as Police Chief Virgilio Sampognaro had done, and/or they had to travel to Buenos Aires, taking advantage of the extradition loophole. Decriminalization did away with these impediments, allowing government ministers and other functionaries to accept duels without needing to abandon their posts, enabling attorneys and their clients to challenge judges who had ruled against them in lawsuits, and even freeing presidents to duel while in office.

In the case of dueling challenges against judges, significant legal issues still remained. The *Revista de Derecho, Jurisprudencia y Administración* ran a series of articles in early 1921 debating whether or not the new law tacitly repealed an article of the Criminal Code that had made it a crime to challenge a government functionary to a duel.[118] The debate was hardly just academic: in at least two instances that year, litigants had sent seconds to the magistrates hearing their cases, claiming that their rulings had contained language or accusations that impugned their honor. In both cases, the judges ordered the arrest of their challengers, arguing – not unreasonably – that the decriminalization of the duel could not possibly be construed to permit intimidation of the judge hearing one's case.[119] Interestingly, however, there were also those who argued that while no judge should ever have to face a duel for properly exercising the duties of his office, judges *should* be bound by the gentlemanly laws that demanded self-restraint in their public utterances, and that it was entirely proper for an aggrieved litigant to recur to dueling protocol and for an honor tribunal to decide whether or not the judge had crossed the line.[120] This kind of debate never would have occurred prior to decriminalization, giving credence to the idea that the dueling law had pushed the climate of tolerance to unprecedented levels.

The most dramatic evidence of a new permissiveness was President Baltasar Brum's decision in 1922 to provoke a duel with National Party leader Luis Alberto de Herrera. Given Uruguay's supercharged political climate, it should come as no surprise that presidents had often found themselves at the center of polemics that would have ended up on the field of honor had they involved anyone else. But no Uruguayan president had ever fought a duel while in office. As we have already seen, José Batlle y Ordóñez had accepted challenges with the stipulation that he would only meet his adversary after his presidential term ended, and despite much grumbling in print, his political enemies had had little recourse but to accept.[121] After all, no president could be asked to violate the law, and no opponent could be asked to run the risk of killing the president, even under the duel's unique conditions. Back in January 1920, when President Baltasar Brum had considered himself offended by words pronounced by Gerardo Sienra, he had allowed his brother to challenge Sienra in his stead. Alfeo Brum's letter to his seconds explained that he had taken on the responsibility because his brother was "unable to demand personally the same reparation, by virtue of his office."[122]

But two years later, when Luis Alberto de Herrera published a manifesto yet again accusing Brum's government of employing police and military to cast fraudulent votes, Brum deliberately provoked a duel by insulting Herrera in print, using terms that no honor tribunal could fail to consider an offense.[123] The prospect of a first-ever presidential duel was much criticized, though trepidation about what might happen – and about the precedent being set – was matched by the breathless excitement of it all. The papers ran speculative and often inaccurate stories about where and when the duel was going to take place, which weapons had been chosen, and more.[124] When the day of the duel arrived, police and army mobilized a convoy of some thirty cars to escort the duelists to the Melilla airfield, about fifteen kilometers from the city center. The military cordoned off the five-hundred-strong crowd of newsmen, photographers, and privileged spectators, keeping them at a distance of few hundred meters while inside a hangar the men exchanged two shots without consequence, emerging afterwards to applause and expressions of relief.[125] In the aftermath, a rumor that the guns had only been loaded with blanks was quickly denied, and the newspapers took stock of what it meant for a president to provoke a duel in response to public criticism of his public actions, and to fight a duel without first resigning. What would have happened to Herrera if he had managed to kill Brum? Although dueling had been decriminalized, laws against magnicide remained on the books. Could they have been applied? Would anything have happened to Brum if he had killed or wounded Herrera? What if he had fired before the signal, violating dueling rules? Could a president now legally commit murder? Did the president's special status before the law give him an advantage on the dueling ground, in violation of the Code of Honor? None of these questions had been thought through.[126]

The incident also reignited the long-standing argument that duels resolved nothing. After all, both sides had accused the other of fraud in an election decided by approximately 5,000 votes out of 240,000 cast. Nonpartisan observers agreed that the charges and countercharges, while possibly exaggerated and not at all new in Uruguay, were sufficiently credible to warrant an investigation and a hearing in the courts. By responding instead with provocations, seconds, and bullets (or powder at least), President Brum and opposition leader Herrera had done nothing to find the truth, nothing to end corrupt electoral practices, and nothing to protect or improve the integrity of Uruguayan democracy.[127] The account published in the Socialist paper was entitled "Yesterday's Farce": "It turns out that Dr Herrera, the losing presidential candidate, accused Dr Brum of being an empresario of electoral fraud, while Dr Brum retorted that Dr Herrera had committed as much fraud or more. And of course, as both men were telling the truth, there had to be a duel ... The spectacle was prepared with great care. The mise en scene was appropriate for the event and there was no shortage of spectators. There were even doctors, not one but three! Naturally, nothing happened."[128]

The Brum-Herrera duel illustrated another unintended consequence of decriminalization: the transformation of the duel into spectacle. For as long as people could remember, opponents of the duel and even many supporters had called for publication bans on information related to duels and *desafíos*. The same argument had appeared and reappeared decade after decade: that if people were denied the publicity they craved, there would be far fewer duels, limited to the most serious of motives.[129] In several European and Latin American countries, the press had a sort of implicit agreement to keep silent about duels, particularly when they feared that publicity might create legal problems for the protagonists. But this had never been the case in Uruguay, where in the absense of a publication ban it had always been something of a spectator sport among the political class to follow polemics in the press, waiting for that incendiary phrase that would push things over into dueling territory. When the papers fell silent, people knew or sensed that seconds were now in secret negotiations, and rumors flew furiously until the *actas* of the duel appeared in print a couple of days later. To that extent, Uruguayan duels had always been high theater.

But prior to the 1920 Ley de Duelos, the *actual moment of combat* had usually – not always, but usually – proceeded with circumspection. The honor codes made quite clear that duels were supposed to be private matters with only nine or ten people in attendance: two duelists, four seconds (two for each), two physicians (one for each), the master of combat, and maybe a professional gunsmith to load the dueling pistols. The duel's technical illegality, even in times of de facto tolerance, reinforced the codes' message. Of course there had been occasions when word got out and small crowds of people in the know, especially journalists, tailed the duelists and set up at some not-so-discreet distance – far enough away to preserve the fiction of a private duel, but close enough to witness what happened and maybe get some decent pictures. Post-decriminalization, people presumed that what had once been the exception would now become the norm.[130] Indeed, during the August 1920 debate on the revised dueling bill, Representative Celestino Mibelli had yet again raised this issue of publicity, forcefully arguing that legalization made the need for a publication ban even more pressing. His proposed amendment to that effect failed to win approval.[131]

So, sure enough, the publicness of high-profile duels fairly quickly got out of control, leading duelists and the press alike to come under criticism and to engage in self-examination. Even before the Brum-Herrera spectacle, a much-anticipated duel between Blanco caudillo Villanueva Saravia and José Urrutia, the police chief of Cerro Largo, had been attended by reporters and photographers from several dailies and a glossy weekly magazine.[132] In subsequent days, *La Mañana* had criticized the event and called on the press to stop giving duelists so much publicity: "The practical application of the new legislation on private combat has lately introduced a novel phenomenon: gentlemanly duels with the character of public spectacle, or if not public, at least *publicized*, with profuse photographs to satisfy readers' curiosity ... This now legal means of settling personal and sometimes intimate matters becomes, thanks to the photographic publicity, not just a spur to curiosity but also a stimulus, so that those who fight duels to show off – likely a good percentage – get the attention they crave [and therefore] multiply their quarrels and their challenges."[133] Responding to the critique, *Diario del Plata* called it hypocritical, pointing out that *La Mañana* had itself published photos of the Batlle-Aguirre duel back in January 1920 when dueling was still illegal.[134] *El País*, one of the papers whose coverage of the Saravia-Urrutia affair had been splashiest, did appear a bit chastened and began to talk about the press's need for voluntary self-restraint.[135]

In discussion of the alleged dueling "epidemic" of 1921–22, critics repeatedly asserted that legalization had removed the last constraints that kept the duel from becoming a spectator event. They exaggerated for comic effect – no one was really about to start renting out theaters and charging admission – but some pundits genuinely believed that the 1920 law had taken the country across a Rubicon, and that dueling had become legal blood sport in the same Uruguay that in recent years had abolished bullfighting and cockfighting.[136]

Implicit in those arguments was the belief that trivial duels and duels for show were on the rise, that seconds needed to do a better job of prevention and conciliation, and that honor tribunals were too quick to permit duels. These critiques gained some urgency after an unexpectedly fatal saber duel between two military officers over an offense that few believed had justified a duel in the first place, followed a few months later by a close shave in a pistol duel where one of the two combatants took a bullet in the collarbone, again for motives that in retrospect did not seem particularly grave.[137]

THE DUEL AS SPECTACLE FOR THE PUBLIC AND THE PRESS

Fig. 3.4 César Batlle Pacheco and Eduardo de Castro, date unconfirmed (possibly 1918)

Fig. 3.5 Baltasar Brum and Colonel Alberto Riverós, January 1924. Archivo Fotográfico de *El País*.

On the other side, however, it was also true that honor tribunals *were* refusing to give some duels their blessing. Several high-profile challenges in 1921 never made it to the combat stage because the law functioned as its advocates hoped and promised it would.[138] Other incidents were settled directly by the seconds in likely anticipation that honor tribunals would not authorize them. At the one-year anniversary of the decriminalization law, Ramírez's paper *Diario del Plata* took stock of the law's impact:

> In vain, the honor codes ... teach that it is not dishonorable for a gentleman [to] retract a phrase that someone considers offensive but which had not been uttered with ill intent. For fear of appearing weak, very few ever practiced this principle. Frequently, they might be willing to admit in private that their intention had not been to offend, but they would not allow that admission to be made public. Other times, the seconds recognized that there was insufficient cause to go to a duel, but they deferred to the contrary instructions of their principals. In the face of this, Dr [Duvimioso] Terra sagaciously found a solution to these problems by placing, above both duelists and seconds, a supreme and impartial authority, free of passion or involvement in the case, as the only one allowed to authorize a duel, only when sufficient motive existed to justify such an extreme measure.
>
> We believe that in the year since its passage, this law has successfully prevented duels that otherwise would have occurred. Even if only one has been so avoided, that would be enough justify its praise; but those who have carefully followed the many cases that have appeared in the press must agree that the salutary effects of the law are far from rare exceptions.
>
> ... It helps that the honor tribunals ... rightly see that they have a higher social mission, to prevent men from jeopardizing their own lives and those of others in the absence of fundamental cause.[139]

El País agreed that many duels had been avoided thanks to the 1920 law, and favorably compared the Uruguayan situation to that of Argentina, where duels continued to take place in violation of the neighboring republic's more repressive legislation, which the daily described as "well-intentioned but useless."[140] Curiously, the same paper just the day before had only half-jokingly warned of the possibility that a new wave of Argentine tourists would cross the Rio de la Plata not only to gamble and get divorced in permissive Uruguay but now also to duel.[141]

Taking a longer perspective strengthens the case that the honor tribunal model may have fulfilled its promise, at least in some ways. In particular, honor tribunals had significant power to protect legitimate investigative journalists from challenges brought by officials hoping to cover up scandal. A 1945 incident is illustrative. Eduardo Víctor Haedo, interim director of *El Debate*, received a challenge from Ángel B. Graña for the contents of an article that had appeared in the paper. The article included accusations against a particular enterprise, Ducar S.A., that was under investigation by a parliamentary commission looking into the allegedly too-cozy and mutually enriching relationship between government officials and certain private firms.[142] Before the 1920 law, if the author of such an exposé had refused to duel, his only possible protection from charges of cowardice and "irresponsibility" would have been the collective weight of public opinion, and public opinion could be unpredictable. But in 1945, the honor tribunal that was convened to hear the case carefully and publicly debated the balance between press freedom in the general interest versus the need for measured language in journalism. Their report, which was published in the press, devoted space to each of the three judges' arguments. Predictably, the judge named by Haedo's seconds defended *El Debate*'s right to editorialize about a problem that "has acquired extraordinary importance, and it is fundamentally useful for the State and for democracy that the public be amply informed, without hinderance or interference."[143] The arbiter chosen by Graña's seconds just as predictably disagreed, noting that the particular *suelto* in *El Debate* "was not a political commentary designed to weigh the facts or clarify the truth in an impersonal way. The violence of the language employed underscores its exceptional character, even compared to the language used by the investigating legislators ... The article that motivated the gentlemanly challenge contains expressions that can only be explained as fruit of a deliberate intention to offend personally."[144] The deciding arbiter joined the first in opting for greater press freedom, and ruled that a duel was not justified.

By 1945, duels had become so infrequent for so long that reformers proposed abolishing the 1920 decriminalization law, arguing that it was no longer needed. In the words of its sponsor, Salvador García Pintos,

> The present law ... has achieved in a quarter century an era of moderation in dueling. Far from its opponents' fears that duels would proliferate ... the Ramírez law has reduced them significantly. In truth it has been exceptional for an honor tribunal to give its authorization for a duel ... Indeed, since the Ramírez law, duels almost never happen.

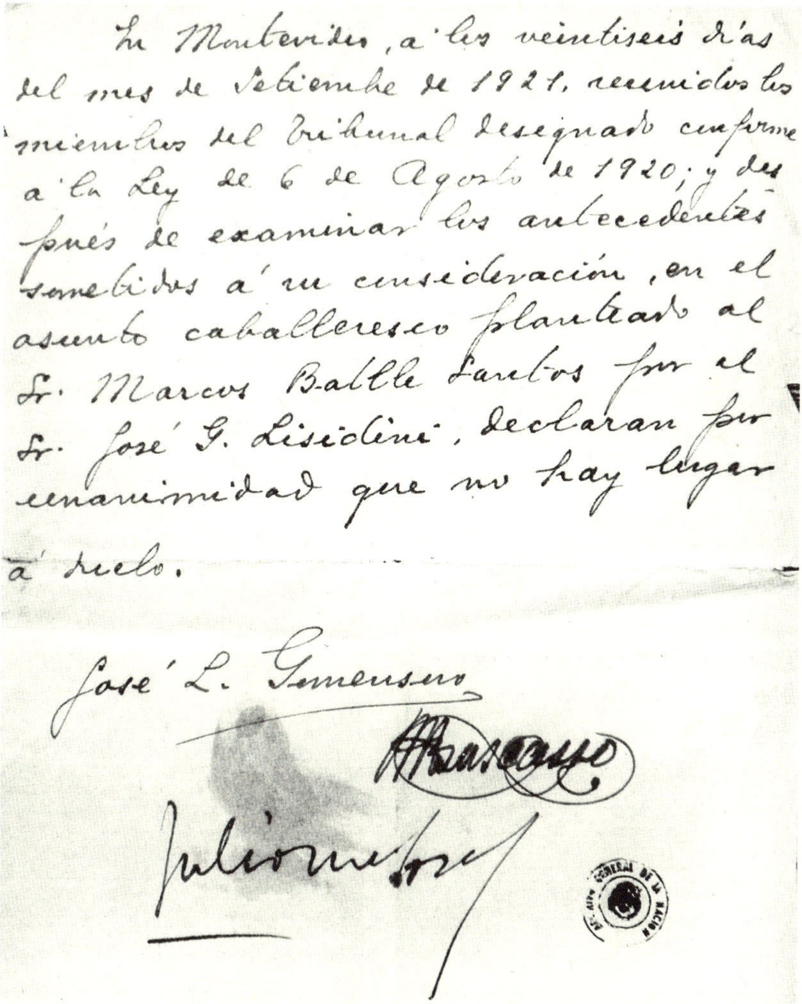

En Montevideo, a los veintiseis días del mes de Setiembre de 1921, reunidos los miembros del tribunal designado conforme a la Ley de 6 de Agosto de 1920; y después de examinar los antecedentes sometidos a su consideración, en el asunto caballeresco planteado al Sr. Marcos Batlle Santos por el Sr. José G. Lisidini, declaran por unanimidad que no hay lugar a duelo.

José L. Gomensoro

Fig. 3.6 Decision of an honor tribunal, convened "in conformity with the Law of 6 August of 1920." The tribunal ruled that José Lisidini's challenge to Marcos Batlle Santos lacked sufficient cause for a duel. This unanimous verdict was unusually brief: honor tribunal *actas* sometimes ran several pages. Archivo General de la Nación, Archivo Histórico, Montevideo, Colección Luis Batlle Berres. Photo by author.

… The time has now come to replace this juridical form of the honor tribunals with another, more in harmony with the present-day national cultural norm, which has dispossessed the duel of its usefulness in repairing offenses against honor.[145]

The prosecutor and criminal law expert Antonio Camaño Rosa, writing in 1957, seconded the assessment that the 1920 law "constitutes practically an effective prevention of the duel, because almost all [honor tribunal] verdicts avoid it."[146] The famed novelist and poet Mario Benedetti agreed, though he saw the tribunals' reluctance to authorize duels as a net negative, lamenting that the purveyors of insult no longer feared the consequences of their words.[147]

Were these analysts correct to attribute the long-term decline in dueling to Uruguay's unique legislation? The argument appears compelling at first glance, but some complicating facts give pause. Duels did decline in the 1930s and 1940s, but not only because honor tribunals were loath to approve them. Just as importantly, there were fewer gentlemanly incidents to begin with, and the principal reason for that appears to lie not in the Ley de Duelos but in changing patterns of Uruguayan politics and journalism. President Gabriel Terra's 1933 self-coup (*autogolpe*), suspending the 1918 Constitution,[148] put a temporary end to the overheated, anything-goes climate that had characterized the 1910s and 1920s, a period so deeply marked by the polarizing figure of José Batlle y Ordóñez and the regular shouting matches in the press and in Congress between Batlle's followers and his many enemies. Terra's 1935 press law furthermore imposed the requirement that all newspapers register with and be approved by the Ministry of Public Instruction, and that papers give free space for corrections and rebuttals. The law greatly expanded the number and variety of press crimes, increasing penalties while lowering the burden of proof needed for prosecution, thus winning restrictions that many governments in the past had sought unsuccessfully.[149]

Partly in response to the new legal climate, partly following worldwide trends in news publishing, and partly adapting to social changes that affected the local market, a number of dailies altered their business model, relying less on subscriptions and more on kiosk sales, cultivating a mass readership rather than catering exclusively to political correligionists. Compare a typical Montevideo daily published in 1935 with a paper published in 1925, and the contrast is evident: the 1935 papers have bigger headlines, wider margins, more pictures, clearer differentiation between news and commentary, and, perhaps most important, vastly expanded sports and international coverage. The years from about 1924 to the mid-1930s were, after all, the famous first golden age of Uruguayan soccer, and foreign news could not help but become more prominent in the polarizing interwar world. Given these trends, it should come as no surprise that proportionally less newsprint was devoted to the kinds of journalistic and political polemics that had once occasioned so many duels.

The scarcity of duels through the World War II era seems also to have generated a momentum of its own. As dueling became less common, fencing skills and knowledge of the honor codes atrophied, as did the social expectation that the duel was a necessary part of public life and that any man who did not guarantee his words on the field of honor was an irresponsible coward, disqualified from politics. Socialists, communists, and Catholics refused to duel and openly challenged the duelist's concept of honor, and increasingly nothing happened to them – a change from the 1920s when a refusal to duel had consequences.[150] Whatever the reason, from the mid-1930s to the early 1950s, Uruguay saw the duel decline almost to insignificance, and many came to believe that its complete disappearance was only a matter of time. The reality would prove a little more complicated.

4

Resurgence and Recriminalization, 1950s–1992

It is time for the sabers to stay inside the fencing clubs or in displays of armor; for the dueling pistols to go into glass cases or museum collections, and for insults and offenses against honor to be regulated by modern legal dispositions, in accordance with the twenty-first century.

    Representative Juan Gutiérrez, House session of 17 July 1990.[1]

So long as the insult is not prohibited, so long as we do not subordinate the solution of our differences to the dominion of serene reason, so long as we are incapable of dominating the impulses of our blood, the duel will be inevitable.

    Juan Andrés Ramírez, House session of 4–5 August 1920[2]

The quality of debate always rises to greatest heights when dealing with trivialities.

    Gonzalo Aguirre Ramírez, Senate session of 16 June 1992,
    quoting Aureliano Rodríguez Larreta, 1919[3]

The decline of dueling in Uruguay over the course of the 1930s and 1940s is consistent with this book's larger argument about the duel's intimate relationship to press freedom and its role in policing the norms of political discourse, and might be taken as further evidence to confirm it. Rather than a remnant of feudal or hispanic ideals of masculine honor stretching back to colonial or medieval times, the Chateauvillard model of speech regulation and conflict resolution – including the duel but encompassing much more than just the duel – was the child of nineteenth-century liberalism, of a robust and contested public sphere, of democracy itself. As a parallel system of customary justice, which its advocates controversially considered more effective than the formal machinery of written laws and courts, the code of honor could count on adherents so long as it appeared to provide a practical answer to the excesses of partisan rhetoric and the perceived failures of defamation law. With the passage of Law no. 7253 of 6 August 1920, legislators chose to fully integrate this Chateauvillard formula of offenses, *cartas-poder*, challenges, *explicaciones*, seconds, sabres, *actas*, and honor tribunals into the formal realm of codified law. Uruguay's revised Código Penal of 1933 went on to absorb and incorporate the 1920 Ley de Duelos as Article 38.[4] Advocates saw this harmonization of law and custom as a victory for the rule of law. The duel's opponents almost certainly disagreed.

Determining how much or how little the introduction of obligatory honor tribunals contributed to dueling's decline, or alternatively, how much or how little decriminalization contributed to the duel's long-term persistence, is no simple task. Nearby Argentina, where dueling remained a crime but generally went unpunished, provides a suggestive comparison and for that reason re-enters the discussion later in this chapter. But the larger point is that when Uruguay's democracy became less vibrant and its public sphere contracted, as it did after 1933 with the "soft" dictatorship of President Gabriel Terra, the conditions that gave rise to a perceived need for the Chateauvillard system diminished, and duels became less frequent. As noted at the end of chapter 3, adapting to Terra's restrictive 1935 Press Law and adopting new technologies and profit models, the newspaper industry dedicated itself less to partisan polemics and attracted readers in new ways, focusing on world events, sports, and for some papers, the local crime beat. Those trends persisted through World War II.

Starting in the late 1940s, the political system gradually reopened and a new generation of Colorado politicians, led by Luis Batlle Berres, took their place on the national stage. These democratic reformers' most significant initiative was the 1952 Constitution, which resurrected the Collegial Executive, the original brainchild of Batlle Berres's uncle, José Batlle y Ordóñez. At first the democratic restoration appeared to usher in a golden age, reconfirming Uruguay's image in the eyes of the world as a model country by Latin American standards, an exceptionalism captured in nicknames and slogans such as "the Switzerland of South America," "Happy Uruguay" (*el Uruguay feliz*), and "Like Uruguay there is no other" (*Como el Uruguay no hay*).[5] Eventually, though, as the political temperature in the country rose to levels not felt perhaps since the 1920s, dueling experienced a mini-renaissance. Through the 1940s and early 1950s, the number of duels that had received an honor tribunal's blessing could almost be counted on the fingers of one hand, but tribunals authorized three high-profile political duels in the late 1950s and four more in the early 1970s.

This development took place in the context of growing political polarization and social unrest, as Uruguay's economy stagnated and the country entered the global Cold War. Militant student and labor strikes in the late 1960s escalated into an armed urban revolutionary movement, the MLN (Movimiento de Liberación Nacional, better known as the Tupamaros); a left-wing electoral alliance (the Frente Amplio, or Broad Front) emerged in 1971 as a challenge to Blanco-Colorado hegemony; and an intensely anticommunist military hierarchy increasingly intervened in day-to-day politics.[6] As men with epaulets took on more power in ostensibly civilian governments facing crises, martial subculture – the duel included – seeped back into Uruguayan political practice, at least temporarily.

But if military participation in politics breathed new life into the culture of dueling, Uruguay's subsequent descent into authoritarianism had the opposite effect. The 1973 military coup, which shut down Congress, criminalized dissent, and tightly censored the press, deprived Uruguay's public sphere of the oxygen that might fuel the kinds of polemics that tended to generate insults and challenges. Indeed, the lack of duels over the twelve years of dictatorship might appear paradoxical given how explicitly the military promoted a discourse of honor and muscular masculinity in its public statements and internal regulations, but such was the case. Only with the 1984 elections and the return to democracy did Uruguayans once again have the freedom to rethink the kinds of laws that should govern the operation of a politicized public sphere. This is the context of the 1990–92 movement to recriminalize dueling, by then a practice that the majority of Uruguayans considered wildly anachronistic. Nevertheless, debate over abolition of the 1920 Ley de Duelos revealed the ongoing relevance of many of the issues addressed by the honor codes, even if the duel itself had been relegated to the status of that curious thing people used to do back in the day.

The 1930s and 1940s: A Nation Forgets How to Duel (or Most of the Nation, Anyway)

On the afternoon of 10 April 1935, four shots – maybe five – rang through the galleries of the Legislative Palace. The targeted victim was Senator Alberto Demicheli; the author of the attack was another senator, Francisco Ghigliani. The two men, former political allies, now estranged, had for some time been insulting one another from the editorial pages of *Uruguay* and *El Pueblo*, respectively. In their most recent exchange, Ghigliani had focused on Demicheli's wife, the feminist jurist Sofía Álvarez Vignoli, who was a driving force behind passage of Uruguay's recently promulgated Código del Niño (Children's Code, 1934). Ghigliani used Álvarez Vignoli's public advocacy as a rhetorical club with which to accuse her husband of hypocrisy, because *Uruguay*, the newspaper that Demicheli edited, included a police page that often ran lurid stories involving children.[7] Launched in recent months by the controversial Uruguayan-Argentine news entrepreneur Natalio Botana, *Uruguay* did indeed employ a quasi-tabloid formula with big headlines and sometimes over-the-top crime coverage,[8] and thus seemed to be following in the steps of Botana's Buenos Aires daily, *Crítica*, with its well-deserved reputation for populist sensationalism.[9] But in extending his critique not just to Botana but to Demicheli and especially to Demicheli's spouse, who also wrote pieces for the paper, Ghigliani touched a nerve. Responding to Ghigliani's ill-fated decision to drag family into their ongoing argument, Demicheli escalated matters with a *suelto* entitled "Francisco Ghigliani, Protector of Minors!" And here he went nuclear: "Having now thrown himself with evangelical furor into the cause of the protection of childhood, Francisco Ghigliani forgets that all of Montevideo has seen him, for months and years, dedicated to the dubious protection of an underage girl, whom he has brazenly paraded arm-in-arm in sight of the entire population."[10]

Days later, Demicheli was in the hospital with four gunshot wounds – from which he luckily recovered – while Ghigliani was detained in the Cuartel Centenario. At first Ghigliani's supporters at *El Pueblo* tried to make a self-defense case, portraying the encounter in the Senate as a face-to-face shootout between two equally armed adversaries.[11] At the same time, Ghigliani signaled his willingness to face justice by sending a letter to the Senate in which he volunteered to renounce his parliamentary immunity.[12]

The question that instantly arises is why Ghigliani did not call upon seconds to insist on a duel with the man who had committed such an egregious offense against his honor, not to mention against the honor of the young woman whom he said was his ward, and whom he claimed to treat like a daughter, nothing more. It was not as if Ghigliani was a stranger to the duel: he had participated in numerous gentlemanly incidents either as protagonist or second, and it was he who had petitioned for reintroduction of the Ramírez bill in order to halt prosecution of José Batlle y Ordóñez.[13] Defenders of dueling had long invoked precisely this kind of incident, involving sensitive matters related to private life, as the reason why the duel was still needed, why the duel could save lives by preventing heat-of-passion violence, and why no other measure – certainly not intervention by the courts or the police – could be as effective. So now that there had arisen just such a textbook attack on the honor of a man and his family, why couldn't Ghigliani discipline his impulses and use the honor code as it had been designed instead of setting out with murder in his heart?

Efforts at explanation are colored by the soap-opera aspects of Ghigliani's subsequent life and death, which included in short order the suicide of his wife, his marriage to the twenty-year-old woman in question, and his own apparent suicide the following year.[14] But training our focus exclusively on the April 1935 confrontation with Demicheli, there are three possibilities: first, perhaps the encounter had indeed been as Ghigliani described it in the pages of *El Pueblo*. Having pushed open the door to the Sala de Ministros in search of a third person, Dr Pujol, Ghigliani unexpectedly found himself facing Demicheli, who stood up and immediately reached into his suit pocket. In this telling, Ghigliani reasonably assumed that Demicheli was going for a gun and in self-defense fired first.[15] Demicheli's paper disputed that scenario in screaming two-inch headlines, describing instead a cowardly, premeditated attack that came from behind and from out of the shadows, rejecting the police report's assertion that the shots were preceded by an exchange of words.[16] (After two days of heated back-and-forth charges and countercharges, the government saw fit to shut down both papers.[17])

A more likely explanation is that Ghigliani had come to hate Demicheli so much, and was so angered by the accusation leveled in public against him – later, seemingly confirmed true – that he balked at the prospect of offering Demicheli an equal chance to kill *him*, as would of course be the case in a proper duel. A third possibility, given the two men's shared political antecedents and overlapping circle of friends, is that Ghigliani feared the seconds might arrive at some conciliation, or that an honor tribunal might refuse to authorize a duel, or that the required deliberations might propagate the scandal further. But if any of these possibilities accurately reflected Ghigiani's state of mind, they would call into question the very proposition, endlessly repeated by the duel's advocates, that Chateauvillard protocols had the power to channel intense emotions onto a more controlled, more equilibrated, more just, and potentially more conciliatory path than that of violent ad hoc confrontation. If the laws of the duel could not tame a man's passion for revenge, if a man whose reputation had been besmirched was not in fact willing to defer to the wisdom and authority of his seconds, then that exposes as either lies or self-delusions the arguments of half the people we have encountered in the course of this book.

The Ghigliani-Demicheli incident at minimum makes a strong circumstantial case that with the ever more regimented formality of the legal duel in Uruguay, dueling had become routinized – almost bureaucratized – in a way that might be appropriate for the partisan journalistic spats that were the bread and butter of honor tribunals most of the time but that no longer provided an adequate forum for venting intense hatreds or dealing with intimate private matters, if indeed they ever had. It is not unreasonable to conclude that the very process of civilizing and domesticating the duel had taken the practice so far from its origins that the machinery of honor no longer knew how to handle *real* enmity, as opposed to the posturing histrionics of ambitious politicos for whom genuine honor was rarely truly at stake.

Or perhaps enough time had passed since the duel's pre-1920s heyday that the infrastructure of honor had begun to atrophy. The continuing health of the duel as an institution depended upon Uruguayans still having places and opportunities to practice fencing and marksmanship. It depended upon their remaining attuned to the complex and sometimes arcane laws of honor, and with ready access to seconds and weapons experts who were equally attuned. In the particular case of Ghigliani and Demicheli, given their ages, histories and connections, they would have had no trouble setting the machinery of the duel into motion, had Ghigliani chosen that route. But over time, particularly in the aftermath of World War II, it becomes easier to imagine a new generation of young journalists and politicians for whom the culture of the duel was something foreign, whose professional training as newspapermen no longer included private sessions with a fencing master, who were no longer schooled in the ins and outs of Chateauvillard and Marqués de Cabriñana rules.

There were still some masters and experts around. South American fencing champion Cándido Dominguez would become a go-to director of combat, serving also on the Special Honor Tribunal for military officers.[18] The Olympian fencer Adolfo Goliardi and his brother José prepped Colorado politicians for their duels. But in general terms, an ever-shrinking number of Uruguayans had the skills inventory, knowledge base, and orientation toward the honor code that prepared them as duelists or seconds. And members of that shrinking class were increasingly likely to wear a uniform, a point that takes on considerable importance moving forward.

The 1950s to 1970s: A Shrinking, Aging Minority Revives the Duel

On 21 November 1957, an honor tribunal chaired by former president José Serrato ruled that an insulting letter published in the press by General Juan P. Ribas – the latest in a series of accusations the general had leveled against the administration of Luis Batlle Berres – constituted an offense and that a duel was justified.[19] Had this been the mid-1920s, back during Serrato's presidency, the news would not have elicited any surprise. Both Ribas and Batlle Berres were serial polemicists with numerous gentlemanly incidents on their resumé; each had fought two previous duels, and the ongoing war of words between them was hardly trivial. Through October and into November of 1957, the retired general and former minister of defense had been publishing a series of long incendiary letters that blamed Batlle's government for the country's economic problems and accused him of violating the autonomy of the armed forces by interfering inappropriately and politically in military promotions and transfers of officers.[20] Batlle Berres responded dismissively in his party organ, *Acción*, leading Ribas to escalate his charges and rhetoric even more, accusing Batlle Berres of a lack of moral sense (*insensibilidad moral*) and openly calling him a liar (*embustero*) – one of the classic fighting words that Julio Herrera y Obes back in 1881 had tried to convince newspapers to voluntarily abstain from using.[21]

But 1957 was not 1883 or 1924. After several decades during which challenges and duels had dwindled in number, news that the country's top civilian political figure would be crossing sabers with a prominent general took people by surprise. One paper captured the sense of the moment:

> This time, yes, a duel is authorized, and the skepticism of the man in the street, who would joke daily about an institution as passé as the political duel, now finds that things are getting serious.
>
> It is necessary to recognize that in recent years it has come to be manifest in public opinion the conviction that the challenge to a duel, as culmination of some bitter polemic or exchange of verbal insults, had lost a lot of its prestige and essential meaning.[22]

Serrato himself appeared keenly aware of how much times had changed and felt the need to set out in meticulous detail why the honor tribunal had arrived at the conclusion that a duel was justified in this instance. Writing for the three-man panel, he explained:

> CONSIDERING: That the duel should be reserved for exceptionally grave cases where our customs and moral sensibility render it indispensible … in order to avoid worse ills;
>
> … That in our country the conception of the kind of offense that merits a duel has changed over past years, … the truth is that expressions

and attitudes are today judged by less exacting standards, which has led in consequence to the number of challenges and duels diminishing, even though at the same time the climate of struggle is one of ever more fervent passion, and the inflammatory nature of attacks is increasingly violent; That the polemic between the gentlemen General Juan P. Ribas and Councillor Luis Batlle Berres developed, from its beginning, in a bitter tone, augured, if it were to continue, a most undesirable outcome;

… We would have preferred that our intervention as a Tribunal of Honor might have impeded the realization of a duel; but it is not possible to remove from the terrain of honor a controversy that has taken this turn and reached this intensity.[23]

On 22 November 1957, Ribas and Batlle Berres fought with sabers, and both incurred minor injuries in the second round.[24] It was the first public political duel in Uruguay in over four years. The last had been on May 1953, a pistol duel between Alfeo Brum and Ulysses Pereira Reverbel that arose out of a public fistfight and had been transmitted "play-by-play" on nationwide radio – a dubious first that led in short order to a government ban on such broadcasts.[25]

The fact that an actual duel had occurred involving some of the most important men in Uruguay – in 1957, if that could be believed – made it onto the wire services worldwide.[26] The Batlle Berres-Ribas duel had been unexpected, but the rising trend in challenges – even if none had made it to the field of honor because the seconds found solutions or honor tribunals refused authorization – provided some indication that duels, too, might continue to occur in Uruguay if the intensely felt passions that characterized the Ribas-Batlle Berres conflict were to repeat. And repeat they did: the following year saw a brief boom in challenges, including two particularly memorable cases that made it to the *terreno* (field of honor). Lieutenant Colonel Luis Joaquín Villar López, apparently unsatisfied after a March 1958 saber duel with fencing expert Ernesto Dodo Pozzolo, followed Dodo to his home later that day, shot him with a revolver, and then turned the gun on himself.[27] As in the 1935 Ghigliani-Demicheli incident, the motives were deeply personal, in this case involving marital infidelity, but after having chosen to control his emotions and channel the conflict via the honor code, Villar López came to the realization that Chateauvillard rules did not offer him the catharsis that he ultimately found in murder-suicide.

In a more conventional confrontation four months later, Minister of Defense Raúl Gaudin and the opposition congressman and journalist Enrique

Erro exchanged two pistol shots without incident.[28] Erro, who had informally appointed himself the Partido Nacional's chief denouncer of corruption, had published in *El Debate* in the run-up to the 1958 elections a series of anti-government exposés entitled "Democracy Continues to be Mutilated." In them he accused high military officials of using a shipment of toys from the United States, earmarked for an exposition at the National Aeronautical Museum, as cover for the illicit diversion of US weapons to an unidentified third country.[29] The charges also incited challenges from two other military officials, including the Uruguayan attaché in Washington, but only Gaudin's received the honor tribunal's approval.[30] In a sign of how the times were changing, one of Erro's seconds remembers the difficulty they had in finding proper dueling pistols in Montevideo in 1958.[31]

Honor incidents continued into the 1960s, though none ended in combat. The most notable came in 1967 when General Oscar Gestido, president of the republic, tendered his resignation in anticipation of a duel with his former finance minister, Dr Amílcar Vasconcellos. Gestido challenged Vasconcellos for criticizing the government, the president, and the foreign minister, after Gestido publicly blamed Vasconcellos for economic policies that had allegedly failed the nation. The honor tribunal ultimately refused to authorize the duel.[32] Other potential duels that failed to receive approval involved figures almost as important as Gestido, some of them – like Vasconcellos – leaders of party factions with presidential aspirations of their own. These included the Blancos Wilson Ferreira Aldunate and General Mario Aguerrondo, and the Colorados Manuel Flores Mora, Julio Maria Sanguinetti, and Juan Luis Pintos. Every person on that list save one would stand for president or vice president in the 1971 elections, while Sanguinetti, the sole exception, was elected president in 1984.[33]

The post-1958 hiatus in actual duels, as opposed to challenges, lasted a dozen years but ended with the explosion of four major political duels over the course of 1970–71. Two of the four were initiated by one man, Senator Manuel Flores Mora, and arose out of a single heated exchange in the press. In the hypersensitive context of a four-day emergency bank holiday decreed by the government, Flores Mora had criticized Jorge Batlle and his political faction for openly promoting the benefits of devaluing Uruguay's currency, at a time when President Pacheco Areco's public stance was that no devaluation was imminent. Flores Mora argued that loose lips by people in power were contributing to downward pressure on the peso from currency speculators, while also creating opportunities for corrupt insider trading, all at the expense of

Fig. 4.1 Julio Maria Sanguinetti. Public domain, courtesy of Guillermo Silva Grucci.

the national credit and the economic well-being of Uruguayans.[34] In countering this denunciation, Jorge Batlle's paper, *Acción*, went ad hominem, characterizing Flores Mora as a paranoid, unreliable political gadfly who had switched parties constantly through his career and was "cowardly to the point of audacity" (*cobarde hasta la temeridad*).[35] Flores Mora assumed that the editorial in *Acción* had been written by Batlle, an intra-party rival with whom he had an acrimonious history, and he sent his seconds only to find out that the article's author was acually the paper's subdirector, Julio Maria Sanguinetti. But the challenge was already delivered, and the honor tribunal agreed it merited a duel. Flores Mora's seconds acceded to a saber duel that favored the well-trained fencer Sanguinetti, and Flores Mora ended up receiving a deep cut to his right hand.[36]

While the Sanguinetti duel was in negotiations, Jorge Batlle had returned to Montevideo and issued identical attacks in his own signed editorial. Flores Mora again sent his seconds, but this time the honor tribunal declared Flores Mora the offender, in recognition that he should have dropped the matter now that one duel had already been fought over the same controversy. Sabers were again the chosen weapon, this time with shorter rounds and less demanding conditions, in deference to Flores Mora's injury and to the fact that Batlle, too, was a fencing novice. The duel took place after a two-week delay to allow Flores Mora's wounds to heal, and he made up in devil-may-care aggressiveness what he lacked in technical skill, scoring a cut on Batlle's cheek in the seventh round.[37]

The third duel once again involved the opposition firebrand Enrique Erro, who by this time had left the Partido Nacional to found a splinter party that ended up affiliating with the Frente Amplio. In this case, the duel arose as a consequence of acts of repression by a government that since 1968 had, with ever-increasing frequency, invoked emergency provisions in the constitution to suspend civil liberties and quash political dissent, all in the name of protecting Uruguay from communist subversion and social unrest. On 1 October 1971, in the midst of a presidential election season that was taking on an increasingly violent tone, Erro's son was captured in a wave of raids against the Tupamaros. Days afterward, police detained and questioned Erro himself and other members of his party, holding them for about half a day without explanation. One can imagine how the combination of guilt by association, zealous counterinsurgency, and the desire to send a message to the parties of the left might have motivated this act of repression, during which Erro reported being roughed up by police. In an angry speech to party followers after his release, he described everything that had happened to him and singled out the minister of interior, General Danilo Sena, as the man behind his arrest, accusing him of being "a great coward" for not showing his face in person while subordinates abused Erro's human rights and physical integrity. Sena read about the speech in the next day's paper, and upon learning that Erro, in his own words, "awaits him whatever place and time he may choose," Sena sent seconds.[38] The honor tribunal of two military officers and one civilian ruled that a duel was in order, with Erro the offender, giving Sena the right to choose a pistol duel, which the two men fought in mid-October 1971, both emerging unscathed.

In this case, the divided vote of the honor tribunal illuminates the widening gulf between civilian and military attitudes toward the duel, and indeed toward all that was going on in the country. Senator Ángel Maria Cusano, the civilian chosen for the honor tribunal by Erro's seconds, took the unusual step of publishing his dissent from the tribunal's majority. In Cusano's view, Erro's detention without charges had been the true offense against honor, not Erro's use of the word "coward" in describing the man who had ordered his summary arrest. Cusano saw Sena's instigation of a duel as a pretext to further escalate the abuse to which Erro had already been subjected.[39] The two generals on the tribunal countered that while Erro had a legitimate right to challenge his alleged mistreatment by the authorities, that complaint involved an official government act and thus had to be pursued via administrative and legal channels; in the eyes of the honor code, it did not constitute an offense by Sena against Erro, and thus Erro was the man at fault for having resorted to the insulting word.[40]

The last duel to be fought in Uruguay took place on 7 December 1971, and like the Erro-Sena duel, it was a product of Uruguay's descent into the Cold War. General Líber Seregni, a former Uruguayan military attaché in Mexico City and Washington, had, like many Colorados on the left, split with the ultraconservative Pacheco Areco government and gravitated toward the Frente Amplio. When the 1971 presidential elections rolled around, the leftist coalition selected Seregni as its presidential nominee. At a time when Pacheco Areco and his cabinet of military men failed to make much distinction between the legal left and Tupamaro so-called terrorists, a time when Salvador Allende had just been elected president in Chile, when the United States and Brazil's military rulers were already discussing in secret whether Brazil might intervene to back a military coup in the event of a Frente Amplio victory,[41] and when – truth be told – the fuzzy line between legal assembly and insurrectionary unrest was regularly tested in the Montevideo streets, it was a short step for Seregni's former colleagues to view his candidacy not as an exercise in democratic politics but as part of the existential Castro-communist threat. General Juan P. Ribas, still politically active in retirement, publicly expressed in radio and TV interviews his belief that Seregni was a traitor to the nation and to the armed forces. In the aftermath of the elections, in which the unpopular Colorados secured a controversial plurality victory and the Frente Amplio placed a disappointing third, Seregni asked the Special Military Honor Tribunal to determine whether Ribas's words had constituted an offense. When the tribunal ruled in the affirmative, the seconds agreed to a pistol duel, two shots apiece in somewhat more dangerous conditions than usual: the duelists would be given a full two-second interval between the second and third handclaps, allowing them more time to aim than was typical in Uruguayan duels. On the field of honor, the director of combat suspended the duel following the first exchange of shots, because Ribas did not fire his weapon until after the third handclap – beyond the two-second window. There was discussion afterward whether this violation of the pacted conditions had been intentional and therefore dishonorable: a man who took longer than permitted could gain a criminal advantage by using the time to aim more carefully. In the end, it was decided that Ribas likely had not heard the sequence of handclaps because of the wind, so his failure to follow the stipulated rules had been accidental, not deliberate. That ruling was not unjustifiable: in 1971 Ribas was, after all, an elderly man, his first duel having taken place forty-nine years earlier.

If we take stock of these late duels and of the incidents that did not make it past honor tribunals in the late 1950s, 1960s, and 1970s, two characteristics stand out above all others: first, the recurrence of the same names in incident after incident, either as duelists, seconds, or honor tribunal members, and second, the preponderance of military men, far more than had been the case in the 1910s or 1920s. The 1971 duel with Seregni was General Ribas's fourth. General Mario O. Aguerrondo, one of Ribas's seconds, had challenged Julio Maria Sanguinetti back in 1961. Ribas himself had served on the honor tribunal that authorized the 1970 Flores Mora–Jorge Batlle duel, and Seregni had chaired the honor tribunal that authorized the Flores Mora-Sanguinetti duel. The community of duelists by 1970–71 was tiny, shrinking, and aging.

The most important corollary to the graying of the dueling class was the comparative freedom that people now had simply to ignore insults that in the 1910s or 1920s would have demanded a challenge, and the growing ease with which civilians could refuse to duel without taking any significant hit to their reputations. Luis Hierro Gambardella, rejecting a challenge from Rubén Menes García in 1960, cited "my condition as a Catholic, and for reasons of culture, education, and common sense." He continued: "In the middle of the 20th century, in the atomic era, this kind of return to primitivism is inconceivable ... Above all, we reject the duel and the false and (for us) archaic conception of chivalry that it implies. Our conception of gentlemanliness resides in correct, responsible, and coolheaded behavior. In cases of doubt or controversy, [society's] moral and juridical institutions, not violence, are the touchstone of the gentleman."[42]

Though anti-dueling sentiments like these were hardly new, by the 1960s their advocates no longer needed to push back against a social consensus that in the 1880s or the 1910s would have branded the non-dueling politician or journalist as cowardly and/or irresponsible. In this particular case, it was now the gung-ho duelist Menes García who came across as out of touch with the sensibilities of the time. Similarly, in June 1970 when Wilson Ferreira Aldunate refused a challenge from the navy commander-in-chief, Rear Admiral Guillermo Fernández, despite a ruling from the navy's Special Honor Tribunal that authorized it, Ferreira cited his Catholic faith and also invoked his innate right as a citizen and a senator to demand Fernández's resignation for official misconduct, a right that the protocol of honor would have obliged him to forfeit had he accepted a duel.[43] In the face of Ferreira's vehement rejection of Fernández's right to challenge him, the navy commander's seconds had no recourse other than to publish in the papers a letter to their *ahijado* declaring his honor intact, a declaration that might have carried significant weight in 1880 or 1918 but which by 1970 mattered to no one other than Fernández himself.[44]

The one major exception, General Líber Seregni's decision to duel with General Ribas, proves the more general rule. Seregni had never fought a duel in his life, and as a politician now committed to the cause of the Frente Amplio, he might have been expected to join his socialist, communist, and other left-leaning colleagues in ridiculing the duel's aristocratic pretentions and its corrupt abuse as a strategem to intimidate the press and suppress legitimate oversight. The socialist icon Emilio Frugoni, deceased in 1969, had made precisely that case with passion and eloquence for some sixty years.[45] Yet Seregni agreed to duel, and it was he who challenged Ribas, not the other way around, in the face of Ribas's offense of calling him a traitor to the nation and a disgrace to the uniform for having affiliated with the left.

The most likely explanation is that Seregni was, in his mind, the Frente Amplio's presidential candidate second and a general in the Uruguayan Army first. Through the 1970s and beyond, the armed forces ran standing Special Honor Tribunals with the mandate to decide whether and when officers were authorized to issue or accept challenges. Although these tribunals had the responsibility to stop frivolous duels just as civilian honor tribunals did, they also fostered a climate in which officers were expected to demand duels under some circumstances.[46] In the face of being called a traitor to the nation and to the armed forces, the worst sort of accusation imaginable against the honor of a high military officer, Seregni presumably saw no other choice but to place the matter before the army's Special Honor Tribunal and to live by its verdict.[47]

The persistence of dueling culture within the armed forces goes far toward explaining the uptick in challenges and duels after 1957 and particularly in 1970–71. To appreciate this point, we need to keep in mind the rising militarization of Uruguayan politics, as generals headed many of the key strategic ministries in the Pacheco Areco government. In retrospect, we can recognize that the early 1970s were a unique moment in Uruguayan history when the country was sliding down the path toward a slow-motion coup d'état. Rocked by social protest and the rise of the revolutionary left, conservative Colorado presidents had responded by gradually but inexorably transferring power to the armed forces. The duels of 1970–71 were a hallmark of this unique transitional moment, when the dueling culture of a politicized officer corps, even though increasingly out of step with society as a whole, contributed to the volatile environment in which a still mostly free and still argumentative press, notwithstanding the government's exercise of emergency powers, poured metaphorical gasoline onto volatile existing tensions.[48]

Fig. 4.2 General Líber Seregni, Frente Amplio 1971 presidential candidate. Ladiaria.com.uy.

Fig. 4.3 Uruguay's last duel, between the generals Líber Seregni and Juan P. Ribas. Archivo Fotográfico de *El País*.

The return of dueling in the late 1950s, and the involvement of some of the nation's most important political leaders in duels or challenges over the subsequent decade and a half, created an anti-dueling backlash and renewed legislative efforts to repeal the 1920 dueling law. On 7 November 1967, in the immediate aftermath of the near-duel between President Gestido and Senator Vasconcellos, Representative Salvador García Pintos, Jr. asked for emergency consideration of the recriminalization bill his father had introduced back in 1945. What had been interesting and attractive about that 1945 proposal was that it explicitly sought to preserve honor tribunals while stripping them of the power to override the anti-dueling articles of the Criminal Code. Article 1 of the 1945 bill, reintroduced in 1967, read as follows: "Honor cannot be repaired by means of arms. It is repaired by the *via judicial* (Articles 333, 334, and 335 of the Penal Code) or by a Tribunal of Honor constituted in the same conditions envisioned by Law #7253."[49]

The tribunals would be preserved but transformed into a quasi-judicial institution for the vetting of honor, in a way that would supplant the duel entirely rather than gatekeeping access to an exemption from the Criminal Code. This conception was consistent with the original thinking of the European anti-dueling leagues of the early 1900s, from whom the idea of obligatory honor tribunals had been borrowed. The *Exposición de Motivos* justifying the 1945 bill, repeated verbatim in 1967, praised the wisdom of the 1920 Ley de Duelos but emphasized how much attitudes had changed, and identified the ongoing threat posed by a law that permitted two separate legal regimes with distinct logics to operate side by side:

> We understand that today there exists a contradiction between the level of culture achieved by our society and the legality of the duel ... It is difficult to argue that our society remains indifferent in the face of a death that goes unpunished just because an Honor Tribunal declared it "gentlemanly."
>
> But the legalized duel – which signifies probable legalized homicide – not only offends our cultural values: it also contradicts the country's juridical norms.
>
> ... Today, just as anachronistic as the duel itself, is the ... existence of a Code of Honor, juxtaposed with the Criminal Code, whose own principles operate independently to the point that the former can anul the latter in a matter as serious as homicide.[50]

Once the Gestido-Vasconcellos crisis had passed and the urgency was gone, the García Pintos proposal was shipped off to committee for further study. The duels of 1970–71 again sparked talk of taking up the issue, but to no avail.[51] The country had bigger problems at the time.

Instead, the temporary recrudescence of dueling came to its end when Uruguayan democracy came crashing down in the year and a half that followed the contested 1971 election of Juan Maria Bordaberry. By early 1973, Bordaberry had closed Congress and suspended the few remaining constitutional guarantees, including freedom of the press.[52] It would thus not be repeal of the 1920 decriminalization law that dealt the death-blow to dueling in Uruguay, but the 1972–73 authoritarian crackdown that suffocated the last remnants of liberty of expression, the freedom that had made possible the sort of escalating rhetoric that culminated in insults that could lead to duels. Repeating the dynamic of 1933 with a vengeance, dueling ended when President Bordaberry instituted a full-on civil-military dictatorship replete with unprecedented surveillance, mass arrests, torture, the exile of up to 380,000 Uruguayans, and the incarceration of a higher percentage of the population for political crimes than in any other country in the world.[53] Under this kind of regime, newspapers had to rely on advertising and/or state patronage to survive; self-censorship inevitably followed, and the country's political leaders – whether capable or incompetent, honorable or corrupt – were rendered untouchable.[54] They had no need to duel.

The Law and the Duel, 1920–1971: Comparative Lessons from Argentina

In explaining the decline, temporary return, and ultimate disappearance of the duel in Uruguay, one needs to ask how much importance to attribute to the duel's unique legal status – on the one hand lawful, but on the other regulated by compulsory honor tribunals with absolute power to authorize a duel or to criminalize it on a case-by-case basis. It is plausible to assume that if the duel had not been legal, it would never have persisted as long as it did: after all, dueling died out entirely in Europe by World War II, never to return. It is equally plausible to assume that in the absence of obligatory honor tribunals, the duel might have returned in the late 1950s with even greater intensity than it did, given the number of challenges that failed to receive authorization. Comparing the case of Argentina, however, calls both of these plausible assumptions into question. When Argentines reformed their Criminal Code in 1922, the legalization of dueling Uruguayan-style was proposed but discarded, in much the same way that it had been discussed and rejected in 1917, 1906, and 1891.⁵⁵ Nevertheless, despite remaining illegal, dueling's post-1922 history in Argentina looks remarkably similar to its trajectory in Uruguay.

Argentina's reformed 1922 Criminal Code imposed modest sanctions for dueling – from one to six months of prison if no one was seriously hurt, one to four years if death or grave injury resulted – but even these penalties were rarely applied.⁵⁶ That is not to say, however, that the toothless prohibition was entirely useless. When a rash of duels threatened to spin out of control or when public sentiment against dueling spiked, Argentine authorities had the legal power to step in and detain duelists, sometimes before they made it to the *terreno*. The potential sanctions also made Argentine duelists somewhat more circumspect in publicizing their actions. Negotiations by seconds were a bit less likely to be discussed in the press than was the case in Uruguay, and when the *actas* of a consummated duel appeared, they would either deliberately omit the location or would declare some city in Uruguay as the venue of a duel that had likely been fought in Buenos Aires.⁵⁷

There were rare cases of successful prosecutions of duelists. In December 1935, Juan Silva Riestra and Carlos Güiraldes were each sentenced to a month of conditional prison for having fought a duel in September of the previous year.⁵⁸ Police may have been trying to stem a rising wave of challenges. They also may have been moved by a fatal June 1934 duel,⁵⁹ or by the high-profile pistol duel in July 1935 between Lisandro de la Torre and the minister of hacienda Federico Pinedo, which arose out of an unprecedented melee in the Congress that had left Senator-elect Enzo Bordabehere dead with two bullets from a revolver.⁶⁰

Did Argentina's mid-1930s crackdown work? The number of reported duels dropped off from six in each of 1932 and 1933 and four in each of 1934 and 1935 to only one in each of 1936 and 1937 and none for several years after.⁶¹ On the other hand, just as in Uruguay under Gabriel Terra, the 1930s and early '40s in Argentina were marked by a "soft" dictatorship, a docile press (when compared to previous decades), and rising reader appetite for sports, international news, the crime beat, and popular radio and film celebrities such as Carlos Gardel and Libertad Lamarque.⁶² Dueling certainly declined in Argentina after 1934–35, but it is impossible to judge whether the prosecution of Güiraldes and Silva Riestra played any role. Perhaps it was just coincidental, or perhaps cause and effect were reversed: prosecution of the duel became possible because the underlying culture of honor was in retreat.

There were a few moments when the high political tensions that characterized the government of Juan Perón manifested themselves in the form of duels: in October 1946, the *New York Times* reported as many as fifty different challenges and conversations among seconds in the aftermath of the non-fatal shooting of former Radical Party senator Agustín Rodríguez Araya,[63] and on 23 June 1950, Radical leader Arturo Frondizi and ex-Radical, now-Peronist John William Cooke confronted one another with pistols. (According to one author, that particular set of dueling pistols had not been used in thirty years.)[64] But it was after the 1955 overthrow of Perón, especially during the presidency of Arturo Frondizi (1958–62), that political duels once again became common national events. The conditions fueling the resurgence again appear to have been similar to those in Uruguay: an intensely partisan press once more comparatively free to publish political invective, combined with the high participation of military officers in everyday politics. As long as those conditions obtained, the criminal prohibition of dueling in Argentina appeared to have little impact.

After General Rodolfo Larcher fought a duel with Rodríguez Araya in late 1959, lawyer Humberto Barraza filed a criminal complaint against the two duelists, but nothing came of it.[65] In 1967, a few months after the coup that brought General Juan Carlos Onganía to power, General Pascual Pistarini sent seconds to challenge Arturo Illía, the civilian president he had just helped to overthrow. Illía refused to duel, and his seconds made the argument that as the duly elected president, *he* remained the legitimate commander-in-chief of the armed forces and hence Pistarini's superior, with the right to talk about his subordinate in whatever manner he chose.[66] In 1968, the former navy commander in chief Admiral Benigno Varela fought a highly publicized duel with newspaper editor Yoliván Biglieri. Police showed up at the country house in which the combat was to occur, knocked on the front door, and asked whether a duel was taking place. "Just a barbecue among friends," came the answer, which apparently satisfied them, and they stood outside while the officer and journalist crossed sabers within. Once it was over, the duelists slipped away through the backyard.[67] The next day, a judge ordered the arrest of everyone, including seconds, doctors, and the director of combat, whose names had all appeared in the papers, but a different judge ruled that there was no proof that any duel had taken place, and that Varela and Biglieri's minor wounds were insufficient cause for judicial action in the absence of a criminal complaint by one of the men involved.[68]

It would be naïve to imagine that any criminal statute could have had an effect on men like Larcher, Pistarini, or Varela. This was but one of countless ways in which they placed their own military code above Argentina's civilian law. Only a decade later, after all, other Argentine military officers would be operating torture factories and throwing drugged political prisoners out of airplanes to their deaths: such men defined the word *impunity*. Does that mean that the duel's legality or illegality was entirely beside the point? Perhaps not. Whereas in the 1920s it was rare to see someone publicly refuse to accept a challenge in Argentina on the grounds that dueling was illegal, by the late 1950s and '60s such sentiments appeared with some frequency.[69] Other rationales for refusing a duel were voiced as well: defense of one's inherent right to criticize public figures for their public acts, loyalty to one's Catholic faith, and in a growing number of cases, contempt for the very idea of the duel as a farce and an anachronism.[70] These diverse arguments against dueling combined to overcome the once-powerful fear of social opprobrium. As in Uruguay at the same time, or in France and Italy decades earlier, the laws of honor were losing their force of moral coercion as the duel went out of fashion. One magazine article, commenting on the 1968 Varela-Biglieri affair, called it "picturesque" and "an anachronistic spectacle in the style of Versailles."[71] The BBC arrived with movie camera and tripod, presumably to regale their viewers with a vision of quaint Argentines and their backward customs.[72] One final duel occurred in Argentina in June 1971, the same year as Uruguay's last.[73]

From the 1940s to the 1990s, and indeed into the 2000s, defenders of Uruguay's Ley de Duelos argued that because of decriminalization and the wisdom of the obligatory honor tribunals, "the number of duels diminished to the point of almost disappearing, transforming the few conflicts that have arisen into a genuine rarity."[74] This belief in the beneficent impact of Uruguay's legislation is supported by the many confrontations that honor tribunals did indeed stop in their tracks by declaring them of insufficient gravity to justify a duel. But Argentina's parallel trajectory raises an alternative possibility: that Uruguayan defenders of the 1920 law were perhaps victims of *post hoc propter hoc* thinking. Both countries, despite taking very different legal approaches, saw the same decline in the 1930s and '40s, and in both countries the explanation appears to lie in the clampdown on competitive politics and on the press, accompanied by changes in the character of the newspaper business and, over time, the rise of a new political generation with different values and assumptions. In both countries, a surge in duels between the late 1950s and early '70s occurred when the same three factors were all simultaneously present: a temporary window of relative political and press freedom; intense political emotions in a climate of polarization; and growing intervention in politics by military men, who (unlike civilian society) preserved and nurtured the culture of the duel. It was crucial, however, that all three factors be present, because once the military took full control and eliminated unfettered debate in Congress and in the media, dueling ended as well.

Uruguay, 1984–1992: Redemocratization and Recriminalization

Uruguay's return to democracy in the 1980s saw a return of press freedom and partisan polemic, and soon enough the return of heated attacks that occasionally escalated into challenges and the sending of seconds. None of these incidents ended up making it past an honor tribunal and onto the field of honor, but they sparked renewed debate about the morality and utility of the duel in the late twentieth century. New and younger voices emerged, particularly but not exclusively on the political left, calling for the repeal of Uruguay's dueling law for once and for all. The first bill was proposed on 7 November 1985, just eight months into the restored democratic government led by Colorado Julio Maria Sanguinetti; it was the work of Colorado representative and law professor Daniel Lamas. In the *Exposición de Motivos*, Lamas drew heavily on European legal theorists and focused on how the 1920 dueling statute violated the fundamental principle of equality before the law, "because nobody fails to realize that the whole mechanism of the dueling law, with the Honor Tribunal and the resulting impunity, is reserved for those who enjoy a determined social position. The common man, who constitutes the majority of our population, cannot take advantage of that mechanism and is therefore subject to the full rigor of the Criminal Code if he takes, in order to vindicate a possible affront to his honor, any action that constitutes a crime."[75] The 1985 Lamas proposal was shipped off to committee without debate, but five years later, it joined three other bills, all written with the identical objective and with almost identical language, that were taken up collectively by the House of Representatives' Commission on Constitution, Codes, General Legislation and Administration, chaired by Representative Jorge Coronel Nieto.[76]

The catalyst for the flurry of new bills was an incident that threatened to become a duel between First Inspector Saúl Humberto Clavería, deputy chief of police for the Department of San José, and journalist Federico Fasano. In late February 1990, Fasano's *La República* had reported that two automobiles observed unloading contraband Brazilian goods were registered in Clavería's name, an accusation that Clavería took as an affront to his honor.[77] His first step was to go to the Special Military Honor Tribunal with what he characterized as documentary proof of his innocence, in order that they might authorize him to challenge Fasano to a duel. When the tribunal gave that authorization, the press office of the Montevideo Police – in coordination with the outgoing minister of interior on one of his last days in the job – published the Special

Tribunal's ruling in the papers, and Clavería proceeded to send his seconds to approach Fasano demanding a retraction or reparation by arms.[78] Fasano, both in discussion with Clavería's seconds and in the pages of *La República*, refused to retract his accusations. He characterized Clavería's demand as an attack on press freedom, impugned the validity of the Special Military Honor Tribunal's ruling because it was comprised entirely of military men and had only heard Clavería's side of the dispute, and commented that he would never agree to participate in the archaic and ridiculous institution of the duel.[79]

Here the story gets more complicated. It appears that soon after Fasano's initial rebuff of Clavería's seconds, he changed his mind when he realized that a proper civilian honor tribunal as defined by the 1920 dueling law was highly unlikely to authorize the duel that Clavería sought, and might even vindicate his inherent right to practice investigative journalism. Fasano's seconds therefore named and publicized their choice of a respected jurist as their representative on the tribunal.[80] Clavería's seconds, however, failed to name a delegate of their own to the civilian tribunal; instead, they communicated that Clavería now refused to duel with Fasano. Clavería issued a statement arguing that he no longer recognized Fasano as a gentleman eligible to duel, because Fasano refused to take back his words, because he continued to repeat his charges in *La República*, and because in prior statements he had said he would not participate in any duel.[81] As all of this was going on, Frente Amplio Senator Leopoldo Bruera petitioned the new incoming minister of interior to intervene and stop a duel from happening. Retired naval captain Oscar Lebel penned an editorial for *La República* explaining in detail why policemen do not, and should not, enjoy the same rights as military officers – the point being that Clavería had had no authority to bring his case before the Special Military Honor Tribunal in the first place.[82] *La República* further made its case by polling reactions from beachgoers in the town of Atlántida, who split evenly between those who thought that Clavería's actions constituted a dangerous attack on press freedom cynically designed to cover up his corruption, and those who declared themselves mystified that a duel might still happen in 1990 and that it would be legal.[83]

In the aftermath of this incident, the House of Representatives took up the cause of abolishing the 1920 Ley de Duelos. At one level, most congressmen's opinions probably differed little from those recorded on the beach boardwalk. But an additional element that may have troubled some of the representatives, even though it was not explicitly mentioned in debate, was the role that the Special Military Honor Tribunal had played in response to accusations of police corruption. The wider context is important here: Uruguay had only recently returned to civilian rule, and over the course of that half decade there had been a national debate over whether or not to give the police and armed forces amnesty for human rights violations they had committed while in power. The Colorado and Blanco party leadership had supported an amnesty law (the Ley de Caducidad) in 1986, the Frente Amplio had vehemently opposed it, and in a 1989 national plebiscite, Uruguayans had voted to uphold the law.[84] Many on the left believed that the plebiscite had been held under conditions of virtual extortion, arguing that the military had indicated their intention to ignore any vote to repeal the amnesty law, and some felt they had implicitly threatened a coup if the vote did not go their way. At issue, in other words, was whether the military was in actual fact subordinate to the recently restored civilian authorities, or whether they remained a law unto themselves.

In such a context, the ability of an official accused of corruption to turn to a Special Military Honor Tribunal for permission to challenge his accuser to a duel could be read as a means that military and police officials might employ to continue exercising the same impunity they had enjoyed when they were in charge of the country. Following internal regulations first harmonized across the various armed branches in 1969 and amended in 1985, the Special Military Honor Tribunals were a *sui generis* adjunct to the duel and expressed values that envisioned the military as a caste apart with unique rights and responsibilities, including the duty to defend their honor even in disputes with civilians.[85] At a time when among the general population dueling culture and its precepts were falling into disuse or being rejected outright, it was not unreasonable for critics to see the military discourse of honor, offenses, challenges, seconds, and sabers not just as a "paleontological" artifact of the past, as one legal scholar put it,[86] but as intimately tied to military presumptions of institutional privilege and exemption from civilian oversight. When one further takes into account that resort to the so-called gentlemanly arena had always been a strategic resource that corrupt men in power had used to control the narrative, to silence critics and to evade legal responsibility – remember, from chapter 2, Colonel Schilemberg's attempt to muzzle *El Negro Timoteo* and Police Chief Juan A. Pintos's habitual challenging of his many accusers – it becomes easy to see why reformers wary of military impunity might be troubled by the continued existence of the dueling law's unique carve-out from the Criminal Code.

Each of the three distinct bills was submitted with its own *Exposición de Motivos*, and the various representatives' concerns were similar and overlapping but also showed subtle differences in emphasis. Frente Amplio congressmen

Daniel Díaz Maynard and José Díaz focused on how the dueling law undermined Uruguay's constitutional principles of equal justice and separation of powers:

> Above and beyond any ethical, philosophical, or even religious questions, this bill is rooted – purely and simply – in a sociological fact, which is the community's profound expressed rejection of the practice of the duel, a sentiment that the legislator must heed. It is also founded in a juridical concern ... it is the Judicial Power that is responsible for intervening in the delucidation of conflicts that deal with honor, correspondently proscribing the *via privada*. The very mandate of the Constitution, encapsulated in the article that guarantees all inhabitants of the Republic protection in the enjoyment of life, honor, and security, among other rights, leads to this.[87]

Representative Agapo Luis Palomeque of the Partido Nacional expanded upon the difference between honor and human dignity, arguing that only the latter is an eternal value, while the former is an artifact of social convention, and social conventions evolve and change:

> The duel does not protect dignity, given that it sees man as a means and not as an end in himself. Yes, it seeks to defend the social category of honor, which is by nature protean and fleeting, and changes with the times.
> ... It is true that part of the patrician sector of our society began to dedicate some of its free time to training in arms (fencing, shooting) for eventual duels, thereby incorporating into its process of moral formation certain martial elements. This came at the cost of human solidarity and authenticity. It also created a false sense of manliness – a kind of showcase virility – typical of an era of ostentatious class markers and intense gender discrimination and sexual taboos.
> Today this artifice no longer has a place in our collective mentality ... The duel is an anachronistic institution because our values and our cosmovision of society have changed.[88]

With the three draft bills to study, the Commission on Constitution, Codes, General Legislation and Administration took up repeal of the Ley de Duelos with considerable seriousness of purpose and in what member José Díaz described as an atmosphere of technical-legal professionalism, with the hope of hammering out a consensus bill that could win approval from both houses of Congress.[89] That consensus was not immediately easy to find, because it soon became clear that the dueling law continued to elicit strong support from those who saw the duel and its accompanying system of customary law as the only effective deterrent against libel, defamation, and out-of-control polemics in the press and electronic media. Back in 1920, in response to critiques from both socialists and Catholics, Juan Andrés Ramírez had argued,

> The anachronism, in reality, is not the duel. The anachronism is *la injuria*; the anachronism is that we still accept, as an instrument of action in public life and sometimes in private life as well, not serene reason and the spirit of justice but the diatribe and the insult. So long as the insult is not prohibited, so long as we do not subordinate the solution of our differences to the dominion of serene reason, so long as we are incapable of dominating the impulses of our blood, the duel will be inevitable. It will either take the form that the gentlemanly laws give it, or it will take a much worse form.[90]

Seventy years later, this was the argument that some Uruguayans continued to find compelling and that any reform to the law would need to address. In order for the duel to be abolished, the members of the commission realized they had to provide convincing legal remedies for slander, libel, character defamation, false accusations, name-calling, and all the other excesses that the partisan press committed all too frequently.[91] Yet an effective, consensus legal remedy for libel and defamation was the holy grail that Uruguayans had sought fruitlessly for most of their history as a constitutional republic.[92] As discussed in chapter 1, there were good reasons why dueling law, not defamation law, had long ago become the forum that Uruguay's public men chose when shopping for a set of rules and institutions to discipline public and political discourse. Back in 1919 during debate on the original Ramírez bill, Duvimioso Terra had clearly set out why he believed that was the case:

> Slander, depending on its severity, is a crime punished by a few months in prison or a monetary fine of some amount. Well, there are cases when the person slandered does not want justice to be done via the intervention of the authorities. Why? Because justice, that authority, is incapable of punishing the crime. For an honorable person, there are cases where

one simply would not recur to that means to resolve the conflict; there are cases in which the members of his family, the society in which he interacts, would consider him worthy of disdain if he appealed to that recourse.

... With a duel, even if he dies in the *terreno*, the act is effective; because this individual has lost his life defending his honor, he continues to be worthy of the society in which he lived, and he continues to be worthy of the family to which he belonged, because ... a name unstained is worth more than a chest full of money.[93]

How much had attitudes changed by 1990? For most Congress members, belief in the morality and efficacy of the duel had plummeted, but belief in the inadequacy of the laws against slander and insult had not.[94] Uruguay's history of dueling and press freedom had demonstrated for years the limits and tradeoffs. Duels could be deterred, and the uncontrolled escalation of partisan rhetoric could be curbed, as they had been in the 1930s and from 1973 to 1985, but only with the implementation of restrictive press laws that came at a cost to democracy itself. The challenge facing legislators in 1990 was nothing less than how to regulate a press culture that still gave rise to insults, character defamation, challenges, and potentially duels, yet also simultaneously to rebuild, in the aftermath of an unrepentant military dictatorship, a flourishing democracy with freedom of expression and active, reasoned, candid debate.

With those concerns very much in mind, the House Commission on Constitution, Codes, General Legislation and Administration hammered out a revised bill that did not limit itself to repealing the 1920 law but also replaced the gentlemanly instrumentality of seconds and honor tribunals with a new set of procedures that on the one hand provided "an agile and public mechanism to safeguard the honor of persons,"[95] but on the other hand would not be a law unto itself, separate from the existing Uruguayan justice system, and would not have the authority to permit single armed conflict in suspension of the Criminal Code. The bill called for individuals who believed that they had been insulted or defamed to take their case before a judge who would bring both parties together, each side with supporting documentation and/or legal counsel if they desired. Although the judge could choose to prosecute the alleged offender, the hearings were designed to encourage reconciliation whenever possible, and the framers of the law foresaw the speedy publication of the judges' decisions in the press, just as the honor tribunals had, in order to serve public witness to the litigant's good name.[96] The legislators clearly wanted the new procedures to fulfil the purpose that seconds, honor tribunals, and published *actas* had served in the past, and the hope was that they would be almost as expeditious.[97]

One complicating wrinkle was Article 6 of the bill, which decreed that when an alleged offense against honor was committed via "a medium of communication" such as print, radio, or TV, the case would fall instead under the jurisdiction of the new press law, Law 16.099 of 3 November 1989, which set up its own distinct process for adjudicating defamation accusations.[98] Law 16.099 was drafted by the executive branch to improve upon an 1984 decree-law promulgated during the transition from military to civilian rule, a law that had incorporated some but not all of the recommendations of an independent expert commission.[99] The new revised press law included among its many liberalizing tweaks the elimination of the earlier decree-law's deference to military tribunals, so that in the juridical vetting of defamation charges, a single set of procedures would apply for all citizens without exception.[100]

In debate on repeal of the Ley de Duelos, the informing representative of the commission, Jorge Coronel Nieto, provided a long juridical treatise on the history of regulation of the duel, drawing on many of the same legal scholars who had been referenced in the 1919–20 debate and quoting heavily from two of the dissenting representatives who had argued most forcefully against decriminalization at that time, Emilio Frugoni and Joaquín Secco Illa. Coronel Nieto's principal argument focused on the how the duel "supplant[ed] the decision of judges for that of arms, to the detriment of the power of justice and the jurisdiction [of the courts]." He continued:

> Representatives Dr José Díaz and Daniel Díaz Maynard manifest "that it is inadmissible in a democratic state of law that there remain private forms of dealing with conflicts – with all the grave consequences that can eventually ensue – that escape the natural course of legal resolution via laws and courts. Existing in our positive law specific norms for the protection of honor – Articles 333 to 339 of the Criminal Code – the authority to intervene in the delucidation of conflicts of honor belongs to the Judicial Power, and it is therefore proper to eliminate the *via privada*.
>
> It has been said that the laws that protect honor are insufficient, and that in relying on the justice system to obtain relief from offenses against honor one cannot obtain the adequate satisfaction.
>
> Those who sustain this position, and who consequently conclude that it is necessary to maintain the duel, are in our opinion mistaken. It is

illogical to think that just because one believes that the sanctions against certain offenses are insufficient, the conclusion should be that the individual must place himself above society and substitute law with force.[101]

Other voices seconded this position. Representative Juan Gutiérrez agreed that "the state should have a monopoly on Justice and on the means of dispensing it. Therefore, respect for duelists goes against the constitutional principle of equality before the law because these citizens would get special treatment and have the privilege of being able to exercise justice by their own hand."[102] He also characterized the duel as "an institution that originates in military circles, not fitting for a civil institutionality such as ours. It is an excess of military influence over civilian society." His conclusion rose to the flight of lyricism that provided the first of this chapter's epigraphs: "It is time for the sabers to stay inside the fencing clubs or in displays of armor; for the dueling pistols to go into glass cases or museum collections, and for insults and offenses against honor to be regulated by modern legal dispositions, in accordance with the twenty-first century."[103]

Because the Commission on Constitution, Codes, General Legislation and Administration had worked out a consensus before bringing the bill to the House floor, little opposition was expressed in general debate. Several congressmen, however, wished to put on the record their conviction that repeal of the 1920 Ley de Duelos did not signify its repudiation but rather the confirmation of its original wisdom. Representative Antonio Morell was most forceful on this point:

> Today we seek the repeal of an institution founded in 1920, that obeyed the logic of channelling the regulation of incidents that frequently occurred in our society, among men who disregarded the penalties that the legislation of the era applied to duelists. In reality, though the duel was prohibited, it was an institution consolidated de facto, to the point that the justice system looked the other way when duels occurred.
>
> ... The operation of this institution, and the guarantees that were derived from it via the honor tribunals, comprised an instrument of undoubted efficacy for the era, bringing order to the existing reality and improving it noticeably, to the point that the few duels that occurred within the guidelines of the 1920 law did not lead to outcomes that society might lament. On the contrary, it is possible to affirm that from the moment the law was passed, the number of duels diminished almost to the point of disappearing ...

> I believe that this process that the nation followed is the greatest homage we can pay to those legislators of 1920, highlighting the unquestionable wisdom of adopting a measure that recognized the existing reality of the era, rationalized it, regulated it, and ultimately achieved the objective of diminishing the duel.[104]

Put to a vote, the bill passed easily and by a large majority, the session's low turnout a testimony to the commission's effective behind-the-scenes work at forging consensus.[105]

But that did not mean that repeal of the 1920 Ramírez law was assured, because resistance in the Senate was somewhat stiffer. The Senate's Commission on Constitution and Legislation unanimously recommended passage of the House bill, but in floor debate it ran into opposition from Gonzalo Aguirre Ramírez, Senate president and former vice president of Uruguay, who was also the grandson of Juan Andrés Ramírez.[106] Although Aguirre Ramírez understood that the commission's unanimous recommendation made repeal a fait accompli, he nevertheless felt it important to detail his objections. He started with a joke, quoting Representative Aureliano Rodríguez Larreta from the original discussion of his grandfather's bill, to the effect that "the quality of debate always rises to greatest heights when dealing with *zonceras* (stupid matters of little importance)." He then went on to explain why the dueling issue was not a *zoncera*, that even if one could perhaps ridicule the duel as it was carried out in practice, the conditions that originally gave rise to the Ramírez proposal were deadly serious. There had indeed been the grave problem of a Criminal Code whose provisions were openly flouted by duelists and routinely unenforced by the authorities, to the discredit of all laws. And on this front, Aguirre Ramírez joined other representatives such as Morell in praising the foresight of the Ley de Duelos and the role of honor tribunals in civilizing, controlling, and essentially ending dueling in Uruguay.[107]

But Aguirre Ramírez went a big step further to argue that the brilliance of the 1920 law had also been in preserving intact the traditional code of honor – duel included – and he made the case that no other law or set of procedures had ever been proven to work as well to deter insults and defamation in the press:

> I believe that the Ley de Duelos of 1920 has been an effective deterrent against the insulters, against those who do not have any respect for the moral integrity of their fellow citizens and compatriots. I consider it an element that leads people to think two or three times before letting their passions loose or sitting down at a typewriter to write some virulent

suelto against another citizen, political leader, or other eminent figure in society. And this is not because they might be denounced in the courts of justice as a slanderer or prosecuted for the crime of *injurias*, but because somebody might demand a reparation by arms. It may be easy to smile or laugh about someone who finds himself in this position, but it really is a very difficult position to be in.

I reiterate that the Ley de Duelos for seventy-two years was incrementally making the duel disappear from our political customs and from the heart of our society, but at the same time it was also moderating those who lacked respect for another's honor and becoming a highly efficacious element, still functioning today, leading people to carefully think things through before offending another.[108]

He pointed out that in the seven or so years that the new press laws had been in operation, "almost no one brings a defamation case to the courts, or if they do, the judge doesn't apply the punishment, does not condemn the accused, because just as Dr Juan Andrés Ramírez explained in 1919, a conviction requires ... not just proof of the defamation or insult but proof of intent, the subjective element called 'animus injuriandi,' which is difficult or impossible to prove."[109] Given Aguirre Ramírez's conviction that the *via legal* remained just as unsatisfactory as it was back then, he asked whether legislators could truly be sure that repeal of the Ley de Duelos would not return Uruguay to the pre-1920 days of duels that were illegal but went unpunished.

Aguirre Ramírez's arguments won over at least one senator who had previously intended to vote for repeal, but they did not prevail. Uruguay's 1920 decriminalization law, unique in the world, was formally invalidated and replaced on 1 July 1992, by a roughly two-to-one margin.[110] Most senators were less moved by Aguirre Ramírez's passionate argumentation than they were by Frente Amplio Senator José Korzeniak's counter, that in the real world at the turn of the twenty-first century, if he were to find himself involved in some sharp political argument "and the next day two people came to tell me that they represent a third person who wants to have a duel with me, I confess that I would have quite a prolonged fit of laughter."[111]

Nevertheless, it is worth noting and paying attention to the remarkable fact that there was still a serious pro-dueling argument to be made in Uruguay in 1992, an argument that continued to be heard even in the 2000s. Former president Julio Maria Sanguinetti, the Colorado politician and ex-duelist who shepherded Uruguay's transition back to civilian rule in 1984–85, was one. In a series of interviews he gave between the late 1990s and early 2000s, just after the end of his second presidential administration, Sanguinetti's message was virtually identical to Aguirre Ramírez's: that the 1989 press law did not work as a safeguard for honor and that without the duel and the procedures set out in the 1920 law there was no "psychological inhibition" operating upon members of the political and journalistic class to keep them from hurling the worst kinds of insults and defamatory accusations, and no effective way to put the brakes on an escalating back-and-forth, tit-for-tat war of words when these vicious cycles broke out, as they all too frequently still did.[112] In 2017, José Mujica, the ex-Tupamaro guerrilla and former president whose Frente Amplio had been more dedicated to the duel's recriminalization than any other party, sounded much like Sanguinetti in the face of what he believed to be spurious accusations of irregularities by the government: "The only thing I lament is that there is no longer a Ley de Duelos ... Some things you need to settle that way and not some other way, conversing and blah, blah, blah, because it's really easy in this country to run your mouth."[113] Asked to comment on Mujica's statement, Sanguinetti reiterated his earlier opinion, pointing out that Mujica was "alluding to an institution that is rationally indefensible, because gunshots don't determine who is right and who is wrong; but what happens is that the judicial process today tends to be slow, and it benefits the defamer more than the person defamed – that's the thing."[114]

None of this means that there is pressure to reinstitute the duel in Uruguay, but it does illustrate the ongoing relevance, even the intractability, of the kind of thinking that for so many years led public men to believe that the duel was necessary. The fact that in 1992 (indeed, in 2017) there were voices arguing that recriminalization of the duel gave insult and defamation free rein highlights some of the unresolved questions inherent to open political competition whenever and wherever public opinion matters. These concerns should not be interpreted as typifying an archaic, patriarchal, authoritarian society or political culture. On the contrary: in liberal Uruguay, the duel was eminently modern, a corollary of a free press and one might even say a precondition or at very least a predictable by-product of democracy itself.

Final Considerations

Washington Beltrán Jr., in an editorial published near the seventieth anniversary of his father's death, wrote: "To challenge someone to a duel or to accept a challenge was, for many citizens, to give a testimony. A testimony of honorable conviction behind one's words, of a total belief in their truthfulness, of actions free of any sinister motive. Neither the challenger, the person presumed to have been offended, nor the man challenged, the presumed offender ...would ever vaccilate, in order to give witness of the rectitude of their conduct, in risking that which is most precious to the human being: life."[115]

The jealous defense of one's own honor and reputation; generous respect for the honor and reputation of others; responsibility for one's words and actions; self-control in the face of passion and conflict; and direct, immediate, personal confrontation with those who would slander: these were the values that politicians and journalists sought to communicate to society at large through the institution of the duel. The duel's run in Uruguay lasted as long as it did because these public men who operated the levers of power believed that the honor code's system of parallel legality provided the least bad means of safeguarding those cherished ideals, and of resolving the conflicts that arose when flawed human beings failed to live up to them. In the duelist's moral imaginary, single armed conflict was never the sought-after outcome, but without the possibility of single armed conflict, there could be no respect, no responsibility, no self-control, no punishment for defamers, no honor. The duel itself might be problematic, but it was the problematic keystone of a greater, necessary, even beautiful social edifice of civil and reasoned democratic debate.

Yet the duel *was* problematic, in part because the laws of honor could themselves be abused. Just as any system of laws and courts can attract vexatious litigants who rape its spirit while instrumentalizing its letter, bullying their way to preferred but undeserved outcomes, committing crimes while exacting nondisclosure agreements to legally silence witnesses and victims, threatening lawsuits bereft of merit to exhaust the resources of less wealthy adversaries – the list of modern-day legal abuses could go on and on – the parallel system of honor jurisprudence similarly and equally attracted vexatious duelists. The duel as an institution, when placed in the wrong hands, was a powerful tool to reward intimidation, to shut down legitimate scrutiny, to silence the press or encourage its self-censorship, to suppress internal dissent within a party or movement, to impose one's will rather than win a debate fairly with convincing reasoned argument. The duel could be an extraordinarily efficacious tool for defending the amoral and protecting the corrupt. The duel was misused in more trivial ways as well: manufacturing controversies to increase newspaper circulation, or provoking silly, first-blood duels for insincere motives in order to call attention to oneself. For the duel's opponents, single armed combat was not the unfortunate but necessary cornerstone of responsibility and decorum: it was the tainted foundation of a barbarous and corrupt regime of intimidation, impunity, and privilege. I would argue that it could be both things at once.

The procedures set down in the codes of honor provided some recourse and defense against their abuse. One of the more intriguing and important conclusions of this book, a focus of chapter 2, is the extent to which the gentlemanly negotiations that preceded duels, whether between the seconds or in honor tribunals, so often litigated crucial issues of politics, governance, and law: how to differentiate between legitimate criticism and illegitimate attack, the line where the public sphere ends and private life begins, the rights and responsibilities of government officials to the citizens they serve, the limits of press freedom, and so much more. These issues were disputed in a forum that was extralegal and by definition private, implicating no one except those directly involved in each dispute, with the voluntary intervention of a tiny group of representatives selected by the participants themselves. Yet these private matters were still extraordinarily public, because a whole society of fascinated observers looked on in judgment of which party was right or wrong, who was a bully, who was a coward, who was claiming a legitimate right, and who was acting irresponsibly. Indeed, a strong case can be made that the laws of honor were every bit as consequential as Uruguay's formal legal codes and statutes, given the centrality of the issues that were preferentially vetted in that gentlemanly sphere.

The uneasy and ever-changing dialogue between the parallel system of gentlemanly jurisprudence and codified written law is one of the things that makes the Uruguayan case distinct, even if many of the issues raised are universal. That dialogue, fascinating in itself, speaks also to larger debates about whether the enlightened legislator can ever use the tool of law to alter entrenched customs, or whether the rule of law can only gain respect by deferring to existing cultural norms. Similarly, debate over the legal status of the duel inevitably brought into focus questions of elite privilege and inequality before the law, when the very definition of the crime encoded a whole set of classed and gendered assumptions about who had honor to defend.[116] It may go without saying, but the effective rule of law requires a commitment by society's leaders to submit to law's rule. An argument can be made that Uruguay's decision in 1920 to decriminalize the duel was an inspired one, not so much because it succeeded in ending dueling – it didn't really, or at least it didn't alone – but because having political elites write a special law for their own benefit was so much less odious than permitting those elites to live and act in open violation of their nation's Criminal Code, as remained the case in neighboring Argentina. The Uruguayan solution at least helped to end one flagrant challenge to the rule of law, until such time as actual social behavior caught up with what people thought the ideal should be. This debate over how best to confront the duel – whether by legalizing or more diligently repressing it – has relevance for all sorts of present-day controversies: abortion, pornography, gambling, drugs, guns, and disinformation, to name just a few.

Popular depictions of the duel often end up having little to do with what dueling was really all about. By training all eyes on swashbuckling swordplay or the sudden turn after the march of twenty paces, they focus attention on the wrong thing. The actual moment of combat was in many ways the honor code's least important element. Or to put it differently, the *potential* for combat was essential, but only insofar as it was the keystone of an all-encompassing system of laws and norms. That system entailed so much more than swords and pistols: it was built on socially constructed understandings of what kinds of speech and action were considered offenses against honor, on procedures for vetting disputes when people did not agree about the intent of a particular word or gesture, on the acceptable universe of reasons for demanding or refusing explanations, on the essential and unappealable duties of seconds, and on the way the duel enforced the guardrails of civility and self-control in journalism and political speech. In providing a historical-legal anthropology of this system of honor as it actually functioned, and by focusing not just on its structures and principles but also on its weaknesses and internal contradictions, I hope that this book has shed some light on the duel, but even more light on what one Uruguayan author called "the drama of a people who seek the course of their liberty."[117]

François Billacois famously wrote that the duel is a "touchstone," offering "an aid to the identification and understanding of a particular period, society and political system, with its moral and aesthetic sensibilities and metaphysical and spiritual background."[118] In the case of Uruguay, those moral and aesthetic sensibilities were for the most part unabashedly liberal and democratic, progressive for the region and for the time. The idea that the duel was not only consistent with liberal democracy but may have contributed in some small way to its success flies against stereotype but is consistent with recent scholarship.[119] One thing that arguably made Uruguay unique was the extent to which the dueling class – which was also the law-making class – actually believed this connection to be true and acted upon that belief. The civilian political elites who most fervently embraced the duel saw themselves not as superior aristocrats with a God-given exemption from the rule of law but as guardians of that law, guardians of enlightenment reason and responsible debate, and guardians of democracy. Yes, many of them believed that they were saving democracy from democracy's own excesses, and some of them refused to acknowledge the patently undemocratic and illiberal motives of the duel's worst abusers. The duel's many opponents also invoked democratic ideals: freedom of speech, freedom from intimidation, freedom to audit and criticize the conduct of government officials, and equality before the law without a special carve-out for a privileged minority. I would probably argue that the anti-dueling position was the more compelling of the two. But the democratic rationale for the duel was still being voiced in 1992 when dueling once again became a crime, and was still being voiced in 2017 by an ex-Tupamaro president. That surely says something important about the duel, and something even more important about Uruguayan democracy.

APPENDIX

Methodology

Determining the frequency of dueling as a practice, based on fragmentary public records, is no easy matter. In the case of Argentina, I relied upon three different compilations of duels and challenges, published between 1928 and 2014. The history and methodology of these sources, and their limitations, are discussed below. No similar compilations exist for Uruguay. The closest approximation is a list of seventy duels that appeared in Juan Andrés Ramírez's newspaper *El Plata* in 1920 in the days following the death of Washington Beltrán.[1] Lacking anything remotely resembling a complete accounting, I have nonetheless compiled a list of every duel or pre-duel negotiation that I examined as part of research for this book. Not all the duels and challenges in the table below are discussed in the text or referenced in footnotes, but the overwhelming majority, with only a few exceptions, are incidents I traced back to contemporary news reports or archived copies of the original *actas*. Chronologically ordered, the list is far from comprehensive and makes no claim to be so, but with over 150 incidents, it constitutes a large enough and diverse enough sample that I have confidence in the interpretive conclusions derived from their analysis.

In the absence of any long-running, digitized, and searchable newspaper of record in Uruguay, I would have needed infinitely more time and resources to find every reported duel and incident over the 140 years that the book covers. Given that limitation, my research methodology went roughly as follows: I started with duels and incidents that were important or memorable enough to appear in secondary sources or in those primary sources that discussed dueling as a general phenomenon. Following leads from these sources, I examined the press for the time periods referenced. Often, based on the biographies of the participants, it was easy to anticipate which newspapers were most likely to carry information about the particular duel or challenge. Over time, it became clear from general discussion in the press that dueling activity rose and fell, with relatively quiet stretches alternating with periods that contemporaries described as epidemics. Sometimes the political conflicts that gave rise to those epidemics were fairly evident. For such peak periods, I went through the press more systematically, looking for duels and challenges not discussed or recorded elsewhere. Over much of the period covered by the book, *La Tribuna Popular* was the paper most likely to record incidents in which its own journalists were not involved. For duels and incidents after 1950, the newspaper clipping collection compiled by the fencing master Cándido Dominguez was invaluable.

General discussion of the duel in the press and in Congress also pointed to those moments when the authorities made the greatest effort to prevent duels or to prosecute duelists after the fact, so these were the time periods for which I paid closest attention to police investigation records and court cases. For those who might wish to build on the work of this book, there is, I suspect, much more still to be found in the AGN's Archivo Judicial and in the records of Uruguay's military honor courts. I chose instead to prioritize the daily papers because the records of challenges, duels, negotiations between seconds, rulings of honor tribunals, and even the doings of police and judges were unusually complete and detailed in the Uruguayan press. Almost every country has accounts of the most famous duels between its most celebrated duelists, but nowhere have I found a richer public record of the day-to-day workings of the honor code's parallel legal system. In some countries, the duel's illegality imposed strict limits on what details could be revealed. Even in relatively permissive Argentina, it was not unusual to find cryptic references in the papers to "a duel last night in Palermo between two very well-known persons," "a pistol duel that secretly took place a few days ago in this city," or "talk around town about a duel yesterday between two young journalists," when fear of intervention by the authorities made discretion prudent, even if clued-in readers could fill in the blanks.[2] Such reticence was the exception in Uruguay in the late nineteenth century and exceedingly rare by the twentieth, even prior to legalization.[3]

The diligence with which Uruguayan newspapers published the full *actas* of challenges, responses, negotiations, and duels, particularly if their own writers or proprietors were involved, bore witness to the fact that in Uruguay, the periodic press was for duelists and seconds what the *Diario de Sesiones* was for congressmen: the public record of their private deliberations. The richness of detail holds not only for duels but equally for those instances when explanations were given, the seconds refused to let a challenge proceed, or an honor tribunal declined to give its authorization. This extraordinary documentation in the daily papers helps to explain why the research and writing of this book was possible in the first place, but it is itself also a central element of the story.

Argentina

Compilations of dueling data for Argentina start with César Viale, *Jurisprudencia caballeresca argentina*, published in three editions – 1914, 1928, and 1937 – with each new edition simply taking the previous one and adding to it. Similar to Iacopo Gelli's dueling statistics for Italy, Viale's methodology consisted of compiling the *actas* of duels and incidents published in *La Nación* and a few other important Argentine newspapers, along with information provided directly by people he knew. He documented 253 "incidents without combat" and 100 duels from 1904 to 1928, and an additional 61 incidents and 31 duels through 1937.[4] Jorge Varangot's *Virtudes caballerescas*, published in 1972, took up where Viale left off and added another 147 duels or incidents between 1940 and 1971, five of them from Uruguay. The third compilation is Hernán Antonio Moyano Dellepiane's "Jurisprudencia caballeresca porteña," published in 2014 as a 550-page special issue of the journal *Cruz de Sur*. Moyano declared that his intention was to complement Viale and Varangot by covering only nineteenth-century duels, and his statistics are incomplete.

Sandra Gayol discusses Viale and Varangot's limitations.[5] First is the issue of gaps: the most poorly reported period is immediately after 1938, the publication date of Viale's third and final edition. Because Varangot went to press thirty-four years later, we might guess that his record keeping for the 1940s is not as good as it was for the 1960s, his memory of those years not as fresh. The events most likely to have faded into oblivion were challenges not leading to duels.

But second and more important is the question of representativity: did these works cover the majority of duels, or were the highly publicized incidents protagonized by the politically well connected just the tip of the iceberg? Robert Nye guesses that the statistics for France, based on official and press sources, undercounted by a factor of three or more.[6] Steven Hughes, judging the completeness of Gelli's compilation work for Italy, posits a smaller undercount, arguing not only that Gelli was a diligent researcher but also that the vast majority of duels *were* publicized in the press because the press was the principal milieu from which they sprung.⁷ For Argentina, as for Uruguay, the commentary of contemporaries supports Hughes's view over Nye's, at least insofar as civilians were concerned. Though duels between social and political unknowns would not have made it into the Viale, Varangot, or Moyano Dellepiane volumes, the reality appears to have been that social and political unknowns did not duel with any great frequency, for reasons that I hope this book has made clear. The one significant exception to this rule appears to have been military officers, who did not need to be high ranking or involved in politics to figure as duelists. There is every indication that military men followed a unique institutional code of comportment with its own rules and procedures.

Uruguay

As mentioned previously, no published compilation of duels exists for Uruguay, the closest being the early 1920 newspaper article naming the protagonists of every duel that Juan Andrés Ramírez and his friends could remember, looking back approximately three decades.⁸ Memories got fuzzier the further back in time, and the list included few or no verified duels from the 1880s or earlier, nor did it include incidents that never made it to the *terreno*. Seventy was certainly a significant undercount. But newspaper coverage was, as we have seen, extraordinarily complete and extensive, thanks to Uruguay's permissive attitude toward the duel, especially after 1920 but even before. And because Uruguayan newspapers so often reported on the actions of their own writers or editors, press reports were the ideal place to follow the evolution of conflicts from first insult to final resolution, with different papers providing informed commentary from a full range of competing perspectives.

There were, of course, exceptions to this norm of high visibility. A desire for secrecy might arise if the original offense was of a particularly sensitive nature, or if the authorities at that specific moment were taking a tougher line against the duel, as occasionally was the case. There surely were also duels that went unreported because the participants were not important enough or well connected enough to make it into the papers. But my strong sense is that the lion's share of private, unpublicized duels in Uruguay, as in Argentina, were between military officers, not civilians, and Uruguayans tended to agree that the overwhelming majority of civilian duels arose from politics and the press rather than from sensitive private matters.⁹ The final main category of underreported duels would comprise those fought in the provinces rather than in the capital, given the Montevideo-centrism of the country in general and the press in particular.

APPENDIX: METHODOLOGY

With all the previous caveats in mind, the tables below provide as full a list of Uruguayan duels and challenges as currently exists, incomplete though it may be. It is my firm hope that future scholars will add to it. The list is in two parts: Table A1, as noted above, includes every duel or incident that I was able to locate, date, and analyze for the purposes of this book. Table A2 adds duels that made Juan Andrés Ramírez's early 1920 list, based on collective memory, but which my own research did not specifically locate for follow-up.

Table A1   Duels or Incidents Researched for this Book, Involving an Uruguayan or Fought in Uruguay

Duels/Incidents, by Date or Date Reported				
Year	M/D	Type of Event	Person 1	Person 2
1856	29 Dec	duel, pistol	Juan Carlos Gómez	Nicolás Calvo
1866	12 Mar	duel, pistol, fatal	José Cándido Bustamante	Servando Martínez
1869	27 Jun	challenge and satisfaction	José Pedro Ramírez	Héctor Varela
1869	20 Dec	police arrest duelists	Julio Herrera y Obes	José Cándido Bustamante
1870	11 Apr	duel, foil and pistol	José Pedro Varela	Benito Neto
1871	1 Jul	refused duel, mutual insults	José C. de Oliveira	Amaro Carvé
1871	11 Aug	duel, pistol	Carlos Maria Ramírez	Francisco Bauzá
1880	5 Jul	challenge and refusal	Lieutenant Schilemberg	Washington Bermúdez
1880	13 Aug	duel, pistol, fatal	Enrique Romero Giménez	José Paul y Angulo
1881	18 May	refused duel	General Máximo Santos	Carlos A. Fein
1881	16 Aug	refused duel	Tomás Jameson	Cheppi
1883	11 Sep	challenge, no duel	Salvatore "Totó" Nicosía	David Buchelli
1883	16 Nov	duel, saber	Salvatore "Totó" Nicosía	Juan Smith
1884	12 Jul	challenge, refusal, arrest	Nicanor García Leguizamo	Alberto Nin
1884	14 Aug	police stop duel	Salvatore "Totó" Nicosía	Savastiano
1888	12 Dec	duel, pistol	Eugenio Garzón	Pedro Pardo
1889	18 Mar	duel, saber	Alberto Palomeque	Samuel Blixen
1892	February	police stop duel	Carlos Blixen	Víctor Arreguire
1893	20 Oct	duel, pistol	José Batlle y Ordóñez	Eugenio Garzón
1893	28 Oct	duel, pistol, fatal	Guillermo Ruprecht	Joaquín Tejera
1905	1 Feb	challenge and satisfaction	officials Silva and De Leon	Carlos Roxlo
1905	13 Mar	duel, rumors of serious injury	unnamed army official	unnamed army official
1905	21 Jul	duel, saber	Ruperto Michaelson	Luis Alberto de Herrera
1905	2 Aug	challenge and satisfaction	Eugenio Garzón	Reyes

Duels/Incidents, by Date or Date Reported				
Year	M/D	Type of Event	Person 1	Person 2
1905	13 Oct	duel, pistol, arrest of two Argentines	Manuel López (Jr.)	Lieutenant Amaro Godoy
1906	24 Apr	duel refused	Luis Alberto de Herrera	José Batlle y Ordóñez
1906	20 Oct	duel, saber, later investigation	Pedro Manini Ríos	Aureliano C. Berro
1908	31 Mar	duel, saber, arrests	Lorenzo Carnelli	Baltasar Brum
1908	12 May	duel, saber	Juan Andrés Ramírez	Alberto Guani
1908	31 May	duel, pistol, fatal	Lieutenant Arturo Gomeza	*Alférez* Alfredo Giordano
1908	25 Aug	duel, saber	José Sienra Carranza	Lieutenant Mitre
1912	27 Mar	refused duel, explanations given	Otto Miguel Cione	Vicente A. Salaverri
1912	12 Dec	duel, saber	Carlos Maria Gurméndez	Julio Maria Sosa
1913	6 Jan	duel, saber	*Alférez* Gustavo Schroeder	Lieutenant Arturo Dubra
1913	13 Jan	refused duel	Justo R. Pelayo	Emilio Frugoni
1913	3 Feb	military honor tribunal, no duel	Ramiro Jouan	Lieutenant Arturo Dubra
1913	14 Apr	challenge postponed	various Blancos	José Batlle y Ordóñez
1913	March	unspecified incident	José Pedro Blixen Ramírez	Orlando Pedragoza Sierra
1914	2 Feb	duel, weapon unknown	Orlando Pedragoza Sierra	Leonel Aguirre
1914	28 Feb	duel, pistol	Washington Paullier	Gastón R. Plaucia
1914	4 Mar	duel, pistol, after mediation	Mario Ferreira Martínez	Eduardo de Castro
1914	28 Apr	police stop duel	Domingo R. Reyes	Enrique E. Buero
1914	28 Apr	challenge and satisfaction	Pedro Oribe	Vicente A. Salaverri
1914	7 May	refused duel (invokes Catholicism)	Eduardo Acevedo Álvarez	José Miranda
1914	17 May	duel, pistol, police intervene	José Pedro Blixen Ramírez	Raúl Martinelli
1914	20 May	challenge and satisfaction	Virgilio Sampognaro	Washington Paullier
1914	3 Jun	duel, pistol	Carlos Rodríguez Larreta	Héctor Miranda
1914	8 Jun	duel, saber	Julio Raúl Mendilharsu	Miguel A. Pringles
1914	1 Jul	challenge and satisfaction	Carlos Maria Gurméndez	Luis Paysée
1914	1 May	duel, pistol	Washington Paullier	José G. Antuña
1915	17 Jan	challenge and satisfaction	Alberto Costa Podestá	José Guerra
1915	20 Jan	refused duel, honor tribunal	General Duchefrou	Guillermo García
1915	27 Feb	refused duel	José Batlle y Ordóñez	Juan Andrés Ramírez
1915	3 Mar	seconds reject duel	Leonel Aguirre	José Batlle y Ordóñez
1915	19 Mar	challenge and satisfaction	Lucas Moreno	Damián Vivas Cervantes
1915	27 Mar	duel, pistol	José Pedro Blixen Ramírez	Haroldo Mezzera

APPENDIX: METHODOLOGY 173

Duels/Incidents, by Date or Date Reported				
Year	M/D	Type of Event	Person 1	Person 2
1915	3 Oct	duel, saber	José Batlle y Ordóñez	Guillermo García
1915	4 Nov	refused duel, mediation	Alfredo Schroeder	Isidoro Viana (Jr.)
1915	29 Dec	seconds disagree, no duel	Baltasar Brum	Carlos Reyles
1916	4 Feb	aborted duel	Alejo Idiartegaray	Manuel Solosona y Flores
1916	9 Feb	unspecified incident	Manuel Solsona y Flores	Alejo Idiartegaray
1916	11 Feb	duel, saber	Washington Paullier	Celestino Mibelli
1916	15 Feb	refused duel	Juan J. Risso	Enrique Piqué
1916	18 Feb	duel, pistol (stopped day earlier)	Juan Andrés Ramírez	Baltasar Brum
1916	1 Mar	duel, pistol	Alfredo Mallarini	Brigido Ríos Silva
1917	24 Mar	challenge, no duel	Enrique E. Buero	Washington Beltrán
1917	24 Mar	duel, saber	Eugenio Martínez Thedy	Washington Beltrán
1917	26 Dec	duel, saber	Enrique F. Areco	Pedro Manini Ríos
1918	9 Apr	challenge, no duel	Andrés Puyol	Enrique Puppo
1918	9 Apr	duel, saber, police	Roberto Mibelli	Lorenzo Carnelli
1918	10 Apr	duel, pistol, serious, police intervene	César Miranda	Lorenzo Carnelli
1918	10 Apr	challenge, no duel	César Miranda	Emilio Rodríguez Brito
1918	17 Apr	duel, saber	Enrique Cornú	José Luis Espalter
1918	6 Jul	duel, saber, dispute, honor tribunal	Julio F. Escobar	José Pedro Blixen Ramírez
1918	23 Aug	duel, saber	Ángel Falco	Enrique Gómez Carrillo
1919	31 Jan	duel, saber	Amadeo Almada	Osvaldo Crispo Acosta
1919	27 Feb	duel, saber	Eduardo Rodríguez Larreta	Luis Otero
1919	6 Mar	duel, pistol, later arrest	Roberto Pietracarpina	Julio Raúl Mendilharsu
1919	14 Mar	refused duel	Virgilio Sampognaro	Emilio Frugoni
1919	15 Mar	duel, saber	Benjamín Capurro	Eduardo de Castro
1919	29 Mar	duel, pistol	Eduardo Arrechavaleta	Juan Barbat
1919	3 Apr	duel, saber	José G. Antuña	José Luis Espalter
1919	4 Apr	challenge and satisfaction	Alejandro Piovene	Luis Beltrán Barbat
1919	20 May	duel, pistol	Álvaro Platero	Lorenzo Carnelli
1919	16 Jun	duel, pistol, investigation	José Batlle y Ordóñez	Juan Andrés Ramírez
1919	31 Jul	seconds disagree	Roberto Mibelli	Horacio Jiménez de Aréchaga
1919	2 Aug	duel, pistol	Washington Paullier	Francisco Ghigliani
1919	30 Aug	duel, pistol	Ismael Cortinas	Humberto Pittamiglio
1919	3 Oct	seconds disagree	Luis M. Otero	Edmundo Castillo
1919	3 Oct	duel, saber	Luis M. Otero	Enrique Doria

Duels/Incidents, by Date or Date Reported				
Year	M/D	Type of Event	Person 1	Person 2
1919	5 Oct	duel, pistol	Eduardo de Castro	César Batlle Pacheco
1919	6 Oct	duel, saber	Juan A. Pintos	Alfredo Bazet
1919	25 Oct	threat in face of refusal to duel	General Duchefrou	Emilio Frugoni
1919	20 Nov	duel, pistol	Carlos Maria Prando	César Miranda
1919	10 Dec	challenge deflected to another	Leonel Aguirre	Francisco Ghigliani
1920	9 Jan	duel, Italian epee	Gerardo Sienra	Alfeo Brum
1920	13 Jan	duel, saber	Leonel Aguirre	José Batlle y Ordóñez
1920	15 Jan	duel, saber	Atilio Narancio	César Miranda
1920	12 Mar	duel, saber	Eduardo Rodríguez Larreta	Francisco Ghigliani
1920	2 Apr	duel, pistol, fatal	José Batlle y Ordóñez	Washington Beltrán
1920	24 Apr	challenge and refusal	Baltasar Brum	Eduardo Rodríguez Larreta
1920	3 Aug	challenge and refusal	Pablo M. Minelli	Celestino Mibelli
1920	5 Sep	duel, saber	Humberto Pittamiglio	Julio Maria Sosa
1920	2 Dec	honor tribunal, no duel	General Sebastián Buquet	Leonel Aguirre
1920	21 Dec	refused duel, honor tribunal	Lieutenant Galati	Julio Maria Sosa
1920	22 Dec	duel, saber	Julio Guani	Francisco Ghigliani
1920	25 Dec	president forbids duel with diplomat	Julio Maria Sosa	Ambass. Maestri Molinari
1920	February	refused duel	unreported	Justino Jiménez de Aréchaga
1921	19 Jan	honor tribunal, no duel	Gabriel Terra	Luis Alberto de Herrera
1921	7 Mar	duel, Italian epee	Miguel Caprio	Romeo Pereyra
1921	14 Mar	duel, revolver	Gotardo Bianchi	Horacio L. Aflijer
1921	19 Mar	honor tribunal, no duel	Juan J. Sanmartín	José M. Lápido
1921	21 Mar	duel, saber, fatal	Miguel Sánchez Gomeza	Cándido Melo
1921	8 Apr	honor tribunal, no duel	José Urrutia	Juan Andrés Ramírez
1921	13 Apr	duel, pistol	Villanueva Saravia	José Urrutia
1921	13 Apr	rumored challenge	Martirena Saravia	Gabriel Terra
1921	14 Apr	duel, saber	Pedro Díaz	Eduardo Rodríguez Larreta
1921	16 Apr	challenge and satisfaction	Manuel Solsona y Flores	Agustín Musso
1921	16 Apr	duel, revolver	Arturo Guarino Fischer	Pablo J. Ros
1921	18 Apr	challenge and satisfaction	Enrique Aguiar	Enrique Rodríguez Fábregat
1921	31 Aug	honor tribunal, no duel	Álvaro Vargas	Luis Batlle Berres
1921	12 Sep	honor tribunal, no duel	Ramón P. Díaz	José Irureta Goyena

APPENDIX: METHODOLOGY

Duels/Incidents, by Date or Date Reported

Year	M/D	Type of Event	Person 1	Person 2
1921	14 Sep	honor tribunal, no duel	Francisco E. Artucio	Genaro Gilbert
1921	26 Sep	honor tribunal, no duel	José Lisidini	Marcos Batlle Santos
1921	12 Oct	refused duel (denied authorship)	Luis Alberto de Herrera	José Batlle y Ordóñez
1921	19 Oct	challenge, refusal, arrest	José Luis Espalter	Judge Marcelino Leal
1921	29 Oct	seconds disagree	Luis Enrique Andreoli	José Batlle y Ordóñez
1921	29 Oct	challenge and satisfaction	Luis Batlle Berres	Luis Enrique Andreoli
1921	27 Oct	duel, pistol, serious injury	Armando Patiño	Marcelino Elgue
1921	18 Dec	duel, saber	Martín Machiñena	Genaro Gilbert
1921	26 Dec	refused duel	Washington Paullier	José Batlle y Ordóñez
1922	14 Mar	duel, Italian epee	Enrique F. Areco	Luis Batlle Berres
1922	21 Mar	duel refused	Juan A. Pintos	Juan Pedro Suárez
1922	28 Mar	duel, saber	Antonio Maria Fernández (Jr.)	Juan F. Guichón
1922	13 Dec	duel, pistol	Luis Alberto de Herrera	Baltasar Brum
1922	unknown	duel, pistol	Raúl Judé	Luis Batlle Berres
1923	22 Mar	duel, saber	Alfredo L. Laenz	Enrique P. Caballero
1924	26 Jan	duel, pistol	Colonel Alberto Riverós	Baltasar Brum
1924	23 Mar	duel, saber	Eduardo Rodríguez Larreta	Juan A. Pintos
1924	26 Mar	duel, pistol	Juan A. Pintos	Domingo Cruz
1933	2 Nov	honor tribunal, no duel	Juan Andrés Ramírez	Col. Alfredo Baldomir
1934	24 Jul	honor tribunal, no duel	Captain A. Carlos Cutinella	Luis Batlle Berres
1935	3 Nov	honor tribunal, no duel	Juan Andrés Ramírez	Col. Alfredo Baldomir
1937	8 Oct	honor tribunal, no duel	Francisco Rodríguez Larreta	Marcelino Elgue
1945	6 Aug	honor tribunal, no duel	Ángel B. Graña	Eduardo Víctor Haedo
1953	3 Dec	honor tribunal, no duel	Héctor Álvarez Cina	Luis Batlle Berres
1953	7 May	duel, pistol (broadcast on radio)	Alfeo Brum	Ulysses Pereira Reverbel
1954	19 May	honor tribunal, no duel	Luis Alberto de Herrera	Luis Batlle Berres
1956	5 Jan	honor tribunal, no duel	Washington Guadalupe	Luis Batlle Berres
1957	22 Nov	duel, saber	Luis Batlle Berres	Juan Pedro Ribas
1958	28 Mar	duel followed by murder/suicide	Lieut. Col. Joaquín Villar	Ernesto Dodó Pozzolo
1958	5 Jul	duel, pistol, leads to heart attack	Raúl Gaudin	Enrique Erro
1958	27 Jul	honor tribunal, no duel	Manuel Flores Mora	Osvaldo Lezama
1958	31 Jul	challenge, no duel	General Emilio Juárez	Enrique Erro

Duels/Incidents, by Date or Date Reported				
Year	M/D	Type of Event	Person 1	Person 2
1960	17 Oct	challenge, no duel	Luis Hierro Gambardella	Rubén Menes García
1961	unknown	honor tribunal, no duel	Col. Mario Oscar Aguerrondo	Julio Maria Sanguinetti
1967	31 Oct	honor tribunal, no duel	Amílcar Vasconcellos	Héctor Luisi
1967	1 Nov	honor tribunal, no duel	General Oscar Gestido	Amílcar Vasconcellos
1970	30 May	challenge and satisfaction	Miguel A Blancazo	Roberto Ares Pons
1970	18 Jun	honor tribunal, no duel	Guillermo Fernández	Wilson Ferreira Aldunate
1970	7 Aug	challenge, no duel	Miguel Restuccia	Julio Lacarte Muró
1970	21 Oct	duel, saber	Manuel Flores Mora	Julio Maria Sanguinetti
1970	11 Nov	duel, saber	Jorge Batlle	Manuel Flores Mora
1970	14 Nov	honor tribunal, no duel	Juan Luis Pintos	Luis Eduardo Machado
1971	17 Oct	duel, pistol	General Danilo Sena	Enrique Erro
1971	7 Dec	duel, pistol	General Líber Seregni	General Juan P. Ribas
1973	31 May	duel refused	Captain Homar Murdoch	Alberto Heber Usher
1984	15 May	challenge, no duel	Alberto Abdala	Rafael Noboa
1990	23 Feb	challenge, then retracted	Saul H. Clavería	Federico Fasano

APPENDIX: METHODOLOGY 177

Table A2 Additional Duels, c. 1890–Early 1920, as Recorded in "Actualidad: Estadística del duelo," *El Plata*, 14 April 1920

Type of Event	Person 1	Person 2
duel, weapon unspecified	Juan Pedro Ribas	Roberto Fontaina
duel, Italian epee	Lieut. Héctor Luisi	Lieut. Domingo Gomensoro
duel, Italian epee	Rodolfo Servetti y Revello	Domingo Mendy
duel, saber	Teófilo Díaz	Andrés Llovet
duel, saber	Rodolfo Fonseca	Víctor Basabe
duel, saber	Emilio Paysée	Col. Luis Fábregat
duel, saber	Luis F. de la Riva	José L. Peña
duel, saber	Carlos Zumarán Arocena	Enrque Buero
duel, saber	Juan Antonio Buero	Rafael Conde
duel, saber	Luis Ignacio García	Col. Antonio Klinger
duel, saber	Vicente Borro	Alberto Bahamonde
duel, saber	Pedro Manini Ríos	Gualberto Ros
duel, saber	Carlos Roxlo	Arturo Pozzilli
duel, saber	Horacio Abadie Santos	Andrés Pacheco
duel, saber	Manuel Solsona y Flores	Eugenio Martínez Thedy
duel, saber	Aureliano Rodríguez Larreta	Carmelo Cabrera
duel, saber	César Batlle Pacheco	Domingo Cruz
duel, saber	Eduardo Acevedo Alvarez	Héctor Lápido
duel, saber	Luis Melián Lafinur	Juan José Segundo
duel, saber	José G. del Busto	Juan José Segundo
duel, saber	Juan José Amézaga	Carlos Martínez Vigil
duel, saber	Eduardo Ros	Francisco Gómez Cibils
duel, pistol	Carlos Maria Ramírez	Eugenio Garzón
duel, pistol	Pablo Minelli	Alfredo García Morales
duel, pistol	Justo R. García	Eduardo Acevedo Díaz
duel, pistol	Vicente I. García	Leopoldo Peluffo
duel, pistol	Juan Andrés Ramírez	Alejo Idiartegaray
duel, pistol	Eduardo Rodríguez Larreta	Francisco Bruno
duel, pistol	Francisco Forteza	Amorós

Notes

Introduction

1. República Oriental del Uruguay, *Diario de sesiones de la Cámara de Senadores*, vol. 349, session of 16 June 1992, 210, 212. Hereafter cited as ROU, *DSCS*. All translations here and elsewhere are by the author, unless otherwise indicated.
2. "Extraña los duelos," *El Pais*, 28 February 1999, 19.
3. "Cerrado por duelo: Mujica lamentó que no exista la Ley de Duelos para resolver ataques al honor," *Montevideo Portal*, 15 June 2017, https://www.montevideo.com.uy/Noticias/Mujica-lamento-que-no-exista-la-Ley-de-Duelos-para-resolver-ataques-al-honor-uc346138. Mujica was being interviewed on the program *En la Mira* for VTV.
4. Salvatore, Aguirre, and Joseph, *Crime and Punishment in Latin America*, provides an introduction to this important subfield in Latin American history.
5. The two major academic books on dueling in Latin America are Gayol, *Honor y duelo en la Argentina moderna*, and Piccato, *The Tyranny of Opinion*. See also Piccato, "Politics and the Technology of Honor," and Gayol, "Honor Moderno." Both authors agree that dueling was a modern institution, but they focus more than I do on the broader cultural meaning of the concept of honor, on how honor was classed and gendered, and on the role of dueling as a strategy of social differentiation, which is the main argument in Braga-Pinto, "Journalists, *Capoeiras*, and the Duel."
6. Works on Europe and the United States that use the duel as a window onto an all-encompassing cultural ethos, or as an indicator of some fundamental process of change in social relations, include Nye, *Masculinity and Male Codes of Honor*; Frevert, *Men of Honour*; McAleer, *Dueling: The Cult of Honor*; Kiernan, *The Duel in European History*; Reddy, "Condottieri of the

Pen;" Hopton, *Pistols at Dawn*; Wyatt-Brown, *Southern Honor*; Greenberg, *Honor and Slavery*; Sánchez, "Honor de periodistas"; Luengo, "Masculinidad reglada."

7   Burkholder, "Honor and Honors in Colonial Spanish America," 34. Undurraga Schüler, "Cuando las afrentas se lavaban con sangre," 165–88, appears to provide an opposing view, but the eighteenth-century Chilean duel that she recounts is hard to describe as between *elites*.

8   Albornoz Vásquez, "Sufrimientos individuales declinados en plural"; Johnson and Lipsett-Rivera, *Faces of Honor*.

9   In this respect, my approach most closely aligns with that of authors such as Hughes, *Politics of the Sword*; Freeman, "Dueling as Politics"; and Chamberlain, *Pistols, Politics and the Press*.

10 Hughes, *Politics of the Sword*, chap. 3, draws similar conclusions for Italy.

11 Sábato, *The Many and the Few*, 127–8.

12 "A batirse en Montevideo: Nueva corriente inmigratoria," *El País* (Montevideo), 24 October 1921, 3.

13 *Tratados y convenios internacionales suscritos por Uruguay*, 427–9.

14 The suburban Belgrano backyard of fencing enthusiast Dr Carlos Delcasse was the venue of 154 duels, many of them falsely attributed to Colonia, Uruguay, if his recollection in a 1929 interview is to be believed. Juan José de Soiza Reilly, "En el mundo de los viejos muchachos porteños: Un viaje alrededor de don Carlos Delcasse," *Caras y Caretas*, 14 December 1929.

15 Paz, *Memorias póstumas*, vol. 1, 175–6; Rivanera, *Código de honor comentado*, 82–4.

16 Rivanera, *Código de honor comentado*, 34. An 1814 decree by Gervasio Posadas, governor of Buenos Aires, threatened the death penalty for both duelists and seconds. Ibid., 36–7. See also Oller and Casado, *Los duelos*, 32–5.

17 Oller and Casado, *Los duelos*, 48; Cristiani, *Reseña histórica del cuerpo de gimnasia y esgrima del ejército*, 11.

18 Oller and Casado, *Los duelos*, 73–5; Gayol, *Honor y duelo*, 177–85.

19 Braun Menéndez, "Un duelo histórico: Mackenna-Carrera," 29–35.

20 On the nineteenth-century resurgence of European dueling, see Nye, "Fencing, the Duel and Republican Manhood," 366; McAleer, *Dueling*, 3; Hughes, *Politics of the Sword*, chap. 1; Hughes, "Men of Steel," 66. The argument that Argentina and Uruguay followed continental patterns is made in "El duelo y el suicidio," *El Siglo*, 3 April 1881, 1.

21 Piccato, "Politics and the Technology of Honor."

22 Cristiani, *Reseña histórica del cuerpo de gimnasia y esgrima del ejército*, 12–16; "La esgrima en Buenos Aires," *Caras y Caretas*, no. 932 (12 August 1916), 31; Francisco José Lucchetti, "Viejo arte, moderno deporte" (article from unidentified magazine provided by Mr Lucchetti), 72–4.

23 Parker, *Uruguayans of To-Day*, 435.
24 See the biographies of immigrant journalists in *La Nación, Número especial para el Centenario de 1916*, "La prensa española," 251–60, and "La prensa italiana," 338–43; also, de la Fuente Monge, "Enrique Romero Jiménez."
25 Nye, *Masculinity and Male Codes of Honor*, 141–5.
26 On Uruguayan duels resulting in serious injuries, see "Duelo entre militares," *La Tribuna Popular*, 13 March 1905, 6.
27 Gayol, *Honor y duelo*, 210–11.
28 See the appendix for a discussion of the quality of sources for and questions about the available data on the number of duels fought in Uruguay. For Argentina, see Gayol, *Honor y duelo*, 104–18.
29 Viale, *Jurisprudencia caballeresca argentina, nueva edición corregida y aumentada*.
30 "Actualidad: Estadística del duelo," *El Plata*, 14 April 1920, 1.
31 Hughes, "Men of Steel," 68.
32 In 1918, which appears to be a reasonably typical year, the Juzgados Letrados de Crimen processed 248 cases for homicide, 80 for *lesiones* (battery causing bodily harm), and 44 for *pelea y lesiones* (fighting and battery), while the Juzgados de Instrucción Criminal processed 42 cases for homicide, 159 for *lesiones*, and 57 for *pelea* or *pelea y lesiones*. Only four were processed for dueling, and even though dueling cases were rarely prosecuted, this was a moment when local authorities were trying, unsuccessfully, to crack down (see chap. 3). *Anuario estadístico de la República Oriental del Uruguay, Año 1918*, 338, 354.
33 See the debates sparked by incidents involving Uruguayan presidents José Batlle y Ordóñez and Baltasar Brum, chaps. 1 and 3. *El Día, 1886–1981*, 38; "Presidential Duels," *Montevideo Times*, 19 December 1922, 3.
34 Fischer, *¡Qué tupé!*"
35 López-Alves, *Between the Economy and the Polity*, 2–3; López-Alves, "State Reform and Welfare in Uruguay," 95.
36 Etchechury Barrera, "Defensores de la humanidad y la civilización."
37 López-Alves, "State Reform and Welfare in Uruguay," 97.
38 López-Alves, *Between the Economy and the Polity*, chap. 2.
39 The "General Staff without an army" quip comes from Floro Costa, *Écos del Partido Colorado*, 64, and was popularized by historian Juan E. Pivel Devoto. Zum Felde, *Evolución histórica del Uruguay*, 157, called these doctores "the most mistaken men in the country," whose abstract ideals were "well-intentioned but went against the reality of the country and against the laws of nature."
40 Hentschke, *Philosophical Polemics, School Reform and Nation-Building in Uruguay*.
41 López-Alves, *State Formation and Democracy in Latin America*, 92–3.
42 López-Alves, *Between the Economy and the Polity*, 44.

43 Chasteen, *Heroes on Horseback*, provides a classic account and sociocultural analysis of these last two great Blanco rebellions.
44 Rilla, *La actualidad del pasado*, chap. 4, contrasts these two opposing foundational narratives by looking at Colorado historian Eduardo Acevedo and Blanco historian Juan E. Pivel Devoto.
45 The literature on Batlle's reformism is too extensive to list here. Three essential texts in English are Ehrick, *The Shield of the Weak*; Vanger, *The Model Country*; and Vanger, *Uruguay's José Batlle y Ordoñez*. For a succinct summary, see Markarian, *Left in Transformation*, 9–18.
46 Creation of the Collegial Executive is a case in point. In order to win support for such a radical change, *batllistas* proposed the 1916 election of a National Constituent Convention to reform the constitution. Unable to secure sufficient Colorado support, they were crushed at the polls, and control of the convention went to the Blancos. Refusing to give up, however, Batlle found a way the following year to coax a crucial Blanco faction into negotiating a grand bargain, securing Nacionalista leader Luis Alberto de Herrera's support for an attenuated version of the Colegiado in exchange for three guaranteed Blanco seats on the nine-seat executive, plus two huge electoral changes for which the Blancos had been fighting for decades: the secret ballot and proportional representation. Vanger, *Uruguay's José Batlle y Ordoñez*, 97–176.
47 Markarian, *Left in Transformation*, 19–21.
48 Caetano, *La república conservadora*, vols. 1 and 2, take as a central theme this interplay of partisan politics and class interest advocacy, focusing on the backlash against Batlle's reforms.
49 The indispensable guide to the periodic press in Uruguay remains Scarone, "La Prensa periódica en el Uruguay."

Chapter One

1 Coral Luzzi, *Código de honor*, 5.
2 "Ultima ora: Codardo! Codardo! Codardo!," *L'Indipendente*, 6 September 1883, 2–3. Translated from Italian to Spanish and reprinted with Buchelli's commentary in "Solicitadas," *El Ferro-Carril*, 6 September 1883, 2.
3 "Grave colpa," *L'Indipendente*, 31 August 1883, 1; "La Nación risponde," *L'Indipendente*, 2 September 1883, 1.
4 "Reportage: Buchelli-Nicosía II," *El Hilo Eléctrico*, 8 September 1883, 2, also reproduced in *La Tribuna Popular*, 8 September 1883, 1. Silva Grucci, *Duelos en el Río de la Plata*, 49–71, traces as much of Nicosía's biography as can be found, from his youthful political activity in Naples to his later years in Chile.
5 "Reportage: Buchelli-Nicosía II," *El Hilo Eléctrico*, 8 September 1883, 2; "Las verdades del barquero," *El Hilo Eléctrico*, 25 September 1883, 1–2.
6 "Reportage: Buchelli-Nicosía," *El Hilo Eléctrico*, 7 September 1883, 2.

7 "Los escándalos de estos días," *El Bien Público*, 12 September 1883, 1; *Los códigos españoles concordados y anotados*, 70–2.
8 "Remitidos," *El Ferro-Carril*, 3 September 1883, 2; "Sueltos," *El Bien Público*, 7 September 1883, 1. On the parliamentary debate in Uruguay about honoring Garibaldi with a statue, see Silva Grucci, *Duelos en el Río de la Plata*, 51–5. For more on the controversial commemoration of Garibaldi upon his death in 1882, see Sanders, *Vanguard of the Atlantic World*, 157–60.
9 "Solicitadas," *El Ferro-Carril*, 6 September 1883, 2.
10 "Ultima ora," *L'Indipendente*, 8 September 1883, 2.
11 "Reportage: Buchelli-Nicosía," *El Hilo Eléctrico*, 7 September 1883, 2.
12 On Bustamante's fatal 1866 duel with Servando Martínez, see chapter 2.
13 "Ultima hora," *El Ferro-Carril*, 10 September 1883, 2.
14 Ibid.
15 Ibid.
16 "Ultima hora," *El Ferro-Carril*, 11 September 1883, 2.
17 "Ultima hora: Cosas del día," *El Ferro-Carril*, 12 September 1883, 2.
18 "Todavía Buchelli," *La Tribuna Popular*, 18 September 1883, 1.
19 "Remitidos," *El Bien Público*, 13 September 1883, 1. For Buchelli's response to Isaza, see "Remitidos," *El Bien Público*, 14 September 1883, 1.
20 "Buchelli-Nicosía III: Epílogo [...] y cola," *El Hilo Eléctrico*, 13 September 1883, 1.
21 República Oriental del Uruguay, *Diario de sesiones de la H. Cámara de Representantes* (hereafter cited as ROU, *DSHCR*), vol. 61 (secret session of 15 September 1883), 112–14.
22 ROU, *DSHCR*, vol. 61 (session of 18 September 1883), 121.
23 "Basta Sr. Buchelli," *La Nación*, 18 September 1883, 2.
24 "Una ocurrencia singular," *El Siglo*, 15 September 1883, 2; "La moral del cuento," *La Tribuna Popular*, 16–17 September 1883, 1; "Solución inesperada," *El Bien Público*, 18 September 1883, 1; "Jacobinismo parlamentario," *El Bien Público*, 19 September 1883, 1.
25 "En la cárcel," *La Tribuna Popular*, 20 September 1883, 1.
26 "¿Quién me compra un lío?" *El Siglo*, 18 September 1883, 1.
27 "El non plus ultra," *El Telégrafo Marítimo*, 18 September 1883, 1.
28 "La Cámara-Tribunal," *El Siglo*, 21 September 1883, 1.
29 "Todavía Buchelli," *La Tribuna Popular*, 18 September 1883, 1.
30 "Los escándalos de estos días," *El Bien Público*, 12 September 1883, 1.
31 *Fiscal* can be translated as "investigating prosecutor," or "investigating public prosecutor." In civil law jurisdictions, a *fiscal* does much the same work that a district attorney or crown prosecutor does, but in a way that must by law be neutral and impartial. The *fiscal* then takes the investigation's findings to a judge, who decides whether or not to bring the case to trial.
32 "Ultima hora," *El Ferro-Carril*, 14 September 1883, 2.

33 "Ultima hora," *La Tribuna Popular*, 18 September 1883, 2.
34 "En la cárcel," *La Tribuna Popular*, 20 September 1883, 1.
35 ROU, *DSHCR*, vol. 61 (session of 18 September 1883), 120–5; vol. 61 (session of 19 September 1883), 127–49.
36 "Crónica policial: Buchelli en la cárcel," *La Nación*, 23 September 1883, 2.
37 "Todavía Buchelli," *La Tribuna Popular*, 18 September 1883, 1; "Ultima hora," *La Tribuna Popular*, 28 September 1883, 2; "Ultima hora," *La Tribuna Popular*, 4 October 1883, 2; "Dese por desairado y archívese," *El Hilo Eléctrico*, 4 October 1883, 3.
38 "La estatua de Garibaldi," *La Tribuna Popular*, 11 October 1883, 1; "El monumento a Garibaldi," *La Tribuna Popular*, 1 March 1913, 2.
39 Candea, "The Duelling Ethic and the Spirit of Libel Law," looks at how the dueling ethic shaped the French Penal Code's treatment of offenses against honor. Speckmann, "Los jueces, el honor, y la muerte," examines tensions between liberalism and legal codification in Mexico.
40 Chateauvillard, *Essai sur le duel*. The 1836 edition has "Chatauvillard" without the letter e, but Chateauvillard is the common spelling by the 1870s. Spanish translations include Borrego, *Ensayo sobre la jurisprudencia de los duelos*; Fors, *Arte del testigo en duelo*, 57–93.
41 Chateauvillard, *Essai sur de duel*, 4. See also Nye, *Masculinity and Male Codes of Honor*, 137, 141–2.
42 What follows is an incomplete list of honor codes published in Spanish, either in Spain or in the Rio de la Plata region, between 1870 and 1972: Yñiguez, *Ofensas y desafíos*; Cabriñana, *Lances entre caballeros*; Sánchez and Panella, *Código argentino sobre el duelo*; Oreiro, *Reglas del duelo*; Ferreto, *Código de honor*; de Menviel, *El médico en los duelos*; Levene, *Duelo: Manual de procedimiento*; Rivanera, *Código de honor comentado*; Varangot, *Virtudes caballerescas*; and the three already cited: Borrego, *Ensayo sobre la jurisprudencia de los duelos*; Fors, *Arte del testigo en duelo*; and Coral Luzzi, *Código de honor*. Argentines and Uruguayans also used several French and Italian honor codes in the original. I have found in libraries, antiquarian bookstores, or private collections all of the following: Gelli, *Codice cavalleresco italiano*; Borciani, *Le offese all'onore*; and Bruneau de Laborie, *Les lois du duel*. Other foreign codes mentioned by name by Argentines or Uruguayans include Saint-Thomas, *Nouveau code du duel*; Tavernier, *L'art du duel*; and Barbasetti, *Codice cavalleresco*.
43 Varangot, *Virtudes caballerescas*, 50n217.
44 Sánchez and Panella, *Código argentino sobre el duelo*, 91–107; Fors, *Arte del testigo en duelo*, 59–60.
45 Coral Luzzi, *Código de honor*, esp. 11–18, 46–57.
46 Fors, *Arte del testigo en duelo*, 41–2.

47 Oreiro, *Reglas del duelo*, 55–6. Similar rules held all over. See McAleer, *Dueling*, 46–53.
48 "Personal," *El Día*, 17 January 1915, 3. Similar examples abound. See, for example, "Personal," *El Día*, 18 April 1921, 5; "Personal," *Diario del Plata*, 16 April 1921, 4.
49 "Satisfacción cumplida," *La Tribuna*, 27 April 1872, 2.
50 "La ley sobre el duelo: Apreciando sus efectos," *Diario del Plata*, 13 September 1921, 3.
51 Fors, *Arte del testigo en duelo*, 22, 50.
52 "Solución de un incidente," *La Tribuna Popular*, 1 February 1905, 4. See also "En Diputados," *Diario del Plata*, 1 January 1915, 11, in which Diputado Areco notes that Diputado Luis Alberto de Herrera is likely to refuse to retract the insults he hurled against members of the Colorado majority, "for fear that it will be interpreted as an act of cowardice."
53 "Incidente Reyes-Garzón, casi duelo," *La Tribuna Popular*, 2 August 1905, 8; "Personal: Solución de un incidente," *El País*, 4 April 1919, 3.
54 Oreiro, *Reglas del duelo*, 64.
55 ROU, *DSHCR*, vol. 271 (session of 28 May 1919), 134.
56 From Argentina: Viale, *Jurisprudencia caballeresca argentina de los últimos treinta y cinco años*, 377–82.
57 "Incidente Idiartegaray-Solsona: Trámite y suspensión del duelo," *La Razón*, 4 February 1916, 9.
58 Chateauvillard, *Essai sur de duel*, 10 (chap. 1, art. 5), also translated in Fors, *Arte del testigo en duelo*, 61; "Personal," *El Día*, 18 September 1919, 4.
59 Oreiro, *Reglas del duelo*, 67–9.
60 McAleer, *Dueling*, 47.
61 Coral Luzzi, *Código de honor*, 15.
62 Fors, *Arte de testigo en duelo*, 26–8.
63 Ibid., 50–5; Levene, *Duelo: Manual de procedimiento*, 54–61.
64 Fors, *Arte del testigo en duelo*, 13–14, citing Chateauvillard.
65 De Menviel, *El médico en los duelos*.
66 Oreiro, *Reglas del duelo*, 107–8, provides one template.
67 "Duelo entre Jose Luis Espalter y el Decano de la Sección de Enseñanza Secundaria, Dr. Enrique Cornú," *La Tribuna Popular*, 18 April 1918, 1.
68 Honor tribunals are described and discussed in Rivanera, *Código de honor comentado*, 63–87; Ferretto, *Código de honor*, 88–90, 130; Levene, *Duelo: Manual de procedimiento*, 44–5. For one of many cases of an honor tribunal deciding just this kind of controversy, see Viale, *Jurisprudencia caballeresca argentina, nueva edición corregida y aumentada*, 422–4.
69 *El Siglo*, 9 February 1913, 3. See also "El lance de honor de ayer," *El Siglo*, 7 January 1913, 3.

70 "Personal," *El Día*, 5 February 1916, 4. Their point was that Solsona's physical handicap did not give him the right to choose the conditions of the duel when he was the offender.
71 "Personal," *El Día*, 8 April 1921, 4.
72 Varangot, *Virtudes caballerescas*, 85. The case came from 1958.
73 Ibid., 119–20.
74 Fors, *Arte del testigo en duelo*, 45–49.
75 "Defensa," *El Ferrocarril*, 2 December 1886, 2.
76 For a case of the legal and gentlemanly paths running more or less on parallel tracks, see the conflict between Alejo Idiartegaray and Manuel Solsona y Flores, which can be followed in several papers through the month of February 1916. "Incidente Solsona-Idiartegaray," *Diario del Plata*, 8 February 1916, 3; "Juicio Idiartegaray-Solsona," *Diario del Plata*, 23 February 1916, 3; "Personal: Incidente Idiartegaray-Solsona Flores," *La Tribuna Popular*, 4 February 1916, 2; "Personal," *La Tribuna Popular*, 7 February 1916, 1; "Personal," *La Tribuna Popular*, 8 February 1916, 2; "Juicio Solsona Flores-Idiartegaray: Pedido desatendido," *La Tribuna Popular*, 23 February 1916, 1.
77 Archivo General de la Nación, Buenos Aires, Argentina. Tribunal Criminal Serie 1, bundle (*legajo*) D-4 (1874–1916), "Cantón Eliseo el Doctor contra Dickmann Enrique el Doctor por calumnia," fol. 3v.
78 ROU, *DSHCR*, vol. 270 (session of 9 May 1919), 410. See also "Libertad y responsabilidad," *El Heraldo*, 26 February 1881, 1.
79 Piccato, *Tyranny of Opinion*, 168, gives succinct legal definitions of *injuria* (an insult or affront in word or deed in the victim's presence), *difamación* (defamation of character in speech or writing, whether the victim is present or not, where there is a third-party audience), and *calumnia* (an aggravated form of defamation that involves the false imputation of a crime). "Slander" and "libel" in English do not quite match up as exact translations of the Spanish terms, so I use the Spanish terms when being precise, or "defamation" more generically.
80 Zuviría, *La prensa periódica*, 46, 85–8.
81 In 1942, the director of Uruguay's Biblioteca Nacional published an entire dictionary of literary and journalistic pseudonyms. Scarone, *Diccionario de seudónimos del Uruguay*.
82 Ramírez, *Conferencias de derecho constitucional*, 309; ROU, *DSHCR*, vol. 8 (1863), 117–30; Fernández y Medina, *La imprenta y la prensa en el Uruguay*, 71.
83 Article 141 of the 1830 Uruguayan Constitution established the principle that the publisher (*impresor*) was liable when no responsible author could be identified, but many scholars and parliamentarians disagreed with this provision, and some judges disregarded it in practice. Ramírez, *Conferencias de derecho constitucional*, 310; ROU, *DSHCR*, vol. 8 (1863), 30–6.

84 Durá, *Del enjuiciamiento en los delitos de imprenta*, 21–7; ROU, DSHCR, vol. 44 (August–September 1881), 125.
85 Ramos, *Los delitos contra el honor*, 27–9.
86 "El valor de un tajo," *El Socialista*, 17 October 1915, 2; "A Futile Duel," *Montevideo Times*, 15 December 1922, 3.
87 "A mis amigos y al público," *La Tribuna Popular*, 29 September 1883, 2; "Cuestión personal: Al Doctor Samuel Blixen," *La Opinión Pública*, 9 April 1889, 4.
88 ROU, DSHCR, vol. 271 (session of 28 May 1919), 132–3.
89 "El duelo," *El Siglo*, 24 May 1914.
90 Ramírez, *Conferencias de derecho constitucional*, 307–10.
91 "La mordaza," *La Tribuna Popular*, 28 October 1886, 1; "La caída del Ministerio," *La Tribuna Popular*, 29 October 1886, 1; "La Conciliación: Los documentos cambiados," *La Tribuna Popular*, 3 November 1886, 1–2; "Oficial," *El Ferro-Carril*, 14 December 1886, 1; see also Aguirre Ramírez, *La Revolución del Quebracho y la conciliación*, 124, 167–79; Acevedo, *Anales históricos del Uruguay*, 4:273–84, 391. Contrast Mexico, where Porfirio Díaz was more successful at muzzling the press. Piccato, *Tyranny of Opinion*, chap. 5.
92 See *El Siglo* and *La Tribuna Popular* throughout late May and early June 1912, and *Diario del Plata* and *La Tribuna Popular* in early 1915. For example, "Colaboración: La ley mordaza," *Diario del Plata*, 25 February 1915, 3; "La ley mordaza: El juicio de la prensa," *Diario del Plata*, 26 February 1915, 3.
93 This argument, which continues below, receives expanded treatment in Parker, "Gentlemanly Responsibility and Insults of a Woman."
94 "Personal," *Diario del Plata*, 6 November 1915, 3.
95 See Police Chief Juan A. Pintos's self-characterization in his denunciation of Socialist Emilio Frugoni's refusal to duel with him. Archivo General de la Nación, Archivo Judicial, Montevideo, Uruguay, Juzgados Letrados en lo Penal (hereafter cited as AGN-AJ-JLP), Juzgado de Instrucción de Segundo Turno, case file (*expediente*) no. 236, arch. no. 58, 1925, "Juan A. Pintos, Querella por abuso de la libertad de imprenta," fols. 126–7.
96 "Personal," *Diario del Plata*, 7 November 1915, 3.
97 Trías, *Batlle periodista*, 41.
98 Viale, *Jurisprudencia caballeresca argentina*, 34–5.
99 Ibid. See also Gayol, *Honor y duelo*, 120–1.
100 Gayol, *Honor y duelo*, 103, 113.
101 For example, "Personal," *Diario del Plata*, 17 February 1916, 3.
102 "Se dice," *La Tribuna Popular*, 27 January 1924, 2.
103 "A paso marcial," *La Tribuna Popular*, 28 January 1924, 1; "El duelo Brum-Riverós," *El Día*, 27 January 1924, 5.

104 For one of countless "true crime" stories about a *duelo criollo* ending in a death and an arrest, see "Tribunales: Un gaucho malo," *La Tribuna Popular*, 12 June 1908, 2. For a sociohistorical analysis, see Chasteen, "Violence for Show."
105 "Responsabilidades: Las gestiones caballerescas y nuestra manera de pensar," *La Tribuna Popular*, 26 March 1924, 1.
106 Dufort y Álvarez, *La prensa irresponsable*, 11, wrote that "society has more effective methods than legal penalties, to limit abuses" of freedom of the press. Dufort focused on public scorn rather than on the duel, but his point was that legal sanctions were as ineffective as they were dangerous, and on this point defenders of the duel agreed.
107 "Libertad y responsabilidad," *El Heraldo*, 26 February 1881, 1.
108 "El duelo," *El Siglo*, 24 May 1914, 3. Chapter 3 covers this debate in more detail.

Chapter Two

1 El duelo," in *Ideas y críticas*, 53.
2 Víctor Soliño, *Crónica de los años locos*, 82.
3 Melián Lafinur, *Semblanzas del pasado: Juan Carlos Gómez*, 124; Moyano Dellepiane, "Jurisprudencia caballeresca porteña," 10–15, reproduces the *acta* of the duel.
4 Melián Lafinur, *Semblanzas del pasado*, 124; Gomensoro, *Crónicas de historia*, 111–14; ROU, *DSHCR*, vol. 271 (session of 28 May 1919), 123–5; "Un duelo célebre: Juan Carlos Gómez-Calvo," *El País*, 30 May 1919, 3.
5 "El maricón delator y los redactores de la 'Reforma,'" *La Reforma Pacífica* (Buenos Aires), 14 July 1858, 2. See also Archivo General de la Nación, Buenos Aires, Tribunal Criminal Serie 1, bundle A2, file 4, 1858, "Agente Fiscal del Crimen contra los Hermanos Guido; Gómez, Carlos; Calvo, Nicolás; Castro, e Pacheco, por duelo."
6 "El maricón delator y los redactores de la 'Reforma,'" *La Reforma Pacífica*, 14 July 1858, 2.
7 "El terror del florete," *La Tribuna* (Buenos Aires), 23 December 1856, 2, quoted in Vidaurreta de Tjarks, "Juan Carlos Gómez, periodista y polemista," 129.
8 In 1862, Calvo attacked Alejandro Pesce with a metal-tipped riding crop after Pesce refused to "be a man" and accept his challenge to a duel. Pesce denied having committed any offense that could justify a duel. "Interior: La verdad de los hechos ocurridos con el Sr. Pesce," *La Reforma Pacífica*, 24 June 1862, 2.
9 Melián Lafinur, *Semblanzas del pasado*, 120–1.
10 "Actuación de los diputados socialistas: El duelo," *Justicia*, 12 August 1920, 2.
11 "El duelo," *El Siglo*, 24 May 1914, 3. The editorial was written by Juan Andrés Ramírez.

12 "El duelo," *El País*, 12 March 1919, 3.
13 "Del momento, parodias del honor," *El Socialista*, 14 May 1914, 2.
14 ROU, *DSHCR*, vol. 271 (session of 28 May 1919), 123.
15 "De Carlos Roxlo: Carta abierta," *La Democracia*, 27 April 1906, 1.
16 ROU, *DSHCR*, vol. 271 (session of 21 May 1919), 55; words of Aureliano Rodríguez Larreta.
17 According to congressman Pablo Blanco Acevedo, "the immense majority of duelists are comprised of journalists, military men and politicians." ROU, *DSHCR*, vol. 271 (session of 4 June 1919), 225.
18 ROU, *DSHCR*, vol. 271 (session of 30 May 1919), 164.
19 Trías, *Batlle periodista*, 51; Mora Guarnido, *Batlle y Ordóñez: Figura y transfigura*, 69, 95.
20 Author's interview with Jorge Cermesone, Buenos Aires, 6 April 1999. The two newspapers were *La Prensa* and *La Razón*. Gayol, *Honor y duelo*, 147–53, lists the various other fencing schools in Buenos Aires, including those run by the Círculo de Armas, Jockey Club, Club Gimnasia y Esgrima, and Club del Progreso.
21 "Cuestiones periodísticas: ¡Se debe polemizar!," *El Siglo*, 2 February 1908, 1. For analysis of a similar dynamic in Mexico, see Piccato, *Tyranny of Opinion*, chap. 2.
22 Herrero y Espinosa, *José Pedro Varela*, 38–9. See also "Prensa argentina: El Sr. Neto, El Sr. Bustamante y yo," *La Paz*, 13–14 March 1870, 1; "Más sobre el duelo Varela y Neto," *El Ferro-Carril*, 14–16 April 1870, 2.
23 Arena, *Escritos y discursos*, 225.
24 Ibid.
25 Ibid.
26 Frequent duelist Washington Paullier, for example, said the following when "clarifying" a statement he had made, noting that his comments had not actually been directed at the man challenging him to a duel: "[I make] this simple clarification, which does not signify the retraction of a comma, above all because I make it a rule of my life to never retract a word ... I remain at the disposition of Mr Crispo on whichever *terreno*, in the event that he persists in considering himself offended." "Personal," *Diario del Plata*, 11 March 1914, 1.
27 Author's interview with Julio Maria Sanguinetti, Montevideo, June 2000.
28 González Arrili, *Vida de Lisandro de la Torre*, 79–80.
29 "El duelo en el Uruguay: Debate instructiva," *Justicia*, 9 August 1920, 1–2.
30 In the so-called "*hecatombe* of Quinteros," defeated Colorado insurgents were executed at the hands of the government of Julio Pereyra in February 1858. At Paysandú in 1865, Colorado revolutionary forces led by Venancio Flores executed Blanco prisoners after a protracted siege of the city, which was bombed by Colorado forces and their Brazilian allies. On Quinteros,

see Acevedo, *Anales históricos del Uruguay*, 2:621–47. On Paysandú, see Acevedo, *Anales históricos del Uruguay*, 3:27–9, 284–5.

31 Mora Guarnido, *Batlle y Ordóñez: Figura y transfigura*, 52; "Las mazorcadas," *La Paz*, 15 February 1870, 1; "La mazhorca," *La Tribuna Popular*, 16 October 1886, 1. The *mazorca* had been the name of Argentine dictator Juan Manuel de Rosas's private security force.

32 Two examples: "Los asesinos regresan (artículo comunicado)," *La Tribuna*, 4 February 1875, 1; Pedemonte, *El año terrible*, 143–5.

33 "A Futile Duel," *Montevideo Times*, 15 December 1922, 3, on pistol duels.

34 Miguel Arregui, "Duelo de gauchos y malevos, la secta del cuchillo y del coraje," *El Observador*, 8 April 2020, https://www.elobservador.com.uy/nota/duelo-de-gauchos-y-malevos-la-secta-del-cuchillo-y-del-coraje-20204517470.

35 Chasteen, "Violence for Show."

36 Chasteen, "Fighting Words," 83–111.

37 "Entre militares: Un duelo a muerte en Paysandú," *La Tribuna Popular*, 2 June 1980, 4.

38 González Conzi and Giudice, *Batlle y el batllismo*, 17.

39 Melián Lafinur, *Semblanzas del pasado*, 116–20.

40 "Al 'Nacional,'" *L'Indipendente*, 13 November 1883, 1.

41 Ibid.

42 "Stampa argentina," *L'Indipendente*, 16 November 1883, 1 (reprinted from *La Libertad* of Buenos Aires); Moyano Dellepiane, "Jurisprudencia caballeresca porteña," 103–33, devotes thirty pages to the duel, reprinting verbatim articles from *El Diario* of Buenos Aires over 14, 15, and 16 November 1883.

43 Silva Grucci, *Duelos en el Rio de la Plata*, 61–2; Moyano Dellepiane, "Jurisprudencia caballeresca porteña," 109–10.

44 "Smith-Nicosía: Primera acta," *El Hilo Eléctrico*, 17 November 1883, 2.

45 "Pentiti ..." and "Arrepiéntete (traducción del artículo anterior)," *L'Indipendente* 16 November 1883, 2.

46 "Smith-Nicosía: Primera acta," *El Hilo Eléctrico*, 17 November 1883, 2.

47 "Ultimatum de Nicosía," *El Ferro-Carril*, 16 November 1883, 1.

48 "Importantes detalles sobre el duelo," *El Ferro-Carril*, 16 November 1883, 2; "Duelo Nicosía-Smith: Detalles completos," *El Ferro-Carril*, 17 November 1883, 1; "Asunto Nicosía-Smith," *L'Indipendente*, 18 November 1883, 1–2; "Il duello," *L'Indipendente*, 18 November 1883, 2 (reprinted from *El Diario* of Buenos Aires, 16 November 1883). More than forty spectators attended, according to the telling of Juan José Segundo, who discussed the event on the floor of Congress thirty-six years later. ROU, DSHCR, vol. 271 (session of 23 May 1919,) 86.

49 "É finita la commedia," *El Hilo Eléctrico*, 17 November 1883, 1.

50 Silva Grucci, *Duelos en el Rio de la Plata*, 64–6.

51 Fernández Saldaña, *Diccionario uruguayo de biografías*, 893–4.
52 "Lance," *La Tribuna Popular*, 13 July 1881, 2, a case where the seconds did not keep the secret.
53 "La epidemia duelistica," *Justicia*, 5 October 1919, 1.
54 "Lances de Mabille," *El Ferro-Carril*, 30 November 1869, 1.
55 Martínez, *José Cándido Bustamante*, 8–9. Accounts of the duel's origins, including who first challenged whom, also vary. See Ramírez, *La muerte de Servando F. Martínez*, 14–15; "Sobre el duelo del Sr. Bustamante," *La Opinion Nacional*, 23 March 1866, 2; "La muerte de D. José Ramírez: O el grito de una conciencia afligida," *La Tribuna*, 25 April 1886, 2.
56 "Un acontecimiento terrible," and "Asunto lúgubre," *La Opinion Nacional*, 12–13 March 1866, 2.
57 Ramírez, *La muerte de Servando F. Martínez*, 27.
58 Escribano, "El duelo en la legislación penal," 17.
59 "Duelo entre Jose Luis Espalter y el Decano de la Sección de Enseñanza Secundaria, Dr. Enrique Cornú," *La Tribuna Popular*, 18 April 1918, 1.
60 Pivel Devoto, "Estudio preliminar," 53–4; "Un puñado de noticias," *El Ferro-Carril*, 13–14 August 1871, 3.
61 "El duelo Ferreira-Castro," *La Razón*, 4 March 1914, 1; "Otro lance de honor," *La Tribuna Popular*, 4 March 1914, 6; "Otro duelo," *La Democracia*, 4 March 1914, 1; "El duelo de ayer entre los Sres. E. Castro y M. Ferreira," *La Democracia*, 5 March 1914, 1; *Uruguay Weekly News*, 8 March 1914, 7.
62 "Personal: Incidente Ramírez-Brum," *Diario del Plata*, 18 February 1916, 3.
63 "Duelo Ramírez-Brum: Su realización," *Diario del Plata*, 19 February 1916, 3.
64 "Duelo Ramírez-Brum: A propósito de una versión," *Diario del Plata*, 20 February 1916, 3.
65 "El duelo entre los Señores Paul de Angulo y Giménez," *El Ferro-Carril*, 13 August 1880, 3; "Ultima hora: Cosas del día," *El Ferro-Carril*, 14 August 1880, 2–3; "Personal," *El Correo Español* (Buenos Aires), 14 August 1880, 1.
66 "Punto final," *El Correo Español*, 16 October 1880, 1.
67 Ibid.
68 "Ultima hora: Cosas del día," and "Duelo entre periodistas," *El Ferro-Carril*, 14 August 1880, 2–3; "Ultima hora," *La España*, 16 August 1880, 2; "Mas sobre el duelo," *La España*, 19 August 1880, 2.
69 "Ultima hora," *La España*, 23 August 1880, 2.
70 "Ultima hora," *El Correo Español*, 18 August 1880, 2; "La ciega del Guadalquivir," *El Correo Español*, 28 August 1880, 1.
71 On the ceremony in Montevideo, see "Ultima hora: Cosas del día," *El Ferro-Carril*, 23 August 1880, 2; in Buenos Aires, "El entierro de Sr. Romero Jiménez," *El Correo Español*, 25 August 1880, 1. Predictably, *El Correo Español*

provided the high estimate, while *La Nación* from the same day was more conservative in its count. See also *El Correo Español*, 26 August 1880, 2.

72 See *El Correo Español* throughout the entire month following Romero Jiménez's death.

73 "Homenaje público a la memoria de Enrique Romero Jiménez," *El Correo Español*, 26 August 1880, 1.

74 Ibid.

75 Ibid. 2. Italics in the original.

76 "Boletín del España Moderna," *El Correo Español*, 29 August 1880, 1–2; "Una súplica," *La Colonia Española*, 1 September 1880, 1–2.

77 "Homenaje público a la memoria de Enrique Romero Jiménez (Continuación)," *El Correo Español*, 1 September 1880, 1. Italics in the original.

78 "Homenaje público a la memoria de Enrique Romero Jiménez (Continuación)," *El Correo Español*, 29 August 1880, 1; *La Nación: Número especial para el centenario de 1916* (Buenos Aires, 1916), 253. Paul y Angulo was thirty-eight or thirty-nine at the time of the duel; Romero Jiménez was forty.

79 "Homenaje público a la memoria de Enrique Romero Jiménez," *El Correo Español*, 1 September 1880, 1.

80 "Homenaje público a la memoria de Enrique Romero Jiménez (Continuación)," *El Correo Español*, 29 August 1880, 1.

81 Ibid.

82 "Homenaje público a la memoria de Enrique Romero Jiménez (Continuación)," *El Correo Español*, 6 October 1880, 1.

83 "Intereses españoles: Carta del Sr. Paul Angulo," *El Nacional* (Buenos Aires), 2 October 1880, 1. The series continued almost daily until it was cut short on 14 October.

84 "Intereses españoles: El envidioso y el envidiado (I)," *El Nacional*, 4 October 1880, 1; reprinted in *La Colonia Española*, 8 October 1880, 1.

85 "Intereses españoles: El envidioso y el envidiado (II)," *El Nacional*, 5 October 1880, 1; also reprinted in *La Colonia Española*, 9 October 1880, 1.

86 "Intereses españoles: El envidioso y el envidiado (III)," *El Nacional*, 7 October 1880, 1.

87 "Intereses españoles: El envidioso y el envidiado (IV)," *El Nacional*, 8 October 1880, 1.

88 "No más silencio," *El Correo Español*, 12 October 1880, 1; "Punto final," *El Correo Español*, 19 October 1880.

89 "Una opinión como cualquiera otra," *La Nación*, 11 October 1880, reprinted as "Acabemos otra vez," in *El Correo Español*, 12 October 1880, 1; "Pierde su tiempo," *La Nación*, 14 October 1880, reprinted as "La Prensa y el Sr. Paul y Angulo," in *El Correo Español*, 15 October 1880, 1.

90 "Al Sr. Paul y Angulo," *El Correo Español*, 12 October 1880, 1, quoting at length from a 10 October 1880 column in *L'Union Française*; and "Otra protesta," *El Correo Español*, 13 October 1880, 1, quoting at length from the German-language *Deutsche La Plata Zeitung*.
91 "El Sr. Paul y Angulo," *El Nacional*, 16 October 1880, 1, defends his conduct both during and after the duel, and denounces his critics.
92 "No puedo más," *El Nacional*, 14 October 1880, 1.
93 "Punto final," *El Correo Español*, 19 October 1880, 1.
94 *La Nación: Número especial para el centenario de 1916*, 253.
95 "*Permanentes*" were typically short and highly inflammatory statements, repeated day after day on a paper's front page, and designed to provoke a response from the targeted individual. *La Nación*, 1, each day from 1 July to 6 July 1880.
96 "Los testaferros," *El Negro Timoteo*, 4 July 1880, 213–15.
97 Ibid.
98 "Remitidos," *La Nación*, 6 July 1880, 1.
99 Papers varied in their spelling of the officer's surname: most used "Chilaber" or "Chilavert," one a hispanicization, the other a gallicization, of "Schilemberg" or "Schellemberg." I use "Schilemberg" following Fernández Saldaña, *Gobierno y época de Santos*, 46–8.
100 "Remitidos," *La Nación*, 6 July 1880, 1.
101 "Opiniones de la prensa," *El Negro Timoteo*, 11 July 1880, 217–27, reprinted pro-Bermúdez accounts published in more than ten different Montevideo papers over the course of the previous week. The confrontation in his home is described almost identically in the versions from *La Tribuna Popular*, *La España*, *La Colonia Española*, *La Razón*, and *Diario del Comercio*. In one account, an alleged witness saw the men on the street with an unidentified third individual. If this was a normal visit of seconds to deliver a dueling challenge, what was that other person doing there? "El incidente de Bermúdez," *La Razón*, 7 July 1880, 2, reprinted in *El Negro Timoteo*, 11 July 1880, 220.
102 "Un incidente desagradable," *La Nación*, 8 July 1880, 1.
103 "¿De qué se trata?," *La Razón*, 6 July 1880 1; "La palabra de un Ministro," *La Razón*, 8 July 1880, 1; "Don Washington Bermúdez," *Diario del Comercio*, reprinted in *El Negro Timoteo*, 11 July 1880, 220.
104 "Una madeja enredada," *La España*, 7 July 1880, reprinted in *El Negro Timoteo*, 11 July 1880, 221–2.
105 "Un incidente desagradable," *La Nación*, 8 July 1880, 1; "La carta de Bermúdez y lo del Ministro," *La Nación*, 9 July 1880, 1.
106 "Los matones," *La Razón*, 7 July 1880, 1; "La palabra de un Ministro," *La Razón*, 8 July 1880, 1; both also reprinted in *El Negro Timoteo*, 11 July 1880, 223–4.

107 This opinion appeared in two articles that made use of the Bermúdez-Schilemberg case to denounce dueling in general, "De actualidad," *El Bien Público*, 7 July 1880; and "Una madeja enredada," *La España*, 7 July 1880, both reprinted in *El Negro Timoteo*, 11 July 1880, 221–2. One critic of Schilemberg invoked the Gómez-Calvo duel: "We do not know what these killers or duelists would do if they were required to duel at a distance of one pace, with just one of the pistols loaded and chosen at random. But it is most likely that rather than facing their adversaries on an equal footing, they would prefer to eliminate them traitorously and at no risk to themselves." Untitled, undated column attributed to *La Colonia Española*, reprinted in *El Negro Timoteo*, 11 July 1880, 225.

108 "El incidente de Bermúdez," *La Razón*, 7 July 1880, 1; "La palabra de un Ministro," "*La Razón*, 8 July 1880, 1; "La carta de Bermúdez y lo del Ministro," *La Nación*, 9 July 1880, 1.

109 "La libertad y el abuso," *El Heraldo*, 18 June 1881, 1.

110 "La prensa bárbara," *La Paz*, 16–17 January 1870, 1–2.

111 "El Siglo tiene razón en parte."*El Día*, 20 September 1886, 2.

112 "Abordo del Rio Negro: Una denuncia gravísima," *La Tribuna Popular*, 13 March 1921, 1.

113 "Por los fueros de la prensa," *La Tribuna Popular*, 21 March 1921, 1.

114 "Hay que aclarar eso: Con los duelos no se ponen a salvo los intereses del páis," *La Tribuna Popular*, 22 March 1921, 1.

115 "Nosotros y Pintos: Detalles de la gestión caballeresca," *La Tribuna Popular*, 24 March 1922, 1.

116 "Con el General Pintos," *La Tribuna Popular*, 23 March 1922, 1.

117 In the *Rio Negro* incident, Sanmartín's seconds had first approached Vicente's brother Héctor, who also worked at the Lápido family paper. According to the *actas* of the incident, Héctor and Vicente drew lots to decide who would represent the paper, and (surprise of surprises) the fencing champion just happened to be the lucky winner. "Por los fueros de la prensa," *La Tribuna Popular*, 21 March 1921, 1. On Vicente's triumphs in competition, see "Un éxito sin precedente en los anales de la esgrima uruguaya," *La Tribuna Popular*, 20 December 1922, 1; "Triunfo de nuestra esgrima," *La Tribuna Popular*, 21 December 1922, 1.

118 Arena, *Escritos y Discursos*, 225.

Chapter Three

1 "News of the Week," *Uruguay News*, 29 October 1893, 4.

2 ROU, *DSHCR*, vol. 271 (session of 23 May 1919), 82.

3 "El duelo del sábado: La persecución de la policía," *El Día*, 2 March 1914, 7; "Un lance personal: Entre los señores Plaucia y Paullier," *La Democracia*,

3 March 1914, 1; "Otro lance de honor," *El Día*, 4 March 1914, 6; "El duelo de ayer: Entre los Sres. E. Castro y M. Ferreira," *La Democracia*, 5 March 1914, 2. On the publishing of false *actas* to fool the police, see "Lance Ramírez-Brum," *La Razón*, 17 February 1916, 1; "El duelo Ramírez-Brum," *La Razón*, 18 February 1916, 1.
4. Schinca, *Boulevar Sarandí*, 150.
5. "El lance Blixen-Martinelli: Una bala cambiada," *La Razón*, 19 May 1914, 3rd ed., 4. A month and a half earlier, Paullier had evaded the police to fight a duel himself, making this his second act of disrespect. "El duelo del Sabado: La persecución de la policía," *El Dia*, 2 March 1914, 7.
6. "La prisión del diputado Paullier: Mensaje del ejecutivo, discusión en la Cámara," *Diario del Plata*, 19 May 1914, 1; "En la cámara: La prisión del diputado Paullier," *El Siglo*, 19 May 1914, 3.
7. "El duelo Sampognaro-Paullier: Su tramitación," *La Razón*, 20 May 1914, 1.
8. "Lo dicho," *El Siglo*, 23 May 1914, 3.
9. "La ley y la costumbre," *Diario del Plata*, 21 May 1914, 1.
10. "El incidente Sampognaro-Paullier: Solución satisfactoria," *La Razón*, 22 May 1914, 2.
11. "Pido la palabra! Sampognaro y la amnistía," *La Razón*, 13 March 1919, 1; "Pido la palabra! Sampognaro y la amnistía II," *La Razón*, 14 March 1919, 1.
12. "Pido la palabra! Reflexiones sobre el duelo," *La Razón*, 19 March 1919, 1.
13. *Código de Instrucción Criminal*; *Código Militar*; *Proyecto de Código Penal*; Vásquez Acevedo, *Concordancias y anotaciones del Código Penal*; Jiménez de Aréchaga, *Código Penal y Código de Instrucción Criminal*.
14. Details and discussion of the Ruprecht-Tejera duel, from virtually all the Montevideo papers, are reproduced in *El Ejercito Uruguayo*, special edition (November–December 1893), 1–72.
15. "News of the Week," *Uruguay News*, 29 October 1893, 4.
16. Ibid.
17. Eduardo Montautti, one of Tejera's seconds, wrote in the funeral visitor's album, "Tejera: The defenders of the nation may only give their lives – if not in her service – to defend their honor. You have fulfilled your duty and fallen as a good man, and your name will live perpetually in the hearts of all." *El Ejercito Uruguayo*, special edition (November–December 1893), 40.
18. "The Recent Fatal Duel," *Montevideo Times*, 31 October 1893, 1.
19. "La sangre humana," *El Nacional*, 2 November 1893, 2.
20. "El duelo y nuestros códigos," *El Telégrafo Marítimo*, 30 October 1893.
21. *Código Militar*, 268.
22. "Duelo Tejera-Ruprecht – Absolución," *La Tribuna Popular*, 19 February 1894, 2.
23. Ibid.; "Duelo Tejera-Ruprecht: Absolución del Teniente Ruprecht," *El Siglo*, 18 February 1894, 2.

24 "Duelo Tejera-Ruprecht: Absolución del Teniente Ruprecht," *El Siglo*, 18 February 1894, 2.
25 "Duelo Tejera-Ruprecht," *El Ejercito Uruguayo* 3 no. 21 (28 October 1893), 634–5.
26 "Duelo Tejera-Ruprecht: Absolución del Teniente Ruprecht," *El Siglo*, 18 February 1894, 2.
27 *Código Militar*, 196, 199.
28 "Duelo Tejera-Ruprecht: Absolución del Teniente Ruprecht," *El Siglo*, 18 February 1894, 2.
29 This was the case in the 1866 José Cándido Bustamante–Servando Martínez duel discussed in chapter 2, and in the 1908 Gomeza-Giordano duel mentioned later in this chapter. "La muerte del alférez Giordano, el proceder del Teniente Gomeza, detalles emocionantes," *La Tribuna Popular*, 21 June 1908, 8.
30 Gallo, *El duelo*, 39–41; see also Coral Luzzi, *Código de honor*, 36–7.
31 See the following published law theses, all from the Universidad de Buenos Aires between 1881 and 1899: Correa, *El duelo*; Estrada, *Del duelo*; Gallo, *El duelo*; Oliver, *El duelo*; Puch, *El duelo*. Similar arguments are covered in Hughes, *Politics of the Sword*, chap. 5; Gayol, *Honor y duelo*, chap. 8; Parker, "Law, Honor, and Impunity," 321–31.
32 Vásquez Acevedo, *Concordancias y anotaciones del Código Penal*; also quoted in ROU, DSCR (session of 17 July 1990), 283.
33 ROU, DSHCR, vol. 61 (session of 18 September 1883), 121.
34 "Caridad cristiana: Los duelistas deben morir como perros," *El Siglo*, 27 December 1912, 3.
35 "El duelo," *El Siglo*, 24 May 1914.
36 Ibid. This common argument also appears in "El duelo," *El País*, 12 March 1919, 3.
37 "La farsa del duelo," *El Socialista*, 15 May 1914, 1.
38 Gayol, *Honor y duelo*, 55.
39 Jiménez de Aréchaga, *Código Penal*, 10.
40 *Código Penal*, 102.
41 The Italian (1889) and Argentine (1886) criminal codes made identical distinctions between "regular" and "irregular" duels, and explictly used those terms, something the Uruguayan Code did not. Hughes, *Politics of the Sword*, 198–204; Rivarola, *Exposición y crítica del Código Penal*, 75–89; *Proyecto de Código Penal para la República Argentina*, 140–7.
42 "Documentos relativos al duelo del Dr. Alberto Palomeque con el Dr. Samuel Blixen, 1889 y s.f.," MHN-AAP. Folio 3 is the handwritten *acta previa*, which includes the agreement to duel "in the neighboring Republic." The file includes telegrams from family and well-wishers in Montevideo

requestingd news, and from Palomeque and second Eduardo Acevedo Díaz in Buenos Aires providing it. The telegram at fol. 6, from Agustín de Vedia in Buenos Aires to Elvira M. de Palomeque in Montevideo, 17 March 1989, reported that Palomeque and the others were detained in Buenos Aires by the chief of police and only released after promising in writing not to duel. They immediately violated that pledge and fought with sabers, resulting in mild injuries, according to the *acta del terreno* (fol. 30).

43 Pelúas, *José Batlle y Ordóñez*, 183; "Duelo Batlle-Garzón: Su realización, pormenores del lance," *La Tribuna Popular*, 21 October 1893, 2.
44 "Tribunales militares: El proceso Ruprecht," *El Ejército Uruguayo* 4, no. 7 (21 February 1894), 112–14.
45 "Del Dr Irureta Goyena: A propósito del duelo," *El Siglo*, 12 February 1908, 1.
46 "El duelo Herrera-Michaelson," *La Tribuna Popular*, 22 June 1905, 4.
47 Barnuevo, "El duelo ante la razón y la ley," 772–3; de Borbón, *Resumen de la historia*; Ferrer, *Documentos de Don Alfonso Carlos de Borbón*; "Contra el duelo," *La Tribuna Popular*, 5 June 1908, 4.
48 Rodríguez, *Civilizing Argentina*.
49 Barrán, *Historia de la sensibilidad*, vol. 2.
50 Barrán and Nahúm, *El nacimiento del batllismo*, 62–79.
51 "Del Dr Irureta Goyena: A propósito del duelo," *El Siglo*, 12 February 1908, 1.
52 Ibid.
53 Ibid.
54 "Del Dr Irureta Goyena: A propósito del duelo II," *El Siglo*, 13 February 1908, 1.
55 "El duelo de esta tarde," *La Tribuna Popular*, 17 March 1908, 8; "Resonancias de un duelo: Iniciación de una causa," *La Tribuna Popular*, 31 March 1908, 1.
56 "Resonancias de un duelo: Iniciación de una causa," *La Tribuna Popular*, 31 March 1908, 1.
57 "Resonancias de un duelo," *La Tribuna Popular*, 8 April 1908, 8.
58 "Sobre un supuesto duelo: El Juez Dr Gomensoro, irregularidades de este magistrado," *La Tribuna Popular*, 19 May 1908, 1. The Círculo de Armas was, ironically, a recreational club for fencing and target shooting.
59 "Jueces y duelistas: La actitud del Doctor Gomensoro," *El Siglo*, 21 May 1908, 1.
60 "Sobre un supuesto duelo: Prisiones injustas," *La Tribuna Popular*, 17 May 1908, 8.
61 "A las vueltas con los duelos: Exhumando lances personales," *La Tribuna Popular*, 7 June 1908, 8.
62 "El Dr Irureta Goyena: Su prisión," *El Siglo*, 5 June 1908, 1; "La prisión del Dr Irureta Goyena," *El Siglo*, 10 June 1908, 1; "Un atropello," *El Siglo*, 12 June 1908, 1; ROU, *DSHCR*, vol. 271 (session of 21 May 1919), 54. Other

more obscure motives may also have influenced Irureta Goyena's treatment, or at least that was one congressman's allegation. ROU, *DSHCR*, vol. 271 (session of 28 May 1919), 128.

63 ROU, *DSHCR*, vol. 194 (session of 16 May 1908), 167–8.
64 "Entre militares: Un duelo a muerte en Paysandú," *La Tribuna Popular*, 2 June 1908, 4; "Un duelo entre dos oficiales del ejército: Muerte del alférez Giordano," *El Paysandú*, 2 June 1908.
65 It was the victim Giordano who had given the "shot myself by mistake" explanation before he died, but the autopsy said otherwise. "El duelo en Paysandú: Nuevos pormenores," *La Tribuna Popular*, 3 June 1908, 8; "El duelo en Paysandú: Cómo van a declarar los oficiales," *La Tribuna Popular*, 4 June 1908, 8; "El duelo trágico: Las últimas novedades," *La Tribuna Popular*, 9 June 1908, 8; "Fatal Duel," *Montevideo Times*, 3 June 1908, 1; "The Fatal Duel," *Montevideo Times*, 4 June 1908, 1; "La muerte de Giordano, ¡Fiat lux!," *El Paysandú*, 15 June 1908, 2; "El duelo Giordano-Gomeza: Prisión preventiva de los padrinos," *El Pueblo* (Paysandú), 2 July 1908, 3.
66 "Sobre el duelo: Carta del Diputado Giribaldi Heguy," *El Pueblo*, 6 June 1908, 1–2.
67 "La farsa del duelo," *El Socialista*, 15 May 1914, 1; "Nuestra encuesta sobre el duelo: Opiniones favorables y adversas," *La Razón*, 2 June 1914, 1; "El duelo," *El Siglo*, 24 May 1914, 1; "El duelo," *El País*, 12 March 1919, 3; "La legislación del duelo, *La Razón*, 26 April 1919, 1; "La legislación del duelo: Principios a que debe atenerse," *El País*, 27 April 1919, 3. In "La nota: Sección desafíos," *La Razón*, 16 February 1916, 1, a columnist joked about the need for a permanent duels section of the paper.
68 "Lances y desafíos: Estadística interesante," *El Día*, 16 June 1914, 5.
69 This conflict is further explored in Parker, "Gentlemanly Responsibility and Insults of a Woman," 121–5.
70 "Incidente personal," *La Democracia*, 24 April 1906, 1; "De Carlos Roxlo: Carta abierta," *La Democracia*, 27 April 1906," 1; "Al campo de don Nuño voy," *La Tribuna Popular*, 15 April 1913, 10; "El Presidente de la República y los periodistas," *La Tribuna Popular*, 16 April 1913, 1; "Batlle juzgado en Buenos Aires," *El Siglo*, 18 April 1913; "Responsabilidades a largo plazo," *La Democracia*, 16 April 1913, 1.
71 "Sobre el mensaje," *El Día*, 20 February 1916, 4.
72 "Para él," *El Siglo*, 16 April 1913, 3, reprints Batlle's charge followed by Ramírez's defense. Batlle eventually sent seconds to Ramírez in 1915, alleging four years of offenses in the press. "Incidente Batlle-Ramírez: Las cartas cambiadas," *La Tribuna Popular*, 27 February 1915, 8; "Guarda e Passa," *El Día*, 27 Feb. 1915, 4.

73 Viale, *Jurisprudencia caballeresca argentina: Nueva edición corregida y aumentada*, 515–16. See also "Dos duelos," *La Tribuna Popular*, 9 April 1918; "Duelo Carnelli-Miranda: El caballeresco legislador nacionalista resulta herido," *La Tribuna Popular*, 10 April 1918, 1; and on the incident that sparked the duel, ROU, DSHCR, vol. 260 (session of 8 April 1918), 4–14, 31–2.

74 ROU, DSHCR, vol. 271 (session of 21 May 1919), 40.

75 ROU, DSHCR, vol. 259 (session of 15 March 1918), 294. The bill and its justificatory preamble (*Exposición de Motivos*) is also repeated in ROU, DHSCR, vol. 279 (session of 9 May 1919), 390.

76 Ramírez, *Selección de discursos*, 265–93.

77 ROU, DSHCR, vol. 270 (session of 9 May 1919), 390–7.

78 ROU, DSHCR, vol. 270 (session of 9 May 1919), 400.

79 ROU, DSHCR, vol. 270 (session of 9 May 1919), 390–411; ROU, DSHCR, vol. 271 (sessions from 21 May 1919 through 4 June 1919), 38–59, 77–89, 121–35, 155–67, 213–34.

80 ROU, DSHCR, vol. 270 (session of 9 May 1919), 392.

81 Ibid.

82 ROU, DSHCR, vol. 271 (session of 21 May 1919), 42.

83 ROU, DSHCR, vol. 271 (session of 28 May 1919), 127.

84 Ibid., 129.

85 ROU, DSHCR, vol. 271 (session of 23 May 1919), 82.

86 Ibid.

87 ROU, DSHCR, vol. 270 (session of 9 May 1919), 408.

88 ROU, DSHCR, vol. 271 (session of 21 May 1919), 57–8.

89 Ibid.

90 ROU, DSHCR, vol. 270 (session of 9 May 1919), 398.

91 Archivo del Poder Legislativo, Cámara de Representantes, Comisión de Códigos, folder (*carpeta*) no. 589/1918, includes the original manuscript documents, some handwritten and some typed with handwritten annotations.

92 "Embuste," *El Día*, 15 June 1919, 4. "El duelo de ayer: Batlle Ordóñez-Ramírez," *El Día*, 17 June 1919, 4. "Duelo Ramírez-Batlle," *La Tribuna Popular*, 17 June 1919, 1.

93 "Colazos de un duelo: Se procederá a la prisión del Sr. Batlle: Actitud del Dr. Minelli," *La Tribuna Popular*, 18 June 1919, 1; "Duelo Ramírez-Batlle: Intervención del Juez Dr. Minelli," *El País*, 19 June 1919, 3; "El Dr Minelli y el duelo," *La Tribuna Popular*, 20 June 1919, 1; "Colazos del duelo Ramírez-Batlle: Prisiones decretadas," *Diario del Plata*, 9 August 1919, 3; "1919: Un lance sin heridos pero con varios procesados," *La Mañana*, 17 October 1971, 5. Viale, *Jurisprudencia caballeresca argentina*, 517–18.

94 Sr. Representante Juan Andrés Ramírez, "Interrogatorio," Num. 1844, 9 July 1919, in Juzgado de Instrucción del Tercer Turno, "Sumario con motivo del

duelo entre don José Batlle y Ordóñez y Dr. Juan Andrés Ramírez." Courtesy of the Biblioteca y Archivo del Poder Legislativo, Montevideo.
95 Fischer, *Qué tupé!*, 15.
96 Manini Rios, *Una nave en la tormenta*, chap. 4.
97 "Duelo Batlle y Ordóñez-Aguirre," *La Mañana*, 14 January 1920, 3. "El Duelo Batlle-Aguirre: Texto de las actas," *El Día*, 14 January 1920, 4; "El Duelo de ayer: Batlle y Aguirre, algunas gotas de sangre lavan una ofensa," *Justicia*, 14 January 1920, 1; "El Poco amigo de sainetes ... Duelo con fotógrafo," *Justicia*, 15 January 1920, 1.
98 "Qué Tupet! El campeón del fraude acusa al Partido Nacional: Réplica aplastante," *El País*, 1 April 1920, reproduced in Beltrán, *Cuestiones sociológicas*, 259–62; Fischer, *Qué tupé!*, 238–41.
99 Fischer, *Qué tupé!*, 257–62, reproduces the autopsy.
100 From 3 April 1920 onward, news of the duel, Beltrán's funeral, the public homages, and the legal fate of Batlle received wall-to-wall coverage in most Uruguayan papers. Aguirre, *Una vida al servicio de un ideal*, 46–52, reprints the account published in *El País*. See also *El Plata, La Noche, La Tribuna Popular*, and *El Día*. The one-year anniversary of Beltrán's death was commemorated in *El País* and *Diario del Plata*. Notices in the international press include "El lance Batlle y Ordóñez-Beltrán, muerte del doctor Beltrán, hondo pesar en todo el país," *La Prensa* (Buenos Aires), 3 April 1920, 10; "El Duelo Trágico," *Caras y Caretas* (Buenos Aires), no. 1123, 10 April 1920; "Ex-President of Uruguay Kills Editor in Formal Duel Fought with Pistols," *New York Times*, 3 April 1920, 15; "Slayer of Beltan [sic] Prisoner after Duel: Victim's Body Lies in State – Uruguayan Politics in Ferment, *New York Times*, 4 April 1920, W16; "Formal and Fatal Duel: Details of Affair of Honor in Montevideo Serves as Reminder of Our Own Fire-Eating Politicians of Long Ago," *New York Times*, 16 May 1920, XX8.
101 "El Trágico duelo de ayer: Diligencias judiciales," *El Plata*, 3 April 1920, 10; Expediente no. 7761 del Juzgado de Instrucción del Segundo Turno, "José Batlle y Ordóñez: Duelo," 2 April 1920, fols. 5, 6, 7, quoted in Fischer, *Qué tupé*, 141.
102 Expediente no. 7761 del Juzgado de Instrucción del Segundo Turno, "José Batlle y Ordóñez. Duelo," 2 April 1920, fols. 10, 11, quoted in Fischer, *Qué tupé!*, 149–50.
103 Expediente no. 7761 del Juzgado de Instrucción del Segundo Turno, "José Batlle y Ordóñez: Duelo," 2 April 1920, fols. 12, 13, 22, 23, quoted in Fischer, *Qué tupé!*, 162, 165. "Prisión del Sr. Batlle y Ordóñez: Pedido de excarcelación denegado," *El Día* 3 April 1920, 1; "La libertad del Sr Batlle: Auto del juez," *La Tribuna Popular*, 6 April 1920. Fischer makes the case that Judge Lago reversed Judge Gomensoro's ruling after several high officials,

Supreme Court judges among them, weighed in on Batlle's behalf. But Gomensoro continued the investigation, taking statements from journalists who had covered the duel. Expediente no. 7761 del Juzgado de Instrucción del Segundo Turno, "José Batlle y Ordóñez: Duelo," 2 April 1920, fols. 51–3, quoted in Fischer, *Qué tupé!*, 191–4.

104 Manini Rios, *Una nave en la tormenta*, 148–9; Fischer, *Qué tupé!*, 187–9.
105 Manini Rios, *Una nave en la tormenta*, 149; Fischer, *Qué tupé!*, 195–6.
106 "La farsa del duelo," *El Socialista*, 15 May 1914, 1; "Pido la Palabra! Reflexiones sobre el duelo," *La Razón*, 19 March 1919, 1; ROU, *DSHCR*, vol. 283 (session of 4–5 August 1920), 190–2, 201–3.
107 ROU, *DSHCR*, vol. 283 (session of 4–5 August 1920), 205. Mibelli's history with dueling would later include an extraordinary 1924 incident, the subject of Parker, "Honor Ideology, Dueling Culture, and Judicial Lies." Additional detail about Mibelli can be found in Silva Grucci, *Historias que no nos contaron*.
108 ROU, *DSHCR*, vol. 283 (session of 4–5 August 1920), 192–4.
109 "Political Notes: The Senate and Duelling," *Montevideo Times*, 8 April 1920, 3; ROU, *DSHCS* (session of 6 April 1920), 448–9.
110 "Un montón de duelos en pocos años," *La Tribuna Popular*, 14 April 1920.
111 Later, over the years, conspiracy theories did creep into partisan memories of the duel. Fischer interprets the autopsy pathologists' observation of a star-shaped entry wound to Beltrán's aorta as possible evidence that a bullet might have been deliberately marked to have a hollow-point effect. Fischer, *Qué tupé!*, 167–71. The case of Beltrán's death is addressed in a medical journal report: see Berro and Turnes, "Autopsia histórica," 112–20.
112 Hughes, *Politics of the Sword*, 191–211, traces the idea of a permanent honor court back to the Italians Paolo Fambri in 1869, Guiseppe Zanardelli in 1887, and Iacopo Gelli in 1888. In Spain, the honor tribunal idea was a major feature of proposed reforms that failed to become law, but led to the creation in 1916 of a special tribunal for the press. Mateos Fernández, "Cuestión de honor," 772–3; de Borbón, *Resumen*; Ferrer, *Documentos*, Document LII.
113 ROU, *DSHCR*, vol. 283 (session of 4–5 August 1920), 208. See *Registro Nacional de leyes*, 597–8, for the law's final text.
114 Archivo del Poder Legislativo, Cámara de Representantes, Comisión de Códigos, folder no. 589/1918.
115 ROU, *DSHCR*, vol. 283 (session of 4–5 August 1920), 194.
116 "Parlamento: Cámara de Representantes – Legislación del duelo," *El Día*, 5 August 1920, 5. ROU, *DSHCR*, vol. 585 (session of 7 November 1967), 50–1; ROU, *DSCR*, vol. 648 (session of 17 July 1990), 282–307.
117 ROU, *DSHCR*, vol. 283 (session of 4–5 August 1920), 193.

118 *La Revista de Derecho, Jurisprudencia y Administración* 26, no. 16 (1921), 241–3; no. 17 (1921), 257–8; and no. 19 (1921), 289–95.
119 *La Revista de Derecho, Jurisprudencia y Administración* 26, no. 19 (1921), 289; "Incidente Rodríguez Larreta-Díaz," *La Tribuna Popular*, 14 April 1921, 1; "Incidente Rodríguez Larreta-Díaz," *La Tribuna Popular*, 15 April 1921, 1; "Another Duel," *Montevideo Times*, 16 April 1921; "El duelo y los jueces: La prisión del Dr. Espalter," *Diario del Plata*, 20 October 1921, 3; "Incidente Espalter-Leal, *Diario del Plata*, 21 October 1921, 3; "El duelo y los magistrados," *Diario del Plata*, 23 Ocober 1921, 3: "El duelo y los magistrados," *Diario del Plata*, 25 October 1921, 3; "Del Dr José Luis Espalter, *Diario del Plata*, 26 October 1921, 3; "El duelo y los jueces: Sentencia del Dr Vescovi," *Diario del Plata*, 27 October 1921, 3; "Detención del Dr. Espalter," *La Democracia*, 20 October 1921 1; "El desafío a los magistrados: Constituye el delito de desacato?," *El País*, 23 October 1921, 3.
120 "El duelo y los magistrados," *Diario del Plata*, 23 October, 3.
121 Parker, "Gentlemanly Responsibility and Insults of a Woman," 121–3.
122 "Duelo Sienra-Brum," *La Mañana*, 10 January 1920, 3; "Duelo en trámite," *La Mañana*, 9 January 1920, 1.
123 "Un documento patriótico y valiente: Manifiesto del doctor Luis Alberto de Herrera a sus 120,00 electores," *La Tribuna Popular*, 11 December 1922, 1. Brum countercharged that Herrera had overseen the falsification of electoral rolls in the areas *his* party controlled. "Del Dr Brum: Una respuesta al Dr Luis Alberto de Herrera," *El Día*, 12 December 1922, 4. For the highly detailed *actas* of the duel, see "El duelo de ayer," *El Día*, 14 December 1922, 5. Also Pintos Diago, *Luis Alberto de Herrera*, 453; Lacalle Herrera, *Herrera: Un nacionalismo oriental*, 63–4; Manini Ríos, *Una nave en la tormenta*, 243–6.
124 "Duelo Herrera-Brum," *La Tribuna Popular*, 13 December 1922, 8; "Incidente Herrera-Brum," *La Tribuna Popular*, 14 December 1922, 1.
125 "Incidente Herrera-Brum," *La Tribuna Popular*, 14 December 1922, 1–2. The figure of five hundred to six hundred spectators comes from the *Uruguay Weekly News*, 17 December 1922, 6. Also "Uruguay President in Duel Hundreds See: Cabinet Officers, Diplomats and Others Witness Bloodless Exchange with Dr. Herrera," *New York Times*, 14 December 1922, 3.
126 "La actitud del Presidente Brum: Poniendo en ridículo al país," *La Tribuna Popular*, 14 December 1922, 1; "El Presidente duelista," *La Tribuna Popular*, 15 December 1922, 1; "Presidential duels," *Montevideo Times*, 19 December 1922, 3. On the rumor that the guns were loaded with blanks, see "Ecos del duelo Herrera-Brum: Una versión estúpida," *La Tribuna Popular*, 15 December 1922, 1.
127 "A Futile Duel," *Montevideo Times*, 15 December 1922, 3.

128 "La farsa de ayer," *Justicia*, 14 December 1922, 1.
129 "Las cartas y los desafíos," *El Ferro-carril*, 12 April 1871; "La nota: Sección desafíos," *La Razón*, 16 February 1916, 1.
130 "Guani-Ghigliani: Declárase que hay lugar a duelo," *La Tribuna Popular*, 22 December 1920, 1.
131 ROU, DSHCR, vol. 283 (session of 4–5 August 1920), 206–8.
132 "Notas gráficas del lance de ayer," *El País*, 14 April 1921, 3; "El duelo de ayer," *El Día*, 14 April 1921, 5; "Los duelos de la semana," *Mundo Uruguayo*, 21 April 1921. This duel sparked so much interest because it had a long buildup involving an out-of-town duelist who had to come to Montevideo; because the conditions imposed, pistols at twenty paces with time to aim, were more severe than was typical; and because Villanueva Saravia was not a run-of-the-mill Montevideo politician but an old-style Blanco caudillo famed as a fighter and marksman. "A propósito de los dos incidentes," *El País*, 15 April 1921, 3.
133 "La fotografía y el duelo," *La Mañana*, 15 April 1921, 1.
134 "Con motivo a los recientes duelos: Críticas injustas a la ley vigente," *Diario del Plata*, 17 April 1921, 3.
135 "A propósito de los dos incidentes," *El País*, 15 April 1921, 3.
136 "El duelo en solfa," *La Tribuna Popular*, 16 April 1921, 1; "Vamos bien: Un hombre quiere batirse," *La Tribuna Popular*, 18 April 1921, 1. The 1918 ban on bullfights, cockfights, and other spectacles of animal cruelty is covered in Vanger, *Uruguay's José Batlle y Ordóñez*, 251.
137 On the fatal Melo-Gomeza duel, see "Un duelo trágico" and "Un trágico lance de honor entre 2 oficiales del ejército," *El País*, 22 March 1921, 3, 5; "El duelo trágico de ayer," *La Tribuna Popular*, 22 March 1921, 2. On the nearly fatal Patiño-Elgue duel, see "Duelo sangriento," *La Tribuna Popular*, 31 October 1921, 4; "Duelos a pistola," *El País*, 31 October 1921, 3.
138 For two examples of verdicts of honor tribunals, declaring no cause for a duel and presenting their reasoning, see "Por los fueros de la prensa: Una cuestión de honor," *La Tribuna Popular*, 21 March 1921, 1; "Personal: Incidente Díaz-Irureta Goyena," *Diario del Plata*, 13 September 1921, 3.
139 "La ley sobre el duelo: Apreciando sus efectos," *Diario del Plata*, 13 September 1921, 3.
140 "Los duelos acá y en Buenos Aires," *El País*, 25 October 1921, 3.
141 "A batirse en Montevideo," *El País*, 24 October 1921, 3.
142 Cerrano, "La campaña presidencial del herrerismo." This was the so-called *implicancias* scandal in the run-up to the presidential elections of 1946.
143 "Personal: Incidente Angel Graña-Eduardo V. Haedo," *El Plata*, 7 August 1945, 3.
144 Ibid.

145 ROU, *DSHCR*, vol. 463 (session of 21 August 1945), 115–17. Also reprinted in ROU, *DSCR*, vol. 585 (session of 7 November 1967), 50–1. For commentary, see Greco, *Ante el duelo*, 34–7.
146 Camaño Rosa, *Derecho penal*, 141.
147 Benedetti, *El país de la cola de paja*, 19.
148 Taylor, "The Uruguayan Coup d'État of 1933," 301–20.
149 *Ley reglamentando la publicación de los pensamientos por medio de la imprenta, 28 de junio de 1935*, 3–20.
150 Parker, "Honor Ideology, Dueling Culture, and Judicial Lies," 13–15.

Chapter Four

1 Representative Juan Gutiérrez in ROU, *DSCR*, vol. 648 (session of 17 July 1990), 297.
2 Juan Andrés Ramírez, in ROU, *DSHCR*, vol. 283 (session of 4–5 August 1920), 194.
3 Senate President Gonzalo Aguirre Ramírez, in ROU, *DSCS*, vol. 349 (session of 16 June 1992), 205–7, quoting Aureliano Rodríguez Larreta from 1919.
4 *Código penal* (Ley número 9155); Greco, *Ante el duelo*, 7–10, 15–16.
5 Kierszenbaum, "Between the Accepted and the Legal," 36–7. Rilla, *La actualidad del pasado*, chaps. 7–9, makes the case for the fragility of that mythology.
6 Weschler, *A Miracle, a Universe*, 83–172; Markarian, *Left in Transformation*, chap. 2.
7 "Pobres Botijas!" *El Pueblo*, 3 April 1935, 5. *La Tribuna Popular* provides a good summary of the incident and its antecedents: "Bajo el plomo de cuatro balazos cayó abatido el doctor Demichelli," *La Tribuna Popular*, 11 April 1935, 1.
8 Ghigliani and others charged that blackmail was an element of Botana's business model. "La escuela del 'chantage' no va a instalarse sin que la combatamos," *El Pueblo*, 18 October 1934, reprinted as "Un editorial que será histórico," *El Pueblo*, 11 April 1935, 5; "El verdadero culpable es el gangster Botana," *La Tribuna Popular*, 13 April 1935, 1.
9 Saítta, *Regueros de tinta*; Lila Caimari, *While the City Sleeps*, chap. 2.
10 "¡Francisco Ghigliani protector de menores!," *Uruguay*, 4 April 1935, 1.
11 "Un caso claro de legítima defensa" and "No fue a traición," *El Pueblo*, 11 April 1935, 1; also "El suceso de ayer" and "Estructura moral del Dr Ghigliani," p. 5 of the same issue.
12 "El defensor del Doctor Ghigliani," *El Pueblo*, 11 April 1935, 1. Debate on stripping Ghigliani of his parliamentary immunity, and the Senate's decision not to do so, appears in ROU, *DSHCS*, vol. 160 (session of 11 April 1935), 85–8.

13 For three of Ghigliani's previous duels, see Viale, *Jurisprudencia caballeresca argentina: Nueva edición corregida y aumentada*, 511, 516, 519.
14 The ruling of suicide in Ghigliani's case was disputed, but a historical autopsy by medical investigator Augusto Soiza Larrosa reconfirmed that conclusion. Silva Grucci, *Duelos en el Rio de la Plata*, 134–40.
15 "El Dr Ghigliani formula declaraciones a una agencia telegráfica extranjera," *El Pueblo*, 11 April 1935, 5.
16 "Ghigliani es asesino: Alevosamente, por la espalda, quiso matar a Demicheli: La indignación que produjo el atentado ha sido unánime," *Uruguay*, 11 April 1935, 1; "Las heridas prueban la forma cobarde y alevosa en que se perpetró la agresión," *Uruguay*, 11 April 1935, 2.
17 "Fueron clausurados 'El Pueblo' y el diario botanista: Una medida conveniente," *La Tribuna Popular*, 12 April 1935, 1.
18 "Cándido Domínguez, 'el maestro de maestros,'" *ToucheWorld*, 15 February 2019, https://toucheworld.com/candido-dominguez-el-maestro-de-maestros-uru/.
19 "Verdict of the Tribunal de Honor, 21 Nov. 1957," AGN-AH, Luis Batlle Berres collection, box 2.3.11 ("Duelos: Reparación por las Armas"), folder 2.3.11.9 ("LBB-Rivas"). Also published as "El proceso del lance de honor a través de las actas de los árbitros y padrinos del mismo," *La Tribuna Popular*, 23 November 1957.
20 Professor Yvette Trochón summarizes the content of Ribas's epistolary campaign in the Papico Cibils documentary series *Uruguay de Duelo*, episode 3.
21 "Para terminar," *Acción*, 14 November 1957, 1; "Ambos duelistas resultaron heridos: El proceso del lance de honor a través de las actas de los árbitros y padrinos del mismo," *La Tribuna Popular*, 23 November 1957. See chapter 2 on Herrera y Obes's 1881 effort to get the press to eliminate specific offensive words.
22 "Hubo lugar," *El Diario*, 22 November 1957, Cándido Dominguez private archive, newspaper clipping collection, Montevideo (hereafter cited as CDA-NCC).
23 "Verdict of the Tribunal de Honor, 21 Nov. 1957," AGN-AH, Luis Batlle Berres collection, box 2.3.11, folder 2.3.11.9. The ruling was signed by all three members; the text was likely Serrato's, as the honor tribunal's chair.
24 "Batiéronse Luis Batlle y Ribas," *Acción*, 22 November 1957, 1; "Ambos duelistas resultaron heridos: El proceso del lance de honor a través de las actas de los árbitros y padrinos del mismo," *La Tribuna Popular*, 23 November 1957; newspaper clipping "¡Viva Luis Batlle!," *Batlle: Periódico Político* 3 no. 57 (November 1957), 1, in AGN-AH, Luis Batlle Berres collection, box 2.3.11, folder 2.3.11.9.

25 "Duel Broadcast, Both Men Miss in Uruguay Feud," *Globe and Mail* (Toronto), 7 May 1953, 2; "Uruguay Bans Radio Broadcasts of Duels," *Washington Post*, 23 July 1953, 1; Benedetti, *El país de la cola de paja*, 19.
26 "Ex-President and Rival Cut in Uruguayan Duel," *New York Times*, 23 November 1957, 17.
27 "Slaying Follows Duel: Match Halted, Contestant Kills Foe and Himself," *New York Times*, 29 March 1958, 6. A photo of Dodó, taken for a newspaper interview after the duel and just before Villar López arrived to kill him, appears in "Medio siglo de duelos en el campo de honor," newspaper clipping from an unidentified publication, CDA-NCC.
28 "Resultaron ilesos Gaudin y Erro en duelo de ayer," *La Mañana*, 6 July 1958, 3; "Dos disparos se cambiaron resultando ilesos ambos" *La Tribuna Popular*, 6 July 1958, 3.
29 "Uruguayans Duel to a Draw," *New York Times*, 6 July 1958, 6. Information on the origin and context of the challenge comes from interviews with Enrique Erro (*hijo*) and Walter Santoro (one of Erro's seconds) in *Uruguay de Duelo*, episode 4.
30 According to Enrique Erro's son, his journalism had also incited three failed attempts on his life. *Uruguay de Duelo*, episode 4.
31 Walter Santoro (one of Erro's seconds) in *Uruguay de Duelo*, episode 4.
32 "Sin lugar a duelo: Se reintegró el Gral Gestido a sus funciones," *Extra*, 3 November 1967, 2, CDA-NCC. Aníbal Arguello, "Uruguay President to Fight Duel ... Honest! It's Perfectly Legal ... Leader Challenged by Ex-Minister," *Boston Globe*, 31 October 1967, 2.
33 CDA-NCC has press reports of all of these challenges. For a contemporary analysis of the 1971 electoral campaign from a US perspective, see United States Central Intelligence Agency, Directorate of Intelligence, Weekly Summary Special Report, "Uruguay's Elections: Tradition vs. the Left," 12 November 1971, no. 0396/71B, Approved for Release 2009/01/21, in CIA Freedom of Information Act Electronic Reading Room.
34 *Uruguay de Duelo*, episode 5, interview with Flores Mora's daughter.
35 "Proceso a una mentira," *Acción*, 18 October 1970, 4.
36 "No hubo reconciliación luego del tenaz duelo," *La Mañana*, 22 October 1970, 1.
37 "Duelo: Con heridas Flores y Batlle," *El País*, 12 November 1970, 1; "Dictámen de los médicos: 'Imposibilidad de ambos,'" *Acción* (2nd ed.), 12 November 1970; "Detención por lesiones a ambos," *El Día*, 12 November 1970, 2; "Cuestión caballeresca Batlle-Flores Mora," *Acción*, 13 November 1970, 5, in CDA-NCC.
38 "El acta final que decidió el lance caballeresco de ayer," *La Mañana*, ca. 16–18 October 1971, in CDA-NCC.

39 *Uruguay de Duelo*, episode 5.
40 "El Acta final que decidió el lance caballeresco de ayer," *La Mañana* (exact date unknown, ca. 16–18 October 1971), in CDA-NCC.
41 The National Security Archive, electronic briefing book no. 71, "Nixon: 'Brazil Helped Rig the Uruguayan Elections,' 1971," https://nsarchive2.gwu.edu/NSAEBB/NSAEBB71/.
42 "Gestión caballeresca," *Acción*, ca. 18–20 October 1960, in CDA-NCC.
43 "Rechazó el duelo Ferreira Aldunate," *La Mañana*, late June or early July 1970, in CDA-NCC. The conflict stemmed from a radio broadcast on 16 June 1970, in which Ferreira Aldunate demanded the rear admiral's resignation after a theft of weapons from the Naval Training Centre.
44 Ibid.
45 Emilio Frugoni, *Obras de Emilio Frugoni*, 7:237–46, 281–5.
46 *Diario Oficial de la República Oriental del Uruguay* 255, no. 18078 (27 May 1969); "Poder ejecutivo: Ministerio de Defensa Nacional," Decreto 243 969, "Se aprueba el Reglamento de los Tribunales de Honor de las Fuerzas Armadas," in CDA-NCC.
47 My intuition is based on reading between the lines of accounts that do not *explicitly* confirm that such was the case. See, for example, "El Gral Ribas no aceptaría el duelo," *El Eco*, 3 December 1971, in CDA-NCC. Markarian, *Left in Transformation*, 62, sees masculine honor consciousness in "the language of leftist heroism" but also reports that both Seregni and Enrique Erro gave contemporary and subsequent justifications for their decisions to duel that are consistent with the argument presented here.
48 Interview by author with Julio Maria Sanguinetti, Montevideo, June 2000. Sanguinetti attributes the wave of duels in the early 1970s to the intensity of political polarization at that moment. Rico, "1, 2, 3 … Apunten, ¡Fuego!," 135–74, provides a detailed analysis of dueling in this period.
49 ROU, *DSCR*, vol. 585 (session of 7 November 1967), 51.
50 Ibid., 52.
51 "Inician contactos para derogar Ley de Duelos," *La Mañana*, 23 October 1970, 1; "Escribe el Dr. José Pedro Aramendía: La ley de duelo de 1920," *La Mañana*, 8 November 1970, 4.
52 Ley nNo. 14068, "Ley de Seguridad del Estado y del Orden Interno, 12 July 1972," IMPO Normativa y Avisos Legales del Uruguay, https://www.impo.com.uy/bases/leyes-originales/14068-1972. Chapter 3 of the law deals with the press.
53 Weschler, *A Miracle, A Universe*, esp. 87–92, 123–50; the estimated number of exiles comes from the Museo de la Memoria, cited in Schelotto, "La dictadura cívico-militar uruguaya," fn. 6.
54 Interview by author with Representative Daniel Díaz Maynard, Montevideo, July 2000.

55 Gayol, *Honor y duelo*, 211–15. Argentina's debate over the legal status of dueling is as rich as Uruguay's; see Moreno, *El Código Penal y sus antecedentes*, 60–103; Escribano, "El Duelo en la legislación penal," 20–1; Gómez, *Tratado de derecho penal*, 216–23; Soler, *Derecho penal argentino*, 176–93.
56 Moreno, *El Código Penal y sus antecedentes*, 101.
57 Rivanera, *Código de honor comentado*, 47–8.
58 Viale, *Jurisprudencia caballeresca argentina de los últimos treinta y cinco años*, 501–2, 701–3.
59 Ibid., 500–1.
60 Ibid., 656–60; Oller and Casado, *Los duelos*, 93–4; González Arrili, *Vida de Lisandro de la Torre*, 225–45; Larra, *Lisandro de la Torre*, 290–4; see also the coverage in *La Prensa* (Buenos Aires), 24 July 1935, 8, 10–11; 25 July 1935, 9–11; 26 July 1935, 9–10.
61 Viale, *Jurisprudencia caballeresca argentina de los últimos treinta y cinco años*; Varangot, *Virtudes caballerescas*. See the appendix for discussion of these sources and their limitations.
62 On the crime beat, see Caimari, *While the City Sleeps*, chaps. 1–2; on radio, film, and popular culture, see Karush, *Culture of Class*, chap. 2.
63 Frank L. Kluckhorn, "50 Duels Pending in Perón Congress," *New York Times*, 5 October 1946, 6.
64 Hamilton, *Duelos: Los sangrientos combates*, chap. 44.
65 Varangot, *Virtudes caballerescas*, 90–1.
66 Ibid., 141–4.
67 "Dramático duelo protagonizaron almirante argentino y un periodista," from unidentified newspaper; and "Con el honor no se juega: Duelos caballerescos en la Argentina," *Siete Días* (exact date unknown, ca. 1968), both in CDA-NCC.
68 Varangot, *Virtudes caballerescas*, 151–3.
69 Ibid., 126.
70 Invocations of the innate right to criticize can be found in ibid., 101–4, 121–3, 169–70; for invocations of Catholicism, see ibid., 112, 126, 145–7, 173; critique of the duel as an anachronistic farce, see ibid., 97–8, 114–15, 126, 172.
71 "Con el honor no se juega," in CDA-NCC.
72 Ibid.
73 Varangot, *Virtudes caballerescas*, 176–7.
74 ROU, *DSCR*, vol. 648 (session of 17 July 1990), 294; *Uruguay de Duelo*, episode 9.
75 ROU, *DSCR*, vol. 648 (session of 17 July 1990), 284.
76 The various proposals all called for the repeal of Law no. 7253 and Articles 38 and 205, but differed in which articles of the Criminal Code they would also repeal.

77 "Autorizaron duelo Clavería-Fasano," *El Día*, 24 February 1990, 14, in CDA-NCC.
78 "Puntualizaciones del Inspector Clavería" and "Ministerio del Interior," *El Día*, 25 February 1990, in CDA-NCC.
79 "Fasano recibió padrinos: No se retracta y pidió 24 horas para responder al retador," *El País*, 27 February 1990, 12, in CDA-NCC.
80 "Clavería no quiso el duelo que quería," *La República*, 4 March 1990, 1. Much of the editions for Saturday, 3 March, and Sunday, 4 March, of *La República* are dedicated to the affair, with articles on multiple pages. For example, "A más de 24 horas de designados los padrinos de Fasano no fueron recibidos," *La República*, 3 March 1990, 5; "En el acta los padrinos de Fasano manifestaron su expreso desacuerdo," *La República*, 4 March 1990; "Fasano analiza la retirada del subjefe de policía," *La República*, 4 March 1990, 3; all in CDA-NCC.
81 "Las 3 razones de Clavería para abandonar el lance," *La República*, 4 March 1990, 3, in CDA-NCC.
82 "El senador Bruera pidió al Ministro del Interior que evite el duelo," and "Punto de vista: Un policía no es un militar," *La República*, 3 March 1990, 5, in CDA-NCC.
83 Luís Aníbal da Silva, "Nueve ciudadanos opinan sobre el duelo," *La República*, 4 March 1990, in CDA-NCC.
84 Weschler, *A Miracle, a Universe*, 173–236.
85 *Reglamento de los tribunales de honor de las Fuerzas Armadas*; "Decreto 55/985, Reglamento de los Tribunales de Honor de las Fuerzas Armadas" (8 February 1985), Normativa y Avisos Legales del Uruguay. See especially chaps. I A and B, and VI A, B, and C in both documents.
86 *Paleontológico* was the word used by the Spanish jurist Luis Jiménez de Asúa in his commentary on Uruguay's 1933 Criminal Code. ROU, *DSCR*, vol. 648 (session of 17 July 1990), 287.
87 Ibid., 285.
88 Ibid., 287. See also "Ley de duelo: El Diputado Palomeque presenta hoy proyecto de derogación," *El País*, 5 March 1990, 11.
89 Interview by author with Representative José Díaz, Montevideo, 30 June 2000.
90 ROU, *DSHCR*, vol. 283 (session of 4–5 August 1920), 194.
91 Interview by author with Representative José Díaz, Montevideo, 30 June 2000.
92 As noted in chapter 1, new press laws were either debated in Congress or implemented by decree in 1829, 1854, 1862–63, 1881, 1886, 1897, 1904, 1912, 1934–35, 1972, and 1984 (this is an incomplete list). Parker, "Gentlemanly Responsibility," 113–17; Zuviría, *La prensa periódica*; Fernández y Medina, *La imprenta y la prensa en el Uruguay*; Durá, *Del enjuiciamiento de los delitos de imprenta*; Regules, *Breves consideraciones sobre la*

93 ROU, *DSHCR*, vol. 270 (session of 9 May 1919), 410.
94 Interview by author with Representative Daniel Díaz Maynard, Montevideo, July 2000.
95 ROU, *DSCR*, vol. 648 (session of 17 July 1990), 296.
96 Ibid., 291; ROU, *DSCS*, vol. 349 (session of 16 June 1992), 202.
97 Interview by author with Representative José Díaz, Montevideo, 30 June 2000.
98 ROU, *DSCR*, vol. 648 (session of 17 July 1990), 291; "Ley 16.099: Ley de Prensa – Libertad en los medios de comunicación," 3 November 1989, IMPO Normativa y Avisos Legales del Uruguay.
99 ROU, *DSCR*, vol. 639 (session of 5 April 1989), 153–4, 202; for the text of the earlier decree-law, see "Ley 15.672: Se aprueba la Ley de Prensa y se deroga la ley 9.480 y sus modificativas y concordantes," 9 November 1984, IMPO Normativa y Avisos Legales del Uruguay.
100 ROU, *DSCR*, vol. 639 (session of 5 April 1989), 206.
101 ROU, *DSCR*, vol. 648 (session of 17 July 1990), 293.
102 Ibid., 297.
103 Ibid.
104 Ibid., 294–5. See also the intervention of Representative Craviotto, in ibid., 299–300.
105 ROU, *DSCR*, vol. 648 (session of 17 July 1990), 299–300, 319–20.
106 "Aguirre defendió en sala la Ley de Duelos," *La Mañana*, 17 June 1992, 4, CDA-NCC.
107 ROU, *DSCS*, vol. 349 (session of 16 June 1992), 205–7.
108 Ibid., 207–8.
109 Ibid.
110 Ibid., 213, 278–9.
111 Ibid., 272.
112 Interview by author with Julio Maria Sanguinetti, Montevideo, June 2000; "Extraña los duelos," *El Pais*, 28 February 1999, 19; Julio Maria Sanguinetti, in *Uruguay de Duelo*, episode 9.
113 "Mujica lamentó que no exista la Ley de Duelos para resolver ataques al honor," *Montevideo Portal*, 16 June 2017, https://www.montevideo.com.uy/Noticias/Mujica-lamento-que-no-exista-la-Ley-de-Duelos-para-resolver-ataques-al-honor-uc346138; Marcelo Ortale, "A Sable, Espada o con Pistolas," *El Día* (La Plata, Argentina), 3 September 1917.
114 "Sanguinetti sobre Mujica y los duelos: 'No se puede simplificar si uno está de acuerdo o no,'" *Montevideo Portal*, 16 June 2017, https://www.montevideo.com.uy/Noticias/Sanguinetti-sobre-Mujica-y-los-duelos--no-se-puede-simplificar-si-uno-esta-de-acuerdo-o-no--uc346218.

115 "El duelo," *El Pais*, 25 March 1990, 6.
116 Other studies that have looked closely at those gendered and classed exclusions include Gayol, *Honor y duelo*; Piccato, *Tyranny of Opinion*; Braga-Pinto, "Journalists, *Capoeiras*, and the Duel"; Parker, "Gentlemanly Responsibility and Insults of a Woman." Because those other works make the case convincingly, in this book I have chosen to focus elsewhere.
117 Tejera, *Retrato de un ciudadano*, 162. "Course" is a rough translation of *cauce*, literally a channel or riverbed.
118 Billacois, *The Duel: Its Rise and Fall*, 1. I thank one of my anonymous referees for reminding me of this quote.
119 Hughes, *Politics of the Sword*; Chamberlain, *Pistols, Politics, and the Press*.

Appendix

1 "Actualidad: Estadística del duelo," *El Plata*, 14 April 1920, 1.
2 Moyano Dellepiane, "Jurisprudencia caballeresca porteña," 39, 83–4, 102.
3 See, for example, two no-names cases in October 1886, a delicate political moment for Uruguay. "Lance de honor," *La Tribuna Popular*, 21 October 1886, 1; "Duelo," *La Tribuna Popular*, 26 October 1886, 2.
4 Gayol, *Honor y duelo*, 258n211.
5 Ibid., 104–13. Gayol estimates an undercount for the twentieth century by about a factor of two, and identifies the 1890s – before Viale started keeping records – as Argentina's busiest decade of duels and *desafíos*, with an estimated 680 incidents.
6 Nye, *Masculinity and Male Codes of Honor*, 184–6.
7 Hughes, *Politics of the Sword*, 112–18.
8 "Actualidad: Estadística del duelo," *El Plata*, 14 April 1920, 1.
9 ROU, *DSHCR*, vol. 271 (session of 4 June 1919), 225.

Bibliography

Archives

Archivo General de la Nación, Archivo Histórico, Montevideo, Uruguay.
    Colección Luis Batlle Berres. Abbreviated in notes as AGN-AH-CLBB.

Archivo General de la Nación, Archivo Judicial, Montevideo, Uruguay. Juzgados
    Letrados en lo Penal. Abbreviated in notes as AGN-AJ-JLP.
    Juzgado de Instrucción del Segundo Turno.
    Juzgado de Instrucción del Tercer Turno.
    Juzgado del Crimen del Primer Turno.

Archivo del Museo Histórico Nacional, Montevideo, Uruguay.
    Archivo del Dr Alberto Palomeque. Abbreviated in notes as MHN-AAP.

Archivo del Poder Legislativo, Montevideo, Uruguay.
    Cámara de Representantes, Comisión de Códigos.
    Cámara de Senadores, Comisión de Constitución y Legislación.
    Miscellaneous.

Cándido Domínguez Ledo, private archive. With deepest gratitude to Dr Rubén
    Domínguez Cabot.
    Newspaper clipping collection. Abbreviated in notes as CDA-NCC.
    Actas of duels.
    Unpublished manuscripts.

Archivo General de la Nación, Buenos Aires, Argentina.
    Tribunal Criminal Serie 1.

Digital Collections

Anáforas, Universidad de la República, Facultad de Información y Comunicación. https://anaforas.fic.edu.uy. Publicaciones Peródicas del Uruguay.
IMPO Normativa y Avisos Legales del Uruguay. https://www.impo.com.uy.
Biblioteca Nacional, Madrid, Spain. Hemeroteca Digital. http://hemerotecadigital.bne.es.
Archivo Histórico Nacional, Madrid, Spain. Fondo Alfonso Carlos de Borbón Austria-Este. http://pares.mcu.es/ParesBusquedas20/catalogo/search.
Central Intelligence Agency Freedom of Information Act Electronic Reading Room. https://www.cia.gov/readingroom/home.
The National Security Archive, George Washington University, Washington, DC. https://nsarchive.gwu.edu/.

Congressional Records

República Oriental del Uruguay. *Diario de sesiones de la Cámara de Representantes.* Abbreviated in notes as ROU, DSCR.
República Oriental del Uruguay. *Diario de sesiones de la Cámara de Senadores.* Abbreviated in notes as ROU, DSCS.
República Oriental del Uruguay. *Diario de sesiones de la H. Cámara de Representantes.* Abbreviated in notes as ROU, DSHCR.
República Oriental del Uruguay. *Diario de sesiones de la H. Cámara de Senadores.* Abbreviated in notes as ROU, DSHCS.

Newspapers and Magazines

(PLACE OF PUBLICATION IS MONTEVIDEO UNLESS OTHERWISE INDICATED)
Acción
Batlle: Periódico Político (Salto, Uruguay)
El Bien Público
Caras y Caretas
Caras y Caretas (Buenos Aires)
La Colonia Española
El Correo Español (Buenos Aires)
El Debate
La Democracia
El Día
El Día (La Plata, Argentina, online)
El Diario
Diario del Comercio

Diario del Plata
Diario Oficial de la República Oriental del Uruguay
El Ejército Uruguayo
La España
El Ferro-Carril
El Heraldo
El Hilo Eléctrico
L'Indipendente
Justicia
La Mañana
Montevideo Portal (online)
Montevideo Times
Mundo Uruguayo
La Nación
La Nación (Buenos Aires)
El Nacional (Buenos Aires)
El Negro Timoteo
La Noche
La Opinión Nacional
La Opinión Pública
El País
El Paysandú (Paysandú, Uruguay)
La Paz
El Plata
La Prensa (Buenos Aires)
El Pueblo
El Pueblo (Paysandú, Uruguay)
La Razón
La Reforma Pacífica
La Reforma Pacífica (Buenos Aires)
La República
El Siglo
El Socialista
El Sol
El Telégrafo Marítimo
La Tribuna
La Tribuna (Buenos Aires)
La Tribuna Popular
Uruguay
Uruguay News
Uruguay Weekly News

VIA PROQUEST HISTORICAL NEWSPAPERS
Boston Globe
Globe and Mail (Toronto)
New York Times
Washington Post

Interviews by author

Jorge Cermesone, Buenos Aires, 6 April 1999.
José Díaz, Montevideo, 30 June 2000.
Daniel Díaz Maynard, Montevideo, July 2000.
Julio Maria Sanguinetti, Montevideo, June 2000.

Published Primary Sources

Anuario estadístico de la República Oriental del Uruguay, año 1918. Montevideo: Tipografía Moderna de Arduino Hermanos, 1920.
Barbasetti, Luigi. *Codice cavalleresco*. Milan: Tipografía Alessandro Gattinoni, 1898.
Barnuevo, José Maria. "El duelo ante la razón y la ley." *Revista General de Legislación y Jurisprudencia* (Madrid), no. 110 (1907): 772–3.
Barrett, Rafael. "El duelo." In *Ideas y críticas*, 53–4. Montevideo: O.M. Bertani, Editor, 1900.
Beltrán, Washington. *Cuestiones sociológicas: Lucha contra la criminalidad infantil, artículos periodísticos y discursos*. Montevideo: Ediciones de la Banda Oriental, 1990.
Borciani, Alberto. *Le offese all'onore: Il duello*. Turin: Unione Tipografico Editrice Torinese, 1927.
Borrego, Andrés. *Ensayo sobre la jurisprudencia de los duelos por el Conde de Chateauvillard, traducido del francés y seguido por comentarios y preceptos adicionales a dicha obra por D. Andrés Borrego*. Madrid: Juan Iglesia Sánchez, Impresor, 1890.
Bruneau de Laborie, Èmile-Louis Bruno. *Les lois du duel*. Paris: Manzi Joyant, 1906.
Cabriñana, Marqués de. *Lances entre caballeros*. Madrid: Sucesores de Rivadeneyra, 1900.
Camaño Rosa, Antonio. *Derecho penal: Parte general*. Montevideo: Editorial Bibliográfica Uruguaya, 1957.
Chat[e]auvillard, Comte de. *Essai sur le duel*. Paris: Bohaire, 1836.
Código de Instrucción Criminal de la República Oriental del Uruguay. Montevideo: Imprenta La Tribuna, 1879.
Código Militar para la República Oriental del Uruguay, Año 1884. Montevideo: Imprenta La Nación, 1885.

Código Penal de la República Oriental del Uruguay. Montevideo: Imprenta El Siglo Ilustrado, 1889.

Código Penal (Ley número 9155): Promulgación: 4 de diciembre de 1933; Vigencia: 1 de Julio de 1934. Montevideo: Imprenta Nacional, 1934.

Coral Luzzi, Pedro Federico. *Código de honor con las leyes relativas al duelo: Ajustado a la codificación penal de las Repúblicas O. del Uruguay, Argentina e Iberoamericanas.* Montevideo: Talleres Gráficos de A. Monteverde y Cía., 1950.

Correa, Eliseo. *El duelo: Tesis presentada para optar al grado de Doctor en Jurisprudencia.* Buenos Aires: Imp. y Litografía "El Porteño," 1899.

De Borbón y de Austria-Este, Don Alfonso. *Resumen de la historia de la creación y desarrollo de las Ligas Contra el Duelo y para la protección del honor en los diferentes paises de Europa desde fines de noviembre de 1900 hasta fines de octubre de 1909.* Barcelona: Emprenta de Henrich y Cía., 1910.

De Menviel, Carlos Maria [Carlos Delcasse, pseud.]. *El médico en los duelos.* Buenos Aires: Talleres Gráficos de J.L. Rosso y Cía., 1918.

Dufort y Álvarez, Anacleto. *La prensa irresponsable: Tesis presentada para optar el grado de Doctor en Jurisprudencia.* Montevideo: Tipografía Renaud Reynaud, 1883.

Durá, Francisco. *Del enjuiciamiento en los delitos de imprenta: Tesis.* Montevideo: Establecimiento Tipográfico de "El Telégrafo Marítimo," 1881.

Escribano, Carlos. "El duelo en la legislación penal." *La Ley* (Argentina), no. 7 (1937): 18–19.

Estrada, José Manuel (hijo). *Del duelo: Tesis presentada para optar al grado de Doctor en Jurisprudencia.* Buenos Aires: Imprenta de Martín Biedma, 1895.

Fernández y Medina, Benjamín. *La imprenta y la prensa en el Uruguay desde 1807 á 1900.* Montevideo: Imprenta de Dornaleche y Reyes, 1900.

Ferrer, Melchor. *Documentos de Don Alfonso Carlos de Borbón y de Austria-Este: Manifiestos, proclamas, órdenes generales, cartas.* Madrid: Editorial Tradicionalista, 1950.

Ferreto, Escipión A. *Código de honor: Compendio de las leyes de honor destinadas a resolver las vertencias caballerescas.* 6th ed. Buenos Aires, 1930. 1st edition, 1905.

Floro Costa, Ángel. *Écos del Partido Colorado: Colección de artículos políticos publicados en La Razón y en La Tribuna Popular.* Montevideo: Imp. a Vapor de La Tribuna Popular, 1885.

Fors, Luis Ricardo. *Arte del testigo en duelo.* Buenos Aires: Juan L. Dasso and Cía. Editores, 1913.

Frugoni, Emilio. *Obras de Emilio Frugoni.* Vol. 7, *Selección de discursos, años 1920–1921.* Montevideo: Ediciones de la Banda Oriental, 1989.

– *La revolución del machete: Panorama político del Uruguay.* Buenos Aires, 1934.

Gallo, Juan Carlos. *El duelo: Tesis presentada para optar al grado de Doctor en Jurisprudencia.* Buenos Aires: Compañía Sud-Americana de Billetes de Banco, 1898.

Gelli, Iacopo. *Codice cavalleresco italiano*. 15th ed. Milan: Hoepli, 1926.
Gómez, Eusebio. *Tratado de derecho penal*. Vol. 2, *Delitos contra la persona*. Buenos Aires: Compañía Argentina de Editores, 1939.
Greco, Carlos A. *Ante el duelo: Estudio de carácter jurídico, ético y social.* Montevideo, 1949.
Herrero y Espinosa, Manuel. *José Pedro Varela*. Montevideo: Posada y Lagomarsino Editores, 1885.
Jiménez de Aréchaga, Eduardo. *Código Penal y Código de Instrucción Criminal*. 5th ed. Montevideo: Barreiro y Ramos, 1926.
La Nación, número especial para el centenario de 1916. Buenos Aires, 1916.
Levene, Horacio. *Duelo: Manual de procedimiento – edición particular para el ejército*. Buenos Aires: Revista Militar, 1924.
Ley de Imprenta: La doctrina y la jurisprudencia nacional, delitos de difamación e injurias, disposiciones legales. Montevideo: Claudio García & Cía., 1937.
Ley reglamentando la publicación de los pensamientos por medio de la imprenta, 28 de junio de 1935. Montevideo: Imprenta Nacional, 1936.
Los códigos españoles concordados y anotados: Tomo décimo – Novísima recopilación de las leyes de España. Vol. 4, *que contiene el libro duodécimo, suplemento e índices*. 2nd ed. Madrid: Antonio de San Martin, Editor, 1872.
Moreno, Rodolfo, Jr. *El Código Penal y sus antecedentes*. Vol. 4. Buenos Aires: H.A. Tommasi, 1923.
Oliver, Ramón. *El duelo: Estudio histórico, jurídico y social presentado a la Facultad de Derecho y Ciencias Sociales*. Buenos Aires: Imp. de Ostwald y Martínez, 1881.
Oreiro, Ventura. *Reglas del duelo: Precedidas de un prefacio sobre el duelo en general y un bosquejo histórico del mismo*. Buenos Aires: Imprenta de Mendia y Martínez, 1890.
Paz, José M. *Memorias póstumas del brigadier general D. José M. Paz*. Buenos Aires: Imprenta La Revista, 1855.
Proyecto de Código Penal. Montevideo: Imprenta Elzeviriana de C. Becchi, 1888.
Proyecto de Código Penal para la República Argentina, redactado en cumplimiento del decreto de 7 de junio de 1890 y precedido de una exposición de motivos por los doctores Norberto Piñero, Rodolfo Rivarola y José Nicolás Matienzo. 2nd ed. Buenos Aires: Taller Tipográfico de la Penitenciaría Nacional, 1898.
Puch, Damián. *El duelo: Tesis presentada para optar al grado de Doctor en Jurisprudencia*. Buenos Aires: Imp. "Europea" de M.A. Rosas, 1898.
Ramírez, Carlos Maria. *Conferencias de derecho constitucional*. 2nd ed. Montevideo: Imprenta y Litografía "La Razón," 1897.
[Ramírez, José Pedro]. *La muerte de Servando F. Martínez*. Montevideo: Imprenta Tipográfica a Vapor, 1866.
Ramírez, Juan Andrés. *Selección de discursos y trabajos parlamentarios, 1914–1943*. Montevideo: Barreiro y Ramos, 1945.

Ramos, Juan P. *Los delitos contra el honor*. Buenos Aires: Abelardo-Perrot, 1958.

Regules, Wenceslau. *Breves consideraciones sobre la libertad de la prensa y de las distintas leyes que se han promulgado al respecto en nuestro país (derecho constitucional): Tesis*. Montevideo: Imprenta a Vapor de El Heraldo, 1881.

Registro Nacional de leyes, decretos, y otros documentos: Publicación oficial, 1920. Montevideo: Imprenta Nacional, 1921.

Reglamento de los tribunales de honor de las Fuerzas Armadas: Decreto no. 24.891 (D. 243/969). Montevideo: República Oriental del Uruguay, Ministerio de Defensa Nacional, Departamento Sec. Central, División Bol. Impr., 1978.

Rivanera, José J. *Código de honor comentado: El duelo en la historia, el derecho y la institución castrense*. Buenos Aires: Ediciones Arayú, 1954.

Rivarola, Rodolfo. *Exposición y crítica del Código Penal de la República Argentina*. Vol. 2. Buenos Aires: Félix Lajouane Editor, 1890.

Saint-Thomas, Comte Charles Du Verger. *Nouveau code du duel: Histoire, legislation, droit contemporain*. Paris: E. Dentu, 1879.

Sánchez, Samuel F., and José Panella. *Código argentino sobre el duelo*. Buenos Aires: Imp. Moreno, 1878.

Soler, Sebastián. *Derecho penal argentino*. Vol. 3. Buenos Aires: Tipográfica Editora Argentina, 1951.

Tavernier, Adolphe. *L'art du duel*. Paris: C. Marpon et E. Flammarion, éditeurs, 1885.

Tratados y convenios internacionales suscritos por Uruguay en el período enero de 1871 a diciembre de 1890. Vol. 2. Montevideo: Secretaría del Senado, Documentación y Antecedentes Legislativos, 1993.

Varangot, Jorge. *Virtudes caballerescas*. Buenos Aires: Ediciones P. S. Carra, 1972.

Vásquez Acevedo, Alfredo. *Concordancias y anotaciones del Código Penal de la República Oriental del Uruguay*. Montevideo: Barreiro y Ramos, 1893.

Viale, César. *Jurisprudencia caballeresca argentina: Nueva edición corregida y aumentada*. Buenos Aires: n.p., 1928.

— *Jurisprudencia caballeresca argentina de los últimos treinta y cinco años*. Buenos Aires: Talleres Gráficos Argentinos L.J. Rosso, 1937.

Yñiguez, Eusebio. *Ofensas y desafíos: Recopilación de las leyes que rigen en el duelo y causas originales de éste, tomadas de los mejores tratadistas*. Madrid: Evaristo Sánchez, 1890.

Zuviría, Facundo. *La prensa periódica*. Montevideo: Imprenta de la República, 1857.

Reference Works

Archivo General de la Nación. *Guía de fondos del Archivo General de la Nación*. Montevideo: Archivo General de la Nación, 2009.

Fernández Saldaña, José Maria. *Diccionario uruguayo de biografías, 1810–1940*. Montevideo: Librería Anticuaria Americana Adolfo Linardi, 1945.

Parker, William Belmont. *Uruguayans of To-Day*. London and New York: Hispanic Society of America, 1921.
República Oriental del Uruguay, Presidencia de la Asamblea General del Senado y Presidencia de la Cámara de Representantes. *Parlamentarios uruguayos, 1830/2005*. Montevideo: Ediciones de la Proa, 2006.
Scarone, Arturo. *Diccionario de seudónimos del Uruguay*. 2nd ed. Montevideo: Claudio Garcia y Cia. Editores 1942.
– "La Prensa periódica en el Uruguay, 1852–1865." *Revista Nacional*, nos. 9–25 (1940–44). Digitized at https://anaforas.fic.edu.uy/jspui/handle/123456789/11934.
– *Uruguayos contemporáneos: Nuevo diccionario de datos biográficos y bibliográficos*. Montevideo: Barreiro y Ramos, 1937.

Secondary Sources

Acevedo, Eduardo. *Anales históricos del Uruguay*. Vols. 2–4. Montevideo: Casa A. Barreiro y Ramos, 1933–1934.
Aguirre, Leonel. *Una vida al servicio de un ideal: Artículos y discursos*. Montevideo: Impresora Uruguaya, 1950.
Aguirre Ramírez, Gonzalo. *La Revolución del Quebracho y la conciliación: De Ellauri a Tajes*. Montevideo: Barreiro y Ramos, 1989.
Albornoz Vásquez, Maria Eugenia. "Sufrimientos individuales declinados en plural: La necesaria singularidad de los pleitos por injurias en Hispanoamérica colonial." *Nuevo Mundo, Mundos Nuevos*, no. 5 (2010). https://doi.org/10.4000/nuevomundo.60138.
Arena, Domingo. *Escritos y discursos del Dr. Domingo Arena sobre el Sr. José Batlle y Ordóñez*. Montevideo: n.p., 1942.
Barrán, José Pedro. *Historia de la sensibilidad en el Uruguay*. Vol. 2, *El disciplinamiento (1860–1920)*. Montevideo: Ediciones de la Banda Oriental, 1990.
Barrán, José Pedro, and Benjamín Nahúm. *Batlle, los estancieros y el imperio británico*. Vol. 3, *El nacimiento del batllismo*. Montevideo: Ediciones de la Banda Oriental, 1982.
Benedetti, Mario. *El país de la cola de paja*. 6th ed. Montevideo: Editorial Arca, 1967.
Berro, Guido, and Antonio L. Turnes. "Autopsia histórica: La muerte de Washington Beltrán Barbat en 1920." *Revista Médica del Uruguay* 27, no. 2 (2011): 112–20.
Billacois, François. *The Duel: Its Rise and Fall in Early Modern France*. New Haven: Yale University Press, 1990.
Braga-Pinto, César. "Journalists, *Capoieras*, and the Duel in Nineteenth-Century Rio de Janeiro." *Hispanic American Historical Review* 94, no. 4 (2014): 581–614.

Braun Menéndez, Armando. "Un duelo histórico: Mackenna-Carrera." *Mapocho* (Santiago, Chile), no. 28 (1980): 29–35.

Burkholder, Mark. "Honor and Honors in Colonial Spanish America." In *The Faces of Honor: Sex, Shame and Violence in Colonial Latin America*, edited by Lyman L. Johnson and Sonya Lipsett-Rivera, 1–17. Albuquerque: University of New Mexico Press, 1998.

Caetano, Gerardo. *La república conservadora, 1916–1929*. Vol. 1, *El "alto" a las reformas*. Montevideo: Editorial Fin de Siglo, 1992.

– *La república conservadora, 1916–1929*. Vol. 2, *La "guerra de posiciones."* Montevideo: Editorial Fin de Siglo, 1993.

Caimari, Lila. *While the City Sleeps: A History of Pistoleros, Policemen, and the Crime Beat in Buenos Aires before Perón*. Oakland: University of California Press, 2017.

Candea, Mattei. "The Duelling Ethic and the Spirit of Libel Law: Matters and Materials of Honour in France." *Law Text Culture*, no. 23 (2019): 171–97.

Caulfield, Sueann, Sarah C. Chambers, and Lara Putnam, eds. *Honor, Status, and Law in Modern Latin America*. Durham: Duke University Press, 2005.

Cerrano, Carolina. "La campaña presidencial del herrerismo en 1946 desde *El Debate*." *Nuevo Mundo, Mundos Nuevos*, no. 12 (2017). https://doi.org/10.4000/nuevomundo.70697.

Chamberlain, Ryan. *Pistols, Politics and the Press: Dueling in 19th Century American Journalism*. Jefferson, NC: McFarland & Co., 2009.

Chasteen, John Charles. "Fighting Words: The Discourse of Insurgency in Latin American History." *Latin American Research Review* 28, no. 3 (1993): 83–111.

– *Heroes on Horseback: A Life and Times of the Last Gaucho Caudillos*. Albuquerque: University of New Mexico Press, 1995.

– "Violence for Show: Knife Dueling on a Nineteenth-Century Cattle Frontier." In *The Problem of Order in Changing Societies: Essays on Crime and Policing in Argentina and Uruguay*, edited by Lyman L. Johnson, 47–64. Albuquerque: University of New Mexico Press, 1990.

Cristiani, Roberto J. *Reseña histórica del cuerpo de gimnasia y esgrima del ejército y su proyección en la vida nacional: Algunos aspectos de su evolución entre 1897–1960*. Buenos Aires: Servicio de Informaciones del Ejército, 1968.

De la Fuente Monge, Gregorio. "Enrique Romero Jiménez: Un presbítero revolucionario entre España y Argentina." In *Patriotas entre naciones: Élites emigrantes españolas en Argentina (1870–1940)*, ed. Marcela García Sabatini, 17–57. Madrid: Editorial Complutense, 2010.

Ehrick, Christine. *The Shield of the Weak: Feminism and the State in Uruguay, 1903–1933*. Albuquerque: University of New Mexico Press, 2005.

El Día, 1886–1981: 95 años al servicio de la libertad. Montevideo: Imprenta Artegraf, 1981.

Etchechury Barrera, Mario. "'Defensores de la humanidad y la civilización': Las legiones extranjeras de Montevideo, entre el mito cosmopolita y la eclosión de las 'nacionalidades' (1838–1851)." *Historia* 50, no. 2 (2017): 491–524.

Fernández Saldaña, José Maria. *Gobierno y época de Santos*. Montevideo: Litografía e Imprenta "Del Comercio," 1940.

– *La violencia en el Uruguay del siglo XIX (Crónicas de muertes, duelos, atentados y ejecuciones)*. Montevideo: Cal y Canto, 1996.

Fischer, Diego. *Qué tupé!: Batlle-Beltrán, ¿Duelo o asesinato?* Montevideo: Editorial Sudamericana Uruguaya, 2010.

Freeman, Joanne B. "Dueling as Politics: Reinterpreting the Burr-Hamilton Duel." *William and Mary Quarterly* 53, no. 2 (1996): 289–318.

Frevert, Ute. *Men of Honour: A Social and Cultural History of the Duel*. Cambridge, MA: Polity Press, 1995.

Gayol, Sandra. "'Honor Moderno': The Significance of Honor in Fin-de-siècle Argentina." *Hispanic American Historical Review* 84, no. 3 (2004): 475–98.

– *Honor y duelo en la Argentina moderna*. Buenos Aires: Siglo Veintiuno Editores, 2008.

Gomensoro, José L. *Crónicas de historia: Episodios, anécdotas y frases*. 2nd ed. Montevideo: Ediciones de la Sociedad Amigos del Libro Rioplatense, 1937.

González, Ariosto D. *De la revolución del Quebracho a la conciliación de noviembre*. Montevideo: La Revista Nacional, 1939.

González Arrili, Bernardo. *Vida de Lisandro de la Torre*. Buenos Aires: Talleres "Orientación," 1940.

González Conzi, Efraín, and Roberto B. Giudice. *Batlle y el batllismo*. 2nd ed. Montevideo: Editorial Medina, 1959.

Greenberg, Kenneth S. *Honor and Slavery*. Princeton: Princeton University Press, 1996.

Hamilton, Mariano. *Duelos: Los sangrientos combates por el honor en la historia argentina*. Buenos Aires: Planeta, 2019.

Hentschke, Jens. *Philosophical Polemics, School Reform and Nation-Building in Uruguay, 1868–1915: Reforma Vareliana and Batllismo from a Transnational Perspective*. Baden-Baden: Nomos, 2016.

Hopton, Richard. *Pistols at Dawn: A History of Duelling*. London: Piatkus Books, 2007.

Hughes, Stephen C. "Men of Steel: Dueling, Honor, and Politics in Liberal Italy." In *Men and Violence: Gender, Honor, and Rituals in Modern Europe and America*, edited by Pieter Spierenburg, 64–81. Columbus: Ohio State University Press, 1998.

– *Politics of the Sword: Dueling, Honor, and Masculinity in Modern Italy*. Columbus: Ohio State University Press, 2007.

Johnson, Lyman L., and Sonya Lipsett-Rivera, eds. *The Faces of Honor: Sex, Shame and Violence in Colonial Latin America*. Albuquerque: University of New Mexico Press, 1998.

Karush, Matthew B. *Culture of Class: Radio and Cinema in the Making of a Divided Argentina, 1920–1946*. Durham: Duke University Press, 2012.

Kierszenbaum, Leandro. "Between the Accepted and the Legal: Violence in Honor Disputes in Uruguay (1945–1970)." *International Journal of Politics, Culture, and Society* 25, nos. 1–3 (2012): 35–48.

Lacalle Herrera, Luis Alberto. *Herrera: Un nacionalismo oriental*. Montevideo: Ediciones de la Banda Oriental, 1978.

Larra, Raúl. *Lisandro de la Torre: El solitario de Pinas*. Buenos Aires: Hyspamerica, 1988.

López-Alves, Fernando. *Between the Economy and the Polity in the River Plate: Uruguay, 1811–1890*. London: ILAS, University of London, 1993.

– *State Formation and Democracy in Latin America, 1810–1900*. Durham: Duke University Press, 2000.

– "State Reform and Welfare in Uruguay, 1890–1930." In *Studies in the Formation of the Nation-State in Latin America*, edited by James Dunkerley, 94–111. London: ILAS, University of London, 2002.

Luengo, Jordi. "Masculinidad reglada en los lances de honor: Desafíos burgueses en el cénit de un fin de época (1870–1910)." *Rúbrica Contemporánea* 7, no. 13 (2018): 59–79.

Manini Rios, Carlos. *Anoche me llamó Batlle*. 2nd ed. Montevideo: Talleres de Imprenta Letras, 1973.

– *Una nave en la tormenta: Una etapa de transición, 1919–1923*. Montevideo: Crónica Política del Uruguay Contemporáneo, 1972.

Markarian, Vania. *Left in Transformation: Uruguayan Exiles and the Latin American Human Rights Network, 1967–1984*. New York: Routledge, 2005.

Martínez, José Luciano. *Corazones y lanzas (episodios-anécdotas)*. Montevideo: Tall. Graf. Prometeo, 1943.

– *José Cándido Bustamante*. Montevideo: Ediciones Ceibo, 1943.

Mateos Fernández, Juan Carlos. "Cuestión de honor: Los periodistas se baten en duelo." *Historia y Comunicación Social*, no. 3 (1998): 323–41.

McAleer, Kevin. *Dueling: The Cult of Honor in Fin de Siècle Germany*. Princeton: Princeton University Press, 1994.

Melián Lafinur, Luis. *Semblanzas del pasado: Juan Carlos Gómez*. Montevideo: "El Anticuario" de Brignole y Cía., 1915.

Mora Guarnido, José. *Batlle y Ordóñez: Figura y transfigura*. Montevideo: Impresora Uruguaya, 1931.

Moyano Dellepiane, Hernán Antonio. "Jurisprudencia caballeresca porteña." *Revista Cruz de Sur* 4, special issue, no. 7 (2014): 9–558.

Nye, Robert A. "Fencing, the Duel and Republican Manhood in the Third Republic." *Journal of Contemporary History* 25, nos. 2–3 (1990): 365–77.

– *Masculinity and Male Codes of Honor in Modern France*. Berkeley: University of California Press, 1998. 1st ed., Oxford University Press, 1993.

Oller, Raúl, and Raúl F. Casado. *Los duelos*. Buenos Aires: Centro Editor de América Latina S.A., 1972.

Parker, David S. "El código penal y las 'leyes caballerescas': Hacia el duelo legal en el Uruguay, 1880–1920." *Anuario IEHS*, no. 14 (1999): 295–311.

– "Gentlemanly Responsibility and Insults of a Woman: Dueling and the Unwritten Rules of Public Life in Uruguay, 1860–1920." In *Gender, Sexuality, and Power in Latin America since Independence*, edited by Katherine Elaine Bliss and William E. French, 109–32. Lanham, MD: Rowman & Littlefield, 2007.

– "Honor Ideology, Dueling Culture, and Judicial Lies in 1920s Uruguay." *Oxford Research Encyclopedia of Latin American History*. Oxford University Press, 2016. https://doi.org/10.1093/acrefore/9780199366439.013.382.

– "Law, Honor, and Impunity in Spanish America: The Debate over Dueling, 1870–1920." *Law and History Review* 19, no. 2 (2001): 311–41.

Pedemonte, Juan Carlos. *El año terrible: Hombres y hechos de su tiempo, Latorre, Santos, Tajes*. Montevideo: Barreiro y Ramos, 1956.

Pelúas, Daniel. *José Batlle y Ordóñez: El hombre*. Montevideo: Editorial Fin de Siglo, 2001.

Piccato, Pablo. "Politics and the Technology of Honor: Dueling in Turn-of-the-Century Mexico." *Journal of Social History* 33, no. 2 (1999): 331–54.

– *The Tyranny of Opinion: Honor in the Construction of the Mexican Public Sphere*. Durham: Duke University Press, 2010.

Pintos Diago, César. *Luis Alberto de Herrera: Su vida, sus obras, sus ideas*. Montevideo: Claudio García Editor, 1930.

Pivel Devoto, Juan E. "Estudio Preliminar," introduction to reprint edition of Francisco Bauzá, *Historia de la dominación española en el Uruguay*. Vol. 1, part 1. Montevideo: Ministerio de Instrucción Pública y Previsión Social, Biblioteca Artigas, 1965.

Real de Azúa, Carlos. *El impulso y su freno: Tres décadas de batllismo y las raíces de la crisis uruguaya*. Montevideo: Ediciones de la Banda Oriental, 1964.

Reddy, William M. "Condottieri of the Pen: Journalists and the Public Sphere in Postrevolutionary France (1815–1850)." *American Historical Review* 99, no. 5 (1999): 1546–70.

Rico, Álvaro. "1, 2, 3 … Apunten, ¡Fuego! (El duelo, el honor y la épica en los '60)." *Encuentros*, no. 7 (2001): 135–74.

Rilla, José. *La actualidad del pasado: Usos de la historia en la política de partidos del Uruguay (1942–1972)*. Montevideo: Editorial Sudamericana, 2008.

Rodríguez, Julia. *Civilizing Argentina: Science, Medicine, and the Modern State*. Chapel Hill: University of North Carolina Press, 2006.

Sábato, Hilda. *The Many and the Few: Political Participation in Republican Buenos Aires*. Stanford: Stanford University Press, 2001.

Saítta, Sylvia. *Regueros de tinta: El diario "Crítica" en la década de 20.* Buenos Aires: Sudamericana, 1998.

Salvatore, Ricardo D., Carlos Aguirre, and Gilbert M. Joseph, eds. *Crime and Punishment in Latin America: Law and Society since Late Colonial Times.* Durham: Duke University Press, 2001.

Sánchez, Raquel. "Honor de periodistas: Libertad de prensa y reputación pública en la España liberal." In *La cultura de la espada: De honor, duelos y otros lances,* edited by Raquel Sánchez and José Antonio Guillén Berrendero, 305–32. Madrid: Editorial Dykinson, 2019.

Sanders, James E. *The Vanguard of the Atlantic World: Creating Modernity, Nation, and Democracy in Nineteenth-Century Latin America.* Durham: Duke University Press, 2014.

Schelotto, Magdalena. "La dictadura cívico-militar uruguaya (1973–1985): La construcción de la noción de víctima y la figura del exiliado en el Uruguay post-dictatorial." *Nuevo Mundo, Mundos Nuevos,* no. 5 (2015). https://doi.org/10.4000/nuevomundo.67888.

Schinca, Milton. *Boulevar Sarandí: 250 años de Montevideo, anécdotas, gentes, sucesos.* Montevideo: Ediciones de la Banda Oriental, 1976.

Silva Grucci, Guillermo. *Duelos en el Río de la Plata.* Montevideo: Fin de Siglo Editorial, 2018.

– *Historias que no nos contaron.* Montevideo: Fin de Siglo Editorial, 2017.

Soliño, Víctor. *Crónica de los años locos.* Montevideo: Ediciones de la Banda Oriental, 1983.

Speckmann Guerra, Elisa. "Los jueces, el honor y la muerte: Un análisis de la justicia (Ciudad de México, 1871–1931)." *Historia Mexicana* 55, no. 4 (2006): 1411–66.

Taylor, Philip B. "The Uruguayan Coup d'État of 1933." *Hispanic American Historical Review* 32, no. 3 (1952): 301–20.

Tejera, Adolfo. *Retrato de un ciudadano: Apuntes para la biografía de Juan Andrés Ramírez.* Montevideo: Barreiro y Ramos, 1945.

Trías, Walter. *Batlle periodista.* Montevideo: n.p., 1958.

Undurraga Schüler, Verónica. "Cuando las afrentas se lavaban con sangre: Honor, masculinidad y duelos de espadas en el siglo XVIII chileno." *Historia* 41, no. 1 (2008): 165–88.

Vanger, Milton I. *The Model Country: José Batlle y Ordóñez of Uruguay, 1907–1915.* Waltham, MA: Brandeis University Press, 1980.

– *Uruguay's José Batlle y Ordóñez: The Determined Visionary, 1915–1917.* Boulder: Lynne Rienner, 2010.

Vidaurreta de Tjarks, Alicia. "Juan Carlos Gómez, periodista y polemista," *Revista Histórica* 34, nos. 100–2 (1963): 1–137.

Weschler, Lawrence. *A Miracle, a Universe: Settling Accounts with Torturers.* New York: Pantheon Books, 1990.

Wyatt-Brown, Bertram. *Southern Honor: Ethics and Behavior in the Old South.* New York: Oxford University Press, 1982.

Zum Felde, Alberto. *Evolución histórica del Uruguay y esquema de su sociología.* Montevideo: Librerías Maximino García, 1941.

Visual Media

"Uruguay de Duelo: Ofensores y Ofendidos." Television documentary series by Papico Cibils, aired in 2003 on Tevé Ciudad, Montevideo. 9 episodes. Courtesy of Tevé Ciudad.

Index

acceptable speech, 5, 11, 132, 136, 163; disputes over the boundaries of, 61, 85–9, 164; enforcing the norms of, 29–30, 50–1
Acción, 138
Acevedo Díaz, Eduardo, 9
actas (of duels), 38–42, 71, 124, 167; *acta del terreno*, 41–2, 49, 73; *acta previa*, 38–41, 74, 98; publication of, 41–2, 103, 149, 168
Aguerrondo, General Mario, 140, 144
Aguirre, Gil, 65
Aguirre, Leonel, 9, 117
Aguirre Ramírez, Gonzalo, 3, 160–2
Allende Gossens, Salvador, 143
Álvarez Vignoli, Sofía, 134–5
Andreoli, Enrique, 106
anti-dueling leagues, in Europe, 104, 120
Aparicio, Timoteo, 65
Arena, Domingo, 37–9
Argentina, frequency of duels in, 6, 148–51
Aróstegui, Abdón, 21–3, 25, 99

Barrán, José Pedro, 104

Barraza, Humberto, 150
battery (*lesiones corporales*), 9, 102, 181n32
Batlle Berres, Luis, 9, 33, 37–9, 133, 137–9
Batlle Pacheco, César, 41, 126
Batlle Santos, Marcos, 129
Batlle y Ordóñez, José, 9, 14–16, 50, 52, 60–2, 91–2, 103, 116, 130, 133; against self-censorship, 88, 90, 108; duel with Washington Beltrán and arrest, 10, 116–21, 135; opinion on dueling in general, 67, 90; postponement of challenges while president, 108–9
Batlle, Jorge, 9, 140–1, 144
batllismo, 16
Bauzá, Francisco, 9, 74
Bay, Juan, 8
Belinzón, Juan, 44
Beltrán, Washington, 9, 10, 114, 116–20, 167
Beltrán, Washington (*hijo*), 162–3
Benedetti, Mario, 130
Bermúdez, Washington, 82–8, 154, 193n101
Bien Público, El, 17, 25, 27, 83

Biglieri, Yolivan, 150–1
Billacois, François, 165
Blanco and Colorado Parties: clientelism of, 14–16, 53, 64; partisan conflict between, 12–13, 16, 18, 64–5; power sharing, 13, respective positions in 1920 on legalizing the duel, 115, 118–20
Blanco Party: internal factionalism in, 13–14, 16–17, as long-standing party of opposition, 13–15; party self-image, 13, 15
Bocage, Judge, 106
Bordabehere, Enzo, 149
Bordaberry, Juan Maria, 148
Botana, Natalio, 135
Brazil, 13, 143
Bruera, Leopoldo, 153
Brum, Alfeo, 122, 139
Brum, Baltasar, 9, 53, 74–6, 82, 122–6
Buchelli, David, 19–29, 31, 34–6, 44, 68, 95, 99, 101–2
Buenos Aires, as venue for duels between Uruguayans, 6, 69, 196n42
bullfighting, abolition of, 125
Buquet, Sebastián, 116
Bustamante, José Cándido, 8–9, 21–3, 25, 72–3, 82

calumnia, 45; legal definition of, 186n79
Calvo, Nicolás, 55–9, 61, 68, 82
Camaño Rosa, Antonio, 130
Cantón, Dr Eliseo, 44
Carnelli, Lorenzo, 105–6, 110
carta-poder (dueling power of attorney), 32–5
Castillo, Judge Narciso del, 25, 28
Castro, Eduardo de, 41, 74, 126
Catholic Church, 20
Catholic Workers' Circle, 100
caudillos, 13–15, 60, 64–5

Cesario, Andrés Facundo, 8
challenges (*desafíos*), 9; involving public functionaries, 93–4, 122; of judges, 122
Chateauvillard, Comte de, 8, 30–1, 132, 136, 139
chivalry. *See* honor
Clavería, Saúl Humberto, 152–3
Code of Criminal Procedure (*Código de Instrucción Criminal*) of 1867 (Uruguay), 28, 95
Cold War, 134, 143
Colegiado (Collegial Executive), 16, 118, 133, 182n46
Colonia, Uruguay, 6
Colorado Party: as governing party, 13, 15; internal factionalism in, 13–14, 16–17; party self-image, 15, 18
Constitution, of 1830 (Uruguay), 50, 186n83; of 1918 (Uruguay), 130; of 1952 (Uruguay), 133
Constitutional Party, 14
Cooke, John William, 150
Coronel Nieto, Jorge, 158–9
Correo Español, El, 76–82
Cortinas, Ismael, 114–15
Costa Podestá, Alberto, 32
Criminal Code (*Código Penal*) of 1890 (Argentina), 47; of 1922 (Argentina), 148–9; of 1889 (Uruguay), 94–5, 101–3, 106–7, 114, 119, 121; of 1933 (Uruguay), 133, 158, 209n86
Crítica (Buenos Aires), 135
criticism of dueling: as against modern progress and civilization, 96–7, 99, 111, 144, 155; as anti-Christian, 20, 96, 99–101; as class privilege, 111, 152, 155, 159, 163; as defending the corrupt, 54–5, 163; as pointless, 48; as usurpation of authority, 94, 99, 101, 154–5, 158–9

criticism of specific duels: as disproportionate, 72–3, 125; as trivial, 70–1, 73–6
Crivellari, Guilio, 111–12
Cusano, Ángel Maria, 142

Debate, El, 128, 140
de la Torre, Lisandro, 63, 149
defamation laws, 12, 21, 45–9, 80; alleged inadequacy of, 44–5, 49, 51, 132–3, 156–62, 188n106; in Argentina, 47; burden of proof in, 45–8; intent (*animus injuriandi*) in, 47; proposed reforms to, 147, 157–9; truth defense in, 46–7. See also press law
Delcasse, Dr Carlos, 180n14
Demicheli, Alberto, 134–7, 139
democracy, return to (1984), 134, 152
Día, El, 17, 52, 60–1, 108, 116
di Santi, Miguel, 52
Diario del Plata, 17, 75, 93, 125, 127
Díaz, José, 155–6, 158
Díaz, Porfirio, 117
Díaz Maynard, Daniel, 155, 158
Dickmann, Enrique, 44
director of combat, 40–1, 73
Dodo Pozzolo, Ernesto, 139
Dominguez, Cándido, 137, 168
Dubra, Lieutenant Arturo, 42
dueling: as damage control, 60, 62–3, 65; in Europe, 8, 9, 148, 151; history (Argentina), 7, 149–51; history (Uruguay), 7–8; as intimidation, 57–8, 61, 67–8, 82–7, 142, 163; as murder, 72–3, 79, 85, 91; as "necessary evil," 49, 67, 114–15, 156; penalties for, 20, 102, 180n16; post-1933 decline, 128–31, 133, 136–7; post-1957 resurgence, 12, 137–47, 151; by a president, 108–9, 122–4; as publicity-seeking, 60, 63–6, 163. See also repression of dueling

dueling codes. See honor codes
duelists, idealized qualities of, 67–8, 82
duelo criollo, 53, 64–5; double standard in legal treatment of, 111–13
duels: fatalities in, 8–9, 64–5, 72, 76–82, 95–9, 107, 119; "first-blood," 64, 71, 73; frequency of, 9, 64, 108, 132–3, 167–77; motives for, 11, 57–8, 59–60, 79–80; as permanent closure of a dispute, 49, 62–4; 81, 141; as public spectacle, 58–9, 62, 82, 122–6; publicity of, 41–2, 82, 124–6, 149, 168–9

electoral fraud, accusations of, 15, 116–17, 123–4
emotions, 65–6, 76
Erro, Enrique, 139–40, 142–3
Erro, Enrique J. (*hijo*), 142
Espalter, José Luis, 73
España Moderna, La, 76–82
Estrada Cabrera, Manuel, 117
exiles, 6, 7, 82, 148
explanations (*explicaciones*), 32–5, 47
extradition treaty, Argentina-Uruguay, 6, 121

Fasano, Federico, 152–3
fencing, 8, 60, 137
Fernández, Rear Admiral Guillermo, 144
Ferreira Aldunate, Wilson, 140, 144
Ferreira Martínez, Mario, 74
Flores, Venancio, 72
Flores Mora, Manuel, 140–1, 144
forum shopping, 28–9, 44–9, 68–9
Frente Amplio (Broad Front), 18, 134, 143, 154
Frondizi, Arturo, 150
Frugoni, Emilio, 18, 63, 94, 119, 121, 158

García Pintos, Salvador, 128
García Pintos, Salvador (*hijo*), 147–8
Garibaldi, Giuseppe, 13, 19–20, 26–7, 29
Garzón, Eugenio, 9, 103
Gaudin, Raúl, 139–40
Gayol, Sandra, 52, 169
Gelli, Iacopo, 42–3, 54, 169–70
gentlemanly jurisprudence (*jurisprudencia caballeresca*), 43
gentlemanly responsibility, 50–1, 60–1, 64, 66–7, 90, 108, 128; and class, 52–4; and exclusion of women, 51–2. *See also* journalism: responsibility in
Gestido, General Oscar, 140, 147–8
Ghigliani, Francisco, 116, 118; attack on Alberto Demicheli, 134–7, 139
Giménez Zapiola, Horacio, 43
Giordano, Alfredo, 107, 119
Giribaldi Heguy, Juan, 106–7, 110, 119
Goliardi, Adolfo, 137
Goliardi, José, 137
Gomensoro, Judge Juan José, 105–6, 118, 200n103
Gómez, José, 83, 85
Gómez, Juan Carlos, 9, 55–9, 61, 68, 82
Gómez, Pantaleón, 9, 101
Gomeza, Arturo, 107, 119
Goñi, Lieutenant, 53
Graña, Ángel B., 128
Guerra, José, 33
Guerra Grande, 12–3, 20
Güiraldes, Carlos, 149
Gutiérrez, Juan, 159

Haedo, Eduardo Víctor, 128
Heraldo, El, 53, 87
Herrera, Luis Alberto de, 9, 103, 108–9, 122–5
Herrera, Tácito, 118
Herrera y Obes, Julio, 15, 61, 87, 138
Herrero y Espinosa, Manuel, 68

Herrero y Salas, Dr, 77
Hierro Gambardella, Luis, 144
Hilo Eléctrico, El, 24, 70
homicide, 9, 181n32
honor: as a cultural norm, 4, 5, 28, 66; disputes over the idea of, 99, 155; erosion of culture of, 130–1, 137–8, 143–5, 151; performance of, 59, 66–76
honor codes, 4, 8, 19, 90; as an alternative/parallel legal system, 5, 10–11, 28–30, 31–49, 95, 102, 132–3, 156, 163–5; coexistence/interaction with criminal law, 28–9, 102, 133, 164–5; conflict with criminal law, 28, 94–5, 102–6, 155; and defamation law compared, 44–9; principles expressed in, 29–32, 36–7, 42–3, 66–8, 74, 124, 156–7, 162–3; texts (European), 8, 42–3, 54; texts (Spanish American), 31, 184n42. *See also* laws of honor
honor tribunals, 42–3, 136–42, 145, 153; alleged role in the decline of dueling, 127–31, 133, 151, 159–61; composition of, 42, 120; history and antecedents, 104, 120–1, 201n112; legalism of rulings, 42–3; and Ley de Duelos, 120–1; as model for defamation law reform, 147, 157–8
House of Representatives (Cámara de Representantes), Uruguay, 24–5, 28, 93, 110, 114; Codes Commission, 107, 111, 115–16, 118, 120–1; Commission on Constitution, Codes, General Legislation and Administration, 152–3, 155–60
Hughes, Steven, 169–70

Idiartegaray, Alejo, 43
Illía, Arturo, 150
implicancias scandal, 128, 203n142
Indipendente, L', 19, 70

INDEX

Ingenieros, Salvador, 21
injuria, 5, 45, 156; legal definition of, 186n79
Irureta Goyena, José, 103–6, 197n62
Isaza, Monsignor, 22–3, 27

Jiménez de Aréchaga, Justino, 119
Jouan, Ramiro, 42
Journalism: culture of, 6, 17, 60–3, 130, 133, 149, 151, 152; cycles of escalating attack in, 60–2, 162; legal regulation of, 46–7, 50, 209n92; pseudonyms in, 46; responsibility in, 30, 50–1, 60–1, 156, 188n106; self-regulation of, 87–8. *See also* gentlemanly responsibility; press freedom; press laws
Justicia, 70–1, 124

Korzeniak, José, 161

Lago, Judge Pedro, 118, 200n103
Lamas, Daniel, 152
Lamas, Dr Alfonso, 110, 116
Lápido, José, 89–90
Lápido, Vicente, 89, 90
Larcher, General Rodolfo, 150
Latorre, Lorenzo, 14
law: nature and purpose of, 102–3, 114–15; respect for rule of, 4, 28, 95, 104–7, 110–11, 114–15, 133, 155–6, 160, 164–5; versus social convention, 93–5, 101–2, 110, 114–15
"laws of honor," 11, 21, 28–9, 134; as a civilizing force, 100–1, 112–13, 136–7, 156; conflicts in interpretation of, 11, 29–30, 84–5; norms and values embodied in, 28, 48–9, 66–7; violations of, 29, 56, 83, 123, 143. *See also* honor codes
Lebel, Oscar, 153
legalization of dueling: debates (Argentina), 6, 148–9; debates (Uruguay) 11, 110–15
Ley de Caducidad, 1989 referendum to repeal, 154
Ley de Duelos (Law #7253 of 1920), 3, 11–12, 118, 120–1, 133; debate on impact of, 121–31, 147–8, 151, 159–61; repeal of, 3, 12, 134, 147–8, 152–61
"Ley Mordaza," 50. *See also* journalism: legal regulation of
liberalism, 5–6, 53–4, 100, 132, 162, 165–6
Lisidini, José, 129
López, Lucio Vicente, 9
López-Alves, Fernando, 12, 14
López Vago, Leopoldo, 61–2

Mackenna, General Juan, 7
Mañana, La, 17, 125
Mansilla, Lucio V., 101
Martínez, Servando, 8, 72–3, 82
masculinity and feminization, 4, 51–2, 61–2, 134, 155, 207n47
Masoller, Battle of, 15
mazorcas, 64, 190n31
Menes García, Rubén, 144
Mibelli, Celestino, 119, 124–5, 201n107
Mibelli, Roberto, 110
Michaelson, Ruperto, 103
military: accountability of, 150–1, 154; participation in civilian politics, 134, 145, 151; role in preserving dueling culture, 137–45, 150
Military Code of 1884 (Uruguay), 95, 98, 102
military courts, 98, 168. *See also* Special Military Honor Tribunal
military dictatorship: Uruguay (1973–85), 134, 148, 151; Argentina (1976–82), 150, 151
Minelli, Judge Juan M., 116

Minelli, Pablo, 92–3,
Miranda, César, 108
Mitre, Bartolomé, 17, 77
Montevideo, 6–7, 13, 16, 170
Montevideo Times, 96–7
Morell, Antonio, 159–60
Moreno, Carlos, 43
Movimiento de Liberación Nacional) (MLN) (Tupamaros), 134, 142–3, 162, 166
Moyano Dellepiane, Antonio, 169–70
Mujica, José, 3, 162, 166
Muñoz Anaya, Carlos (fiscal), 25, 27, 28

Nacional, El (Buenos Aires), 80; (Montevideo), 68, 97
Nación, La (Buenos Aires), 80–1; (Montevideo), 24, 83
Negro Timoteo, El, 82–6, 154
New York Times, 150
Nicosía, Salvatore "Totó," 19–27, 28–9, 34–5, 68–71, 82
November Conciliation, 15, 50
Novísima Recopilación de las Leyes (Spain), 20, 25
Nye, Robert, 8, 169–70

offenses against honor, 32, 79; rights granted to the offended party, 36–8, 84, 98
Ongañía, General Juan Carlos, 150
Oribe, Manuel, 13

Pacheco Areco, Jorge, 143, 145
País, El, 17, 53, 116–17, 125, 127
Palomeque, Agapo Luis, 155
Palomeque, Alberto, 9
Pampillón, José Maria, 65
Paraguayan War (1865–70), 14, 72
parliamentary immunity, 25, 93–4, 106, 116, 118

Partido Nacional. *See* Blanco Party
Pastor, Judge Dr, 103–4
Paullier, Washington, 92–4, 189n26
Paul y Angulo, José, 65, 76–82, 102
Paysandú, 64, 65, 189n30
Paz, José Maria, 7
Paz, La, 87–8
Peace of 1851, 13
Pedernal, Battle of, 65
Pereira Reverbel, Ulysses, 139
Perón, Juan, dueling during government of, 149–50
physicians, in duels, 40, 42, 69, 73
Piccato, Pablo, 8
Pinedo, Federico, 149
Pini, Eugenio, 8
Pintos, General Juan A., 53, 89–90, 154
Pintos, Juan Luis, 140
Pistarini, General Pascual, 150
pistols, dueling (technical characteristics), 74; norms of duels involving, 74–6, 119–20, 143; Remington, 77, 95
Plata, El, 167, 177
police; accusations of corruption in, 89–90, 116, 152–4; duelists' efforts to evade, 69, 92–3, 103; intervention to prevent duels 75, 92–3, 103–4, 108, 110; investigation of duels, 105–6, 108, 110, 116
Polleri, Felipe, 21
postivism, legal, 104, 115
prensa brava. *See* journalism: culture of
press freedom, 50, 54, 148, 152, 156–7; dueling disputes and, 29, 47–8, 82–5, 87–90, 128, 132, 157, 164
press laws: of 1935, 130, 133; decree-law of 1984, 158; Law 16.099 of 1989, 158, 161–2. *See also* journalism: legal regulation of
principismo, 14, 17

public sphere, question of
    defining, 46–7
Pueblo, El, 134–6
Puyol, Dr Andrés Felipe, 136

Quebracho Revolution, 1886, 14, 50
Quinteros, 64, 189n30

Ramírez, Carlos Maria, 9, 74, 87–8
Ramírez, José Pedro, 72–3
Ramírez, Juan Andrés, 9, 74–6, 82,
    108, 116, 118, 120–1, 127, 160–1,
    167, 170–1; legalization proposal
    (1918–19), 110–11, 135; arguments for
    legalization, 111–15, 156
Ramírez, Juan Augusto, 72–3
Razón, La, 17, 83
refusal to duel, explanations for, 144, 151
repression of dueling, 98–9, 168; in
    Argentina, 7, 149–51; clamor for more
    energy in, 104–5, 107; critique of
    capriciousness of, 104, 106–7, 110–11
República, La, 152–3
Revello, Nicolás, 8
*Revista de Derecho, Jurisprudencia y
    Administración*, 122
Revolution of the Lances (1870), 65
Ribas, General Juan P., 137–9, 143–4
Rivera, Fructuoso, 13
Riverós, Colonel Alberto, 126
Rodríguez Anaya, Agustín, 150
Rodríguez Larreta, Aureliano, 160
Rodríguez Larreta, Eduardo, 118
Roldán, César M., 52
Romero Giménez, Enrique, 65,
    76–82, 101, 102
Rosas, Juan Manuel de, 7, 13
Rosselló, P. J., 80, 82
Roxlo, Carlos, 9, 35, 108
Ruprecht, Guillermo, 95–9, 103

Sabat, Mariano, 83, 85
Salgado, José, 111–12, 115
Sampognaro, Virgilio, 92–4, 108, 121
Sánchez, Amador, 60
Sanguinetti, Julio Maria, 3, 9, 12, 140–1,
    144, 152, 161–2
San Martín, José de, 7
Sanmartín, Juan, 89, 90
Santos, General Máximo, 14–15, 50
Saravia, Aparicio, 15
Saravia, Villanueva, 125, 203n132
Schiaffino, Dr Rafael, 100, 116
Schilemberg, Alberto, 82–6, 154
Secco Illa, Joaquín, 18, 119, 158
seconds (*padrinos, testigos*), 9, 32, 35; as
    advocates, 37, 40, 68; conciliatory
    role of, 32, 34; criticism of, 36, 72,
    125, 127; disputes between, 11, 36–7,
    43; duty to determine if cause existed
    for a duel, 35–6; duty to negotiate
    and guarantee duel conditions, 35,
    40, 68, 73; unquestioned authority
    of, 23, 35–6
Sena, General Danilo, 142–3
Senate (Senado), Uruguay, 3, 119, 135;
    Commission on Constitution and
    Legislation, 160–1
Seregni, General Liber, 9, 10, 18, 143–6
Serrato, José, 137–9
Sienra, Gerardo, 122
Siglo, El, 17, 24, 88, 93, 98
Silva Riestra, Juan, 140
Smith, Juan, 68–71, 82
Socialista, El, 101
Socialist Party of Uruguay, 18
Solsona y Flores, Manuel, 43
Sorín, Carlos Maria, 106, 118
Sosa, Julio Maria, 116
Spain, 7, 25, 28, 78, 80, 94–5, 101–2, 120
Special Military Honor Tribunal,
    143–5, 152–4

Suárez, Gregorio, 65
Suárez, Juan Pedro, 89–90

Tajes, General Máximo, 15, 50
Tejera, Joaquín, 95–9, 103
Telégrafo Marítimo, El, 24, 97
Terra, Duvimioso, 45, 68, 110, 112, 116, 118, 127, 156–7
Terra, Gabriel: 1933 coup and dictatorship, 17, 130, 133, 149
testaferro (front man): accusations of duelists being, 68, 83
Tribuna Popular, La, 17, 53, 60, 75, 88–90, 98, 168
Tupamaros. *See* MLN, Movimiento de Liberación Nacional

Urrutia, José, 125
Uruguay (newspaper), 134–5
Uruguay News, 96, 98
US weapons, scandal involving diversion of, 140

Varangot, Jorge, 169–70
Varela, Admiral Benigno, 150–1
Varela, Jacobo, 71
Varela, José Pedro, 9, 61
Vasconcellos, Amílcar, 140, 147–8
Vázquez Acevedo, Alfredo, 99, 114
Viale, César, 169–70
Vidal, Francisco Antonino, 50
Villar López, Lieut. Col. Luis Joaquín, 139
violence, attitudes toward, 5; political, 13–6, 64–5

women. *See* gentlemanly responsibility; masculinity and feminization
World War II, 131, 148

Yrigoyen, Hipólito, 63

Zorrilla de San Martín, Dr Juan, 27